One from the Hart

ONE FROM THE HART

Stefanie Powers

GALLERY BOOKS

NEW YORK   LONDON   TORONTO   SYDNEY

Gallery Books
A Division of Simon & Schuster, Inc.
1230 Avenue of the Americas
New York, NY 10020

First Gallery Books hardcover edition November 2010

GALLERY BOOKS and colophon are trademarks of Simon & Schuster, Inc.

For information about special discounts for bulk purchases,
please contact Simon & Schuster Special Sales at
1-866-506-1949 or business@simonandschuster.com.

The Simon & Schuster Speakers Bureau can bring authors
to your live event. For more information or to book an event
contact the Simon & Schuster Speakers Bureau at
1-866-248-3049 or visit our website at www.simonspeakers.com.

Designed by Level C, Inc.

Manufactured in the United States of America

10 9 8 7 6 5 4 3 2 1

Library of Congress Cataloging-in-Publication Data is available.

ISBN 978-1-4391-7210-0
ISBN 978-1-4391-7212-4 (ebook)

To Big Julie

Contents

———&&&———

One from the Hart

Kenya

———— ⊗⊗ ————

It was 1974 and my first trip to East Africa, and I was in good hands. No, I was in *perfect* hands, the most perfect hands I could have dreamed of, not only for this trip but for my life.

William Holden, tanned and gorgeous at the wheel of his Land Rover, looked more like a movie star at that moment than ever he did on the screen. We were crashing through the bush on and off a dirt track leading far into the northern frontier of Kenya. Bill and his longtime partners Don and Iris Hunt had established a camp for the purpose of capturing Grevy's zebras to be translocated to the south of the country, away from the onslaught of poachers who would render them extinct. I was already in love with the man, so it was easy to love what he loved, because I loved it too.

In spite of the difference in our ages, Bill and I enjoyed a seamlessness in our frames of reference, particularly when it came to our professional lives. Bill had been under contract to Columbia Pictures, I had been under contract to Columbia Pictures. Although quite a few years apart, many of the people Bill knew as apprentices were department heads by the time I got to the studio. The world of the movies was a family affair, where sons and daughters followed fathers and mothers into the studio "shop." While our times and tenures were different, our inductions into the Hollywood firmament were, if not identical, very much the same.

Bill and I spoke the same language in many other ways as well. We had mutual curiosities, mutual interests, mutual passions, and mutual values. Animals, both domestic and wild, had already played a great part in my life, so I too knew intimately the rewards of the human-animal bond. The only thing we did not share was his addiction, an addiction that we kept at bay for most of the nine years we were together, but which, sadly, won in the end.

I AM ALONE now, driving along yet another dusty and bumpy dirt track leading out onto the plains of Laikipia, a landscape familiar to me now. Never could I have imagined as a young actress how my priorities in life would change after Bill was gone, and how much of his legacy would pass on to me. My twenty-four-year-old Toyota Land Cruiser groans under its own weight as we maneuver into and out of the last in a series of deep trenches, once again victorious over the odds of a breakdown or a punctured tire. As I pull into the tattered grounds of Guara Primary School, the headmistress, Anne Murithi, greets me with a smile and embrace of an old friend, sisters in the fight for education relevant to her students and to the future of her country and my adopted home, Kenya.

This trip to Kenya is different. There will be no more nightly calls to my house in California to speak first with my mother's nurses and then with her, when I was fortunate enough to catch her awake. "Hello, baby," she would say in that voice, so sweet and vulnerable that it was almost childlike, even at ninety-six. Our conversations were brief and usually one-sided, yet I knew she was sustained by every word of my trivial report of the day's activities.

She would laugh and say, "Okay, baby, I love you," and I would say, "I love you more." Then she would laugh and we would sign off, my heart temporarily relieved of anxiety.

How could she not be there? The thought is too big to take in all at once. I have to ration my grief or I will crumble under its heaviness, and I must remember my own condition. I have to remain strong, strong enough to function, strong enough to recover from my own lung cancer and the operation to remove it. I must remain positive enough to overcome both events, one after the other within the same month.

I thank God for my family of friends, I thank God for my faith, and I thank God that Tom came into my life.

Surrounded by such love, how could I not carry on?

A Hollywood Childhood

———◦◦◦———

I was not long into this life when I realized that while I had not been born into its upper echelons, I was indeed and most gratefully a product of the lucky sperm club. It was a matter of luck that my forefathers broke from Poland and joined the hopeful masses emigrating to the United States during the early part of the twentieth century. And it was by even greater luck that Julianna Dimitria Golan, third daughter of Zofja and Frederick Golan, broke from the family farm in New York State to venture, as an eighteen-year-old, with her big sister Helena, to the bright lights of New York City to pursue a life in the theater. She eventually found her way to Hollywood, where she married and produced two children, one of whom was me.

My mother was born on July 21, 1912, near Middletown, New York, at home on the family farm with the help of a midwife. Eventually, more of the family came to Middletown from Poland to seek their fortunes, including one person who was a great influence on her. Uncle Leo taught himself English by reading *National Geographic* magazines, which he passed on to young Julie. Adapting quickly to the New World, Uncle Leo brought with him a sense of adventure and style, resplendent in a photo of him wearing wingtip shoes, posing in front of his newly acquired Model A roadster. Uncle Leo had panache.

The countryside provided an idyllic childhood, but as Julie was grow-ing up, the world around her was changing dramatically. Rural America was being introduced to the telephone, to the moving picture show, and to barnstorming aviators, who toured the country, putting on shows and tak-ing young ladies for rides in their open-cockpit planes. Very exciting for the young Miss Golan. But it was the musical films that caught her attention, and the musical theater's traveling shows that caught her fancy and lured her to the big city.

When the time came for Julie and Helena to spread their wings, they found respectable housing at the home of an Italian lady by the name of Carmella on West 69th Street, one block from Central Park. While study-ing dance and going to all the auditions she could find, Julie and her sister both worked part-time as hostesses at the exclusive foreign film cinema on 57th Street called The Little Carnegie Theatre. It was an extremely glamor-ous art house cinema, serving cocktails, tea, and coffee in the foyer lounge, where speakers from the foreign film companies would address their audi-ences. The Little Carnegie was the only venue in New York City at the time where foreign films were shown, making it avant-garde and an attraction for interesting people, many of whom became lifelong friends, including some of the filmmakers themselves from England, France, and Germany.

Much later in life, while I was filming in England, Mom would introduce me to one of those gentlemen who had been a principal at British Gaumont Films.

In 1934, Mom made the giant step to move to Hollywood, following through on her dream to perform in films. Finding the most glamorous way to travel west, she went to Hollywood by boat, via the Panama Canal. She was quite an attractive package, with lots of shipboard admirers. The captain of the vessel even invited her to travel on to the Far East with him, but she gracefully declined. Instead she stepped off the boat and made her way to Hollywood, installing herself at the Lido Hotel just north of Hollywood Boulevard and very close to another landmark glamour spot called the Monticito.

Hollywood Boulevard in the 1930s was still synonymous with the allure of the industry that inspired its development. Stretching from Sunset Boulevard in the east to just west of Laurel Canyon, it switched its name from Prospect Avenue in 1910 when the town of Hollywood was annexed to the city of Los Angeles, and a couple of decades later it was very much the place to see and be seen. Deco-era moviegoers patronized such ornate and palatial establishments as the El Capitan Theatre, the Pantages Theatre, the Warner Brothers Theatre, and Grauman's Egyptian and Chinese Theatres. Visitors, celebrities, and wannabes rubbed shoulders at the Spanish-style Roosevelt Hotel and the landmark Hollywood Hotel. The town's elite actors, directors, producers, and writers dined, imbibed, did deals, and held court at the already legendary Musso & Frank Grill. Not yet threatened by muggers, pimps, and drug dealers, Hollywood Boulevard was a street where couples could take a leisurely stroll, film stars could venture out in public, and aspiring actors might just get noticed.

Gravitating toward the daily parade of hopefuls was an eclectic assortment of eccentrics, including the "dress extras"—whose exaggerated demeanor and immaculate wardrobe ensured them a desirable place in the hierarchy of the background "performers," giving them a natural sense of superiority—and the self-styled "character extras," each with an attitude commensurate with their adopted persona.

"Nature Boy" wore sandals and white gossamer flowing linen robes, giving the impression of an aesthetic mountain-dwelling mystic who walked the boulevard with staff in hand. There was a lady "Robin Hood" in hunter green shoes, tights, dress, and cape, topped by a chapeau worthy of Sherwood Forest, complete with pheasant plume. She strode the boulevard with defiant purpose, going nowhere. "Goldilocks" was the personification of sweetness, sporting platinum ringlet curls in her hair that were completely inappropriate for her age and size, as well as a youthful costume with gold Mary Jane pumps and anklet socks with lace trim to match her lace gloves, gold bag, belt, and cream-colored dress. They were still in place, though somewhat older, when Mom began to take my brother and me to the movie palaces on Hollywood Boulevard and introduced us to these benign but colorful free spirits.

In the lobby of the Lido Hotel, a piano player accompanied tea service that folded into the cocktail hour. Accordingly it was a gathering place for most of the residents, including a young, aspiring photographer. Their relationship began in the romantic atmosphere of those intimate evenings, and slowly my mother became seduced by the lensman whose portraits of her reflected the affection he felt. He became her first husband, and their union resulted in what she considered her greatest joy, my brother, Jeff, and me.

IN SPITE OF the fact that marriage and motherhood inexorably altered the direction of her life and aborted the realization of her artistic dreams, I never, ever heard Mom express any feelings of frustration or incompleteness. While there are always people who have more, there are a hell of a lot of people who have less, was the thought with which she raised me. To her mind, the inevitable price for a happy state of affairs was to earn each privilege through work. The work ethic imbued in the children of immigrants and survivors of the Great Depression was the criteria for all praise or reward; and at the end of the day, no matter how much we complained at the time, I can now say that it did, in fact, make me a better person and undoubtedly more able to bear the weight of responsibilities to come.

My mother was the source of all stability and fun. One of my favorite childhood memories was when she would be going out of an evening wearing a particular black silk taffeta dress that rustled when she walked. As she would lean down to kiss me goodnight, I'd feel the softness of her silver fox stole on my cheek and smell the intoxicating, fragrances of Shalimar perfume on her neck and a gardenia on her purse, thus establishing my sensual criteria for glamour and excitement. I really don't remember many unpleasant times, with the exception of the tension and unhappiness created by my father's presence. Nevertheless, there are two things I can thank my father for: the role he played in my conception and the sister I gained as a result of his marriage to his second—but not his last—wife.

Mom always lifted our spirits and made a game of adversity. That's how she got herself through the rough patches, and as best she could, she did the same for my brother and me. Perhaps that is why I always felt I wanted to do things for her: extravagant, adventurous, glamorous things to make her feel better about herself and about her life.

Both of my parents' relatives were in the East, so aside from occasional visits for weddings I did not grow up in the bosom of aunts, uncles, cousins, or grandparents. Our closest relative was Mom's sister Cioci (the Polish word for "aunt," pronounced "cho-chi") Helena, who followed my mother to California in the late thirties. After the war, Cioci Helena married Uncle Howard, whom I adored. A former vaudevillian song-and-dance man, tall and lithe, who did a mean soft-shoe and played straight man for various comedians, my uncle Howard was handsome and joyful. Following vaudeville, he made a successful career transition, first becoming a casting director at Ziv TV Studios and eventually an executive at Technicolor. However, my favorite memory of my uncle was when he taught me a soft-shoe dance to the song "On the Sunny Side of the Street." I loved him dearly, and I still remember every step.

Throughout those early years, Mom created an environment for us that reflected her active and rich fantasy life, keeping my brother and me constantly amused with stories about the nightly escapades of our teddy bears, Kitty and Tiger. . . . "Did you hear all that racket last night?" Mom would ask at the breakfast table. Wide-eyed, we would respond, "No," and she would embark on the most elaborate tale of how Kitty and Tiger had opened all the cupboards in the kitchen, taken out all the pots and pans, and somehow raced up and down the kitchen floor in vehicles fashioned out of cooking utensils. No matter how preposterous the stories were, we loved them, even when Kitty and Tiger, beaten and battered beyond repair, disappeared overnight and miraculously reappeared the following day in completely new fur, apparently having gone away to some exotic Teddy Bear Spa.

Then there were the nightly dinner table discussions, some of which included visits to other parts of the world. Out would come dictionaries in the appropriate languages while dinner would represent the country of choice. We never went as far as hats and costumes, but we would make up conversations, brutalizing each language and laughing ourselves silly at words like *platz* and *ausfahrt*.

IN THE NEIGHBORHOOD where we lived, not far from the house my parents built before getting divorced, there were three outstanding residents, plus our iconic television family—the Nelsons, Ozzie, Harriet, Ricky, and David. Dr. Famularo a respected physician and a pillar of the community; Miss Woods, a patrician woman of a certain age who had traveled extensively as a foreign correspondent in the Far and Middle East; and the Reverend Norman, who was always referred to in those terms: the Reverend Norman. The Reverend Norman's credentials were greatly enhanced by his long and celebrated missionary service in China, during which time it was assumed—from the impression he gave to all—that he had gathered considerable knowledge of the Chinese people, their customs, and language. In fact, Miss Woods and the Reverend Norman had China in common, although they had engaged in completely disparate pursuits. These three people, to varying degrees, impacted my young life.

It was not uncommon in neighborhoods like ours to have all sorts of door-to-door salesmen ringing the bell. There was the Encyclopedia Britannica salesman, the Fuller Brush salesman, and my all-time favorite, the Electrolux vacuum cleaner salesman, who would carry in his kit all sorts of bags containing sand, dirt, and small, undesirable particles. To my mother's horror, he would deposit these contents on her carpet and then, magically, his new and greatly improved model with extra suction power would vacuum away the offending soil.

The neighborhood children ranged from the very tiny and therefore irrelevant to the nearly-teens. I was one of those who fell within the category of the minimum age to hang out with the "cognoscenti." Naturally, like all red-blooded American youths of the era, we indulged in that time-immemorial game of you-show-me-yours-and-I'll-show-you-mine. Our sexual curiosity was tempered by the morays of society in the 1950s and the relentless lectures given to us at Sunday school on the subject of mortal sin. Therefore, imagine the combination of shock, fascination, embarrassment, and guilt on the day when I first encountered the forbidden phallus on an adult. The Reverend Norman was indirectly responsible for my first encounter with a flasher.

The Reverend Norman and his family, including his extended family of the faithful, lived in a large house that, in hindsight, must have belonged to his parish. The daughter of the family was in my class at grammar school, and we frequently walked home from school together, so it was not unusual for me to see her at her house. There were lots of visitors coming and going at the Reverend Norman's home, and one day there appeared a Chinese boy in his early twenties. My recollection is rather vague concerning the details leading up to the unveiling, but I do recall that he, who is nameless in my memory, was sitting at the breakfast table. This was situated in a sort of nook, in what seemed to be a large kitchen, where He of Great Expectation was reading a newspaper, with more newspapers on his lap, when he motioned to me to approach the table.

There was no reason for suspicion because, after all, we were in the Reverend Norman's house. As I arrived at the table, the young man pointed to his lap, whereupon he lifted the newspaper and, lying there in what I would come to know as a semierect state, was . . . his penis. I must have looked at it long enough for it to have made an indelible impression, because the memory of it is vivid even to this day, obviously indicating, at an early age, my predilection for heterosexuality.

I departed the kitchen and then the house, never to reenter those premises, and ran nonstop down the block, through our back gate, across the garden, to the back door and the safety of our home. It was long after the Reverend Norman and his family left the neighborhood that I told my mother about the incident. I think Mom was hurt that I hadn't trusted her enough to tell her, but trust had nothing to do with it, and neither did harboring some sort of Catholic guilt (which I did, of course). On the contrary, it had everything to do with how my mother might have reacted. She could be a tiger when it came to defending her son and daughter.

The only other time I encountered a flasher was many years later while riding in the hills of Griffith Park. I kept horses at the L.A. Equestrian Center, and I was exercising them on a weekday by charging up the empty trails of the wonderful park that overlooks the entire San Fernando Valley. I was riding one horse and holding two others by lead ropes, one on either side of me. Suddenly a man in a raincoat, wearing nothing else but black shoes and socks, jumped out of the bushes and opened his coat. My horses reared, and I was so mad that I ran at him with all three horses. I gave him such a piece of my mind that he crawled back into the bushes like the insect he was. I realize flashing is some sort of sickness, but the man looked so silly that it was like seeing a scene out of *Laugh-In,* and I couldn't help but have a good laugh once safely back at the barn.

OUR UPBRINGING HAD a definite European flair to it, with Polish being spoken at home just long enough for both my brother and me to have a good understanding of the language. However, as a preteen who was afraid of appearing different, Jeff soon refused to be spoken to in anything other than English, especially in front of his friends, a rejection he would later regret.

As in most quasi-European homes, a small glass of wine might be permitted young people from time to time, so drinking held no mystique for us. Neither did dining rituals. Given this sensibility, it was not surprising that we should become friendly with a family a few blocks away that consisted of a French father, an Italian mother, and a Puerto Rican nanny. Monsieur Bagier was the U.S. representative for Louis Jadot wines; Madame Bagier was the daughter of Countess Mara, famous in the world of fashion for her men's shirts, ties, and accessories. The Bagiers had lived in Puerto Rico, where their son Robin and daughter Mara were born. So, when they came to live in California, they brought their Puerto Rican nanny with them. In short, there were, at all times, four languages spoken simultaneously in their home.

Because Jeff was the oldest, followed by Robin, me, and then Mara, we formed a perfect gang. And when Monsieur Bagier introduced my mother to the idea of expanding our palates—and, accordingly, our level of sophistication—through the appreciation of the art of fine wine, her fair assessment of our safety under his supervision opened the door to the creation of our kiddies' wine-tasting ceremonies.

Monsieur Bagier did everything according to ritual, in miniature: we were seated along one side of a long oak dining table, and in front of each of us there were three or four small cordial glasses; a small, empty bowl; baskets of bite-sized pieces of French bread; a tray of crudités; and the bottles of wine for tasting. It is difficult to recall all but the broad strokes of the ceremony, but I do fondly remember Monsieur Bagier's valiant attempt to give us both geography and science in one go. Not until many years later, when I was married to a Frenchman whose property in Burgundy was one valley removed from the domain of Louis Jadot, did some of the lessons of Monsieur Bagier resonate.

When we were older, we were sometimes invited to the Bagiers' parties, and there were always the most beautiful and sophisticated people in attendance. The Hollywood agent Paul Kohner was a family friend and frequent guest, occasionally bringing his daughter Susan with him. Susan Kohner was one of young Hollywood's up-and-coming stars, making her mark in a movie costarring Lana Turner and teen idol Sandra Dee. The movie was called *Imitation of Life.* The world of films was never more than a whisper away, but I certainly never imagined that one day I too would costar with Lana Turner and Sandra Dee.

Then again, I also could never have imagined a character like Jack Robinson sweeping into our lives and sweeping my mother off her feet. Tall as a mountain, with a John Wayne swagger, he was her second great love and would become the most indelible father figure in my life. "Uncle Jack" raised Thoroughbred racehorses and drove a Cadillac Eldorado and a Mercedes Benz 300 Gull Wing, each with a solid gold horse head on its hood, a shiny Circle JR brand clamped to the front and rear bumpers, and, to add to his larger-than-life persona, no less than two distinctly different cow horns with which he could elect to announce his arrival or embarrass me in front of my peers when he dropped me at school. Quite spontaneously, he might present us with birthday cake for breakfast. Uncle Jack was an overgrown kid and an unlikely stepfather, but I loved him.

Among the animals on the Circle JR ranch in Corona, California (later purchased by Desi Arnaz), were, of course, the blue-blooded Thoroughbred racehorses, who were either sold at auction to equally blue-blooded buyers or raced under the silver and maroon colors of the Circle JR and trained by Buddy Hersh. In addition, there was also an assortment of other critters, most of whom were rejects from the infield garden at Hollywood Park, which once boasted a "Goose Girl," fully turned out in her Dutch ensemble, parading with a flock of geese in a bucolic setting with exotic fowl, monkeys, baby goats, and baby lambs. The whole improbable yet compatible assortment wound up at the Circle JR when Hollywood Park redesigned the infield.

In the 1950s, what passed for security on a Thoroughbred breeding farm with highly valuable horses was a device called an electric eye. This system, antiquated by today's standards, consisted of an electric box clamped to a post on one side of an entry/exit; a beam would shoot across to a mirror that reflected the beam back to the box, and only if that beam was interrupted by someone crossing it and breaking the connection would the bells and buzzers go off.

The Hollywood Park peacocks found a great home at the Circle JR, and they looked majestic as they paraded gracefully around the circular drive, with its centerpiece flagpole and grassy surround encircled by the prized rose garden planted by Jack's mother. Dr. and Mrs. Robinson had come to live with their son and only child, building themselves a house on the entry circle and presiding in an aristocratic fashion over certain details at the ranch. They were an imposing and rather intimidating couple.

The doctor had been one of the most successful physicians in Kansas City and one of the first to experiment with the healing properties of the X-ray. Unfortunately, the price he paid for his innovation was the loss of quite a few fingers, because he couldn't be bothered to slow down long enough to shield himself with lead-covered gloves. Extremely vain, Dr. Robinson always had on hand no less than two hundred pairs of new and beautifully made broadcloth gloves, which he would discard after only a few wearings. His principle occupation was to board his electric-powered golf cart, upon which he would survey the property and all the activities both in the morning and in the afternoon.

For her part, Mrs. Robinson was like the dowager queen mother, serving tea in the afternoon on beautiful china wearing any number of jewelry ensembles in which she took great pride. She lovingly walked among her roses in the afternoon wearing a large picture hat and carrying a cane, and the peacocks only added to the idyllic ambience of the setting. However, the peacocks quickly fell out of favor after they discovered the mirrored side of the security system, in which they could glory in their reflected beauty, inevitably at the morning's first light, setting off all the alarms and generally causing chaos, much to my amusement.

The ranch, for me, was a bit like Eloise at the Plaza, and I created lots of secret places where I would go with the goat, who followed me everywhere, along with the outside dogs. These were my friends who were at the kitchen door every morning, waiting patiently for me to emerge with a loaf of white bread, which they would immediately consume before following me on my rounds to visit all the horses. The goat was never allowed in the entry circle, near the roses, for obvious reasons. That was until one particular day. For some reason all the adults had gone somewhere, as had my brother, who was nearly three years older than me and did not take to either this life or the horses. Normally Jeff would go off with his father while Mom and I spent weekends at the ranch. I must have been somewhere in the area of seven or eight years old, and there were a lot of staff at the ranch to look after me, but being a bit of a tomboy and having all my animal friends to keep me company, I went off on my own. And what did I come across? The doctor's golf cart.

The dogs would have no part of it, but the goat quite liked it and climbed up into the seat next to me. Somehow I got the damned thing started after lots of false stops and starts, and I managed to move forward at quite a nice pace with the goat beside me. I think we ran out of steam halfway around the entry circle, which meant we had to dismount and I had to try to push the golf cart back to where I found it. This was, of course, impossible for me. Running to find help, I completely forgot that I had left the goat behind. I must have been gone for quite awhile, because when I returned with the help they took one look at the roses and gasped in horror.

The goat had done its best to consume most of the flowers, and there was going to be hell to pay.

Henceforth, I was only allowed to visit the goat at the far end of the property, where it was tethered on a long line for most of the rest of its life. Meanwhile, since it appeared that I had so much time to get into trouble, I was given a full schedule of chores, some of which allowed me to put my hands on the horses and begin to learn about how to care for them and, most important, how to commit to the life of the animals in your care. As for the goat, I am consoled by the knowledge that the head gardener promised me that, whenever possible, he would deliver roses to my delinquent friend.

Thus began my great allegiance to the animal kingdom, and a love affair that would last a lifetime.

From Dancer to Actress

———⊗⊗⊗———

Long before my showdown at the Circle JR, it became obvious that I had some sort of internal, almost cellular engine in my body that caused me to physically react to the classical music constantly playing in my parents' home.

My mother's love of the ballet, and the many performances she saw during the nine months of my gestation, might indeed have played a role in determining my emotional response to the music, but how could my physical movements come to mimic those of the dancers I never saw? It must have been somewhere in my DNA, because apparently I danced around the house nonstop. Being an extrovert by nature probably also contributed to my need for self-expression. So, while my older brother chose to retreat at the call of his introversion, I would forever advance into the unknown with guns blazing. Fearlessness, determination, and a voracious curiosity would remain driving forces for most of my life.

———⊗⊗⊗———

POST–WORLD WAR II Hollywood was, for those who lived there, still a really small town where gossip traveled at the speed of light. I remember my mother telling me that once there had been a scandal at the Mocambo nightclub on the Sunset Strip that everyone in town knew about the following morning. Years later, I found out that the scandal she was referring to involved Francis Lederer and Joan Crawford, both household names at the time. He allegedly disappeared under the tablecloth of their banquette seating and was discovered committing fellatio. . . . Well! You can imagine how the tongues wagged. This was before tabloids, the paparazzi, and *Entertainment Tonight.* The studios guarded every word printed about their stars, and nothing of a compromising nature saw the light of day. Then *Confidential* magazine hit the stands and changed all the rules. In that rarefied atmosphere B.C. (Before *Confidential*), people's lives constantly crossed one another. But after all, the population of Los Angeles in the 1950s was just over two million people, as opposed to today's nearly five million.

Michael Panieff was a soloist with the famed Diaghilev company of the Ballet Russe de Monte Carlo, and he was celebrated as the partner of the prima ballerina Danilova. The Ballet Russe was on tour in America when the war in Europe broke out, so returning there was out of the question. When Pearl Harbor was attacked and Congress declared war, every eligible man within the borders of the U.S.A. was drafted, including "Micha," as he was lovingly called. The Army recruited Micha and, with its notorious myopia, placed him in, of all services, the Tank Corps.

Micha emerged from his tank with a new point of view and a great affection for the United States. When he was offered a chance to remain in the U.S., Micha grabbed it with both hands and headed straight for the Riviera-like atmosphere of Hollywood to do what he did best: open a ballet school.

Shirley Temple had long ago made Hollywood a mecca for ambitious parents of adorable dimpled daughters with ringlets. I was neither dimpled nor ringleted, but I did have energy, so much that my mother saw in the ballet both an outlet for my enthusiasm and a training ground for graceful body development. Mom loved the Russian-scented atmosphere of the European ballet school Micha created, fully equipped with accents, attitude, and a live pianist. Three times a week, we would inhabit the world of a nostalgic classical tradition. Even the ballet master's stick Micha taught with was reminiscent of a painting by Degas.

There were two other girls in my ballet class, and even in small-town Hollywood, with its almost incestuously intimate environment, how could we ever have imagined at the time that one day all three of us would be married to Robert Wagner . . . in one way or another. Natalie Wood had begun acting at a very early age, years before we met in ballet class, and even though she was older and an established child star, she was always sweet to me, and I was always in awe of her. As I began to grow up, my feet were too big and my hands were never right and my waistline failed to reveal itself, but Natalie never had an awkward age. She was always simply beautiful. Jill Oppenheimer, who would become Jill St. John, was also beautiful and bubbly, with perfect teeth and an equally perfect smile, and she invariably had the best outfits in the class. Our mothers became friends, at least for the duration of the class and our various recitals.

I carried on dancing and eventually moved on from Micha's junior ballet company to the American School of Dance. Natalie went on to make wonderful movies, and our paths would cross again and again, as they would with Jill's, whose life also took her away from our ballet class and on to greener pastures.

The most wonderful aspects of the world within the walls of Micha's ballet school were the extraordinarily colorful dancers. Every touring ballet company would pay a call on Micha's class, as would all the best dancers in movies and on television: Zizi Jeanmaire, Jacques D'Amboise, Roland Petit, Luigi, Leslie Caron, Michael Kidd, Vera Ellen, Betty Garrett, plus an assortment of highly unusual individuals of decidedly different demeanor.

The ladies' dressing room was unremarkable, except on the occasions when we were visited by a rather unusual "lady" who discreetly changed out of his street clothes into pink tights and tutu. He'd regale us with funny stories, making us all laugh. I liked him, but it did challenge my mother to come up with an explanation for a transvestite. I think she said something like this: "He is a boy who feels like a girl and likes to dress up in girl's clothing, it's nothing to worry about." And so I never did.

In the summer of my fourteenth year, as if by spontaneous combustion, my latent puberty blossomed and a growth spurt shot me to almost my full adult height. This was accompanied by an increase of two bra sizes, harbingers of the realization that the ballet was not to be for me. I carried on taking Micha's Saturday ballet classes from time to time until he stopped teaching, and it was always a treat to reconnect with him and the nostalgia of my childhood, but if I was going to continue to dance, I needed to expand my horizons.

———— ◦⊗◦ ————

IN THE 1950S, Eugene Loring, a dancer, choreographer, and contemporary of Jerome Robbins's, came to Hollywood from New York to establish the American School of Dance in the basement of a large white residential hotel located on Hollywood Boulevard, next to Grauman's Chinese Theatre. New York was the epicenter of modern dance, so the American School became the West Coast focal point for modern dance and magnetized the very best teachers and dancers, one of whom was Matt Mattox.

Matt Mattox was a brilliant dancer, a fabulous teacher, and one of the brothers in the exceptional musical feature *Seven Brides for Seven Brothers*. Matt Mattox's class was my introduction to contemporary dance; he was also so handsome and so popular that you could hardly find a place to move in his class. Eventually, Matt left the States to teach in Paris, the rumor being that he was forced to go due to the many paternity suits he was slapped with. I never asked him about this when, years later, I showed up in his class in the City of Light, and he was kind enough to make me feel as if he actually remembered me.

At the American School of Dance, in keeping with the tradition of New York dancing schools, auditions or "calls" for traveling Broadway shows, movies, or TV variety productions were posted on a bulletin board in the lobby of the school. I was fifteen when I began to go out on those calls. Mom allowed me to go because I would be with Kathy Gale, who was a year and a half older, presumably more responsible, and most important of all, she had a driver's license and a car. What's more, our mothers were friends.

Both Kathy and I were tall and not bad dancers. Our mothers were always prepared for us to return home late from the auditions, largely due to the fact that no one ever looks at a dancer's face, only at the way they move, and we moved rather well (if I do say so myself). Consistently, we would make it through all the eliminations, until in the end the girl with the clipboard would come around prepared to take down our details. Inevitably, after taking a long look at us, she would ask, "How old are you?" Standing very tall, with great assurance, we would lie. "Eighteen," we'd say, prompting her to dismiss us in a huff, accompanied by a variety of comments, mostly unkind, in reference to how we had wasted their time.

ONE DAY, WE went on an audition for the movie *West Side Story*, and this time something magical happened. We were not told to go home. On the contrary, we were told to come back for another audition, during which we would compete with all the other dancers who had made it through the first round. It is safe to say that every dancer in Southern California and some from out of town had come to those auditions. In all, I went to sixteen dance auditions, eventually "surviving" Kathy, so Mom, a reluctant driver, was left to chauffeur me. Finally, I was given a page of dialog and a date to return for a screen test for the role of Velma. My excitement turned to dismay and panic when I read the dialogue.

"Ooo, ooo, ooobley ooo!" Never having seen the play, I had no idea what the line meant, and I certainly didn't know how to say it! Once again, Mom to the rescue. Somewhere in her youth, Mom had become acquainted with the most famous theatrical family in New York's Yiddish theater, the Adlers. Luther Adler was famous for his creation of the title role in *Golden Boy;* Jay Adler was famous as an acting coach and for playing hundreds of supporting character roles onstage, in films, and on TV; and Stella Adler was famous as a teacher of acting whose reputation rose with the success of her star pupil, Marlon Brando.

Mom took me immediately to "Uncle Jay," who found a way to explain the role sufficiently for me to get through the first test. When "Uncle Luther" heard that I was going to "act," he called my mother and said, "I knew it! I knew she was going to be an actress! Whatever you do, don't let her study with Stella . . ." Apparently, he knew that "Aunt Stella" preferred teaching young men rather than young ladies.

The day of the test, I met the actor who would feed me the lines with his back to the camera. Rudy Solari was his name, and he was very generous with me, giving me all sorts of off-camera energy. Later, he opened an acting school, and I would go to work with him when I needed help with a part. The screen test was to be directed by none other than Robert Wise, the director of *West Side Story,* and the editor of no less a film than *Citizen Kane.* Imagine my good fortune—not bad for my first director.

Mr. Wise knew how green I was, but he was patient and explained everything to me carefully. I must have done something right (although I can't imagine what that could have been), as I was called back for two more tests and finally told to go to the Labor Department, get my work permit, and show up for the beginning of rehearsals. Child labor laws then and now require a parent and a teacher on the set at all times, plus a strict adherence to the amount of hours for work and for school. They seemed to be going through an awful lot of trouble to have me around.

Most of the dancers who showed up that first day came from New York, making me one of the few to have been chosen from the West Coast. In addition, almost all of the other dancers had worked for Jerome Robbins before, so on that first day of rehearsals . . . was I nervous? You bet!

The New York dancers had grown their hair long and were already very much in character. When I look at the film today, the cast looks almost clean-cut by our current standards, but times were very different then.

For the first week of rehearsal, we assembled each day on a large sound-stage at the Samuel Goldwyn Studios, which had been set up as a dance studio with a bar and mirrors. We were given a two-hour ballet class conducted by one of Mr. Robbins's "lieutenants." Howard Jefferies was one of those lieutenants; eventually he would become Natalie Wood's secretary and our paths would cross again. But then I was a peon and he was part of the inner circle.

There were not a lot of laughs on that rehearsal stage; in fact, the environment was extremely tense. After the ballet class, we would divide into Sharks and Jets and be taken to an office to listen to taped interviews of juvenile delinquents from New York's Lower West Side. Afterward, Mr. Wise and Mr. Robbins would talk to us about creating our own characters and back stories, along with our relationships to one another and why we hated the Puerto Ricans. We were warned that anytime during dance rehearsals we might be stopped and asked questions, so we had better make sure we created a full and rich character.

I have never forgotten those first acting lessons, and they have remained with me always. Later in life I had many opportunities to be in Mr. Wise's company, and I never failed to remind him that he was responsible for my career. Of course, there were others just as responsible, but he was the first to see something in me, a fact for which I am eternally grateful.

The dance rehearsals were relentless and brutal, as were Mr. Robbins's assaults on us. Mr. Robbins was notorious for his vitriolic displays of bullying. Books have been written about him disclosing the darker side of his genius. I was a victim of a tongue lashing from Mr. Robbins more than once, so I can attest to his nature. On one occasion while rehearsing the number "Cool," at the part of the dance when the girls run together into the center of the ring of boys, Mr. Robbins yelled, "STOP!"

We all froze. Taking his time, the boss walked over to me and looked down at my feet. I had overshot my mark on the floor by about two inches. "Look where you are," he said in a loud and humiliating tone. "Maybe you would like to do this number all by yourself? We could all sit back and watch you do the number." Tears welled up in my eyes, but I forced them not to spill over.

Many years after *West Side Story,* I was rehearsing what would come to be known as "the ill-fated revival of *Applause,*" in a rehearsal room in a building of rehearsal rooms in Lower Manhattan. The top floor housed the Eliot Feld Ballet Company. Eliot had played Baby John, one of the Jets in *West Side Story.* In a moment of misguided enthusiasm, I sent a note up to Eliot saying that I hoped he remembered me and that I was starring in the revival of *Applause,* rehearsing just below him. I did not receive an answer to my note, so one day, on a break, I took the elevator to the top floor to pay him a call. It was lunch hour and there was no one in the entrance lobby of the company studio. One of the rehearsal room doors was open, and I peeked inside to find none other than Eliot himself rehearsing some choreography. I waited quietly by the door. Eventually he stopped dancing, and from the other side of the room he projected his displeasure by saying, "*West Side Story* was such a nightmare for me that I have blacked out the entire experience like a bad dream and I don't want to remember it." He was another of what I imagine is a long line of those who have felt the "wrath of Robbins."

There was a pregnant pause. I apologized for disturbing him and retreated to the sanctuary of the *Applause* rehearsal room.

Rehearsals for the dance numbers in *West Side Story* began long before the final casting of the principal roles was completed, but slowly the lead players began to appear in ballet class: first, Russ Tamblyn, then Rita Moreno and George Chakiris. I remember the day we were visited by Natalie Wood and Robert Wagner, who watched us rehearse the number "Cool." These were genuine movie stars, the real thing.

Natalie and "RJ" were young Hollywood's dream couple, and they graced the covers of all the movie magazines. They were perfect, they dressed beautifully, they smiled beautifully, and they were positively beautiful. We were in awe of them, and they were so kind and appreciative, shaking hands with all of us and thanking us for allowing them to watch. Natalie had already been cast in the role of Maria, but it had not been announced and was top secret. We were instructed not to mention to anyone that they had visited the set. The studio wanted to orchestrate its own press campaign.

As the rehearsals progressed, it became increasingly apparent that I had become an inconvenience, having to stop for school at crucial moments. I was therefore replaced by Carole D'Andrea, the dancer who had played the part of Velma on Broadway. I was brokenhearted, but I remained friendly with some of the dancers, who are happily still very much in my life—Rita Hyde and George Chakiris in particular, as well as Harvey Evans, one of the Jets, who went on to play my boyfriend in *Experiment in Terror*. Carole D'Andrea would eventually marry her then-boyfriend Robert Morse, with whom I would costar in the Disney film *The Boatniks*.

Being able to cross paths throughout life with the people you have worked with and shared experiences with is part of the joy of our business, and the greatest perk of longevity.

ON THE SAMUEL Goldwyn lot, where *West Side Story* was housed, was a young actor/writer/director named Tom Laughlin (later of *Billy Jack* fame), who was in the midst of casting his second film. The euphemism for low-budget independent movies at the time was "art" films. To make his movie, Tom had raised considerable funds from his hometown pals in Milwaukee, Wisconsin, where the film would be shot. He needed a young, virginal, innocent, inexperienced actress for the role of his high school sweetheart, and I was just the type.

I was still working on *West Side Story* when our script supervisor, Bruce Kessler, presented his friend Tom to my mom and me in the commissary at the studio. When Tom asked me to come and read for him, and Bruce verified that he and the offer were legitimate, Mom agreed and we took the pages of the scene I was to read with us. Mom was naturally protective of me, but she did it with humor, so everyone loved her for it. She was, for me, my greatest confidante and friend, always and unconditionally on my side. She might have once wanted a career for herself, but she never pushed me into films. It all just seemed to happen, and we were both along for the ride.

The day before I was "released" from *West Side Story,* I went to Tom Laughlin's office at the Samuel Goldwyn Studios to read for him. Naturally, I had seen "Uncle Jay" for a session, but this scene was not just "Ooo, ooo, ooobley ooo!" It was a dramatic confrontation between two young lovers, and I had absolutely no life experience whatsoever to draw upon. At a certain point in the reading of the scene, I broke down crying and declared, "I'm not an actress, I'm a dancer," and floods of tears descended. "That's exactly what I want," said Tom, and the next day both Bruce Kessler and I were fired from *West Side Story* and hired by Tom Laughlin for his movie, entitled either *Christopher Woton, We Are All Christ,* or *The Young Lovers.* It had all those titles at one time or another.

My mother was a great believer in the adage "When one door closes, another opens," and she imbued me with the same optimism. With that in mind, Mom and I took off for Milwaukee on the first of many locations together, always as pals, never as stage mother and daughter. I think that is why all the people who attended Mom's ninety-fifth birthday were friends of ours, not just friends of mine. There were twenty-five people and there would have been more, but those who were out of town sent cards and flowers. I hope there will be twenty-five real friends, not just nurses, at my ninety-fifth if I make it.

Among the great and benevolent producers in Hollywood was a man called Jerry Wald. Mr. Wald worked at 20th Century Fox Studios and was housed in a charming and tastefully furnished bungalow on the lot. Mr. Wald had an eye for young talent and was well known for discovering new faces, young writers, and directors, and he was a great promoter of Tom Laughlin. It was only natural that Tom should give Mr. Wald the first look at his newly finished film. In an effort to help Tom, Mr. Wald showed the film to everyone in Hollywood at his lovely home in Beverly Hills in his private screening room, the first one I ever saw.

Mrs. Wald, Connie, was and is one of Hollywood's great ladies and definitely one of the most tasteful women I have ever met. Connie Wald had style, real style, effortless, not manufactured, not premeditated, never obvious, with no need of a designer or a lifestyle coach. She was genuine, as was her hospitality, and I will never forget her kindness to me when I was invited to the screenings at her home, peopled with the Hollywood elite, many of whom were household names: Audrey Hepburn, Billy Wilder, Jimmy Stewart, Claudette Colbert. Traditionally, Hollywood entertained at home and went out in public for business reasons. Consequently, the homes were wonderful. The Selznick house up Tower Road, where the producer David O. Selznick and his wife Jennifer Jones held court, was open to the young friends of Jennifer's son, Robert Walker, Jr., for Sunday pool parties. I did a film with Bobby called *The Young Interns,* and on Sundays my friend Tom Mankiewicz and I would visit the Selznicks' home. It was incredibly glamorous.

Thanks to Jerry Wald, I was invited to join the acting classes at 20th

Century Fox, MGM, and Columbia Pictures Studios. Every major studio had what they called contract players, a stable of talent known or unknown, traditionally signed to a standard seven-year contract. The unknown contract players were to be "groomed" for stardom with the aid of the studio machine, which provided a full-service finishing school on the lot. MGM had a famous dentist on full-time duty perfecting a flawless smile for anyone who was deemed to require a redo. There were the makeup and hair departments, where they would experiment with color and style to get the "look" the studio wanted, and there was the wardrobe department, where they would measure you top to bottom and create an entire mannequin shaped for fitting costumes. But it was the talent department, with its acting coaches, where you would be prepared to vault the first hurdle on the course leading to the finish line and the prize of a seven-year contract.

Because of the rising popularity of television, the star system was in its twilight years, but not as far as I was concerned. All the old rules still applied: always be on time and never call anyone by their first name. In accordance with the system, you would attend classes with all the contract players and be given a scene from a Broadway play or a motion picture to prepare. You would be paired with a contract player, work on the scene, and then perform it for the talent department, which might or might not order a screen test that would be shown to the heads of the studio, who would say yea or nay . . . and voila! You would either be in or out. "Out" had very grave consequences. The world was small and everyone would know that you had been turned down by the studio, so it could mean a stain on future prospects. Such was the way of the world.

The acting coaches at the studios I was invited to were stars in their own right. MGM had Stella Adler's protégée, Zina Provendy; Columbia Pictures had Les Mahoney from the San Francisco theatrical firmament; and 20th Century Fox had Sanford Meisner, whose Neighborhood Playhouse was legendary in New York. In attendance at the MGM class, from time to time, was almost the entire cast of *Where the Boys Are*: Yvette Mimieux, Paula Prentiss, and George Hamilton, all of whom have remained friends to this day. But it was the dashingly handsome Italian import, Fabrizio Mioni, who would remain one of my closest and dearest.

⟨⟩

BEFORE MY BROTHER answered the call of his compulsory military service, he sold me his pride and joy, a vintage 1958 Porsche Carrera. I was hot spit and crazy for sports cars. Now I was able to drive my very own car to the studios I was popping in and out of while preparing scenes. At the time, I had no idea how privileged I was.

On one particular occasion, I was late for Les Mahoney's class at Columbia. Having parked my car across the street, I ran in through the front door, and the uniformed officer at the desk who knew me by now buzzed me in. I took a short cut, running down the narrow corridor leading past the editing department to the makeup and wardrobe building, at the end of which was the talent school. I pushed one swinging door after the next until I swung one right into the face of a man who was wearing the same sunglasses as I was.

In those days, any item of fashion popular on the Riviera that season might take three years to reach the shops in California. As he grabbed the door, saving himself from a bloody nose, the dialog went like this:

HIM: Where did you get those sunglasses?
ME: My friend Lance Reventlow brought them to me. He was driving in the Monte Carlo Rally. Where did you get yours?
HIM: I was at the Monte Carlo Rally. What do you do here?
ME: I'm an actress.
HIM: Are you any good?

ME: Why, yes, of course I am!

HIM: I'm directing a film here. You should come and see me.

ME: I can't right now, I'm late for class.

HIM: Okay, then, after class. Oh, by the way, I'm on the fourth floor and my name is Blake Edwards.

A Studio Player

———⬡⬡⬡———

The early 1960s looked very much like the 1950s. Nothing in fashion would substantially alter until midway through the decade when the Brits shook up the bastions of convention, giving birth to Swinging London's Carnaby Street, Mary Quant, Vidal Sassoon, and, of course, the Beatles. In keeping with the times, as with other industries, motion picture studios reflected the formality of dress, and most crew members, except for those in the heavy-lifting sections, reported to work in trousers, shirts, and ties.

The year before my arrival at Columbia, the founder and mastermind of the establishment, who ran his creation with an iron hand, suddenly died, leaving much to conjecture and fable. Harry Cohn, like so many of the visionaries who invented Hollywood, might have had little formal education, but he was literally a genius when it came to the art of intimidation. His office was an audacious contrivance—driven by his own brazen hubris, he conducted business in an oblong space where his desk was elevated on a plinth at the far end, behind which, on slightly curved shelves, was the entire collection of every Oscar ever won by Columbia Pictures. The length of the required walk from the entry door to his desk was often referred to as "The Last Mile" or "The Death March."

To those in power, it seemed wholly appropriate that Harry Cohn's funeral take place on Columbia's two remaining original soundstages, numbers three and four. The interminable parade of disingenuous mourners was observed at the sidelines by a number of well-known Hollywood raconteurs, several of whom were credited with the now famous quote of the day. Whether it was Red Skelton or the agent "Swifty" Lazar, the quote remains a bitter epitaph: "Give the people what they want and they'll all come out for it."

After my brief encounter with Blake Edwards in the hallway, I raced on, arriving breathless and late to acting class, using my run-in as the pretext for my tardiness. Les Mahoney, never without a wily sense of humor and an uncanny nose for truth, sniffed out the lie, pragmatically extracting the remaining value of the incident, and astutely remarked, "So, what are you doing here? Get back to his office and meet with the man!"

Relieved, I found my way to the rarefied atmosphere of the fourth floor, which housed the elite of Columbia's producers and directors: the likes of Otto Preminger, Frederick Brisson, and, of course, Blake Edwards. I entered the outer door of Blake's office to find no secretary on duty and the inner door open. "That was fast, come on in!" He seemed surprised and amused. All I remember is that we talked endlessly about sports cars. Blake loved sports cars and hated authority.

Because I was not officially under contract to the studio, it was going to be tricky to order a screen test for the part of Lee Remick's younger sister, Toby, in his film *Experiment in Terror*. The good news was that no one in Les Mahoney's class, either under contract or working toward a contract, was anything like me. Most of the girls were either former beauty contestants or models and were much more "worldly" than I was. Blake reveled in concocting his plot, which would involve the head of the talent department, Max Arnow.

Blake would describe the role of Toby to Max, asking if there was anyone under contract who might fit the part. Needless to say, he would describe me in such detail, freckles and all, that Max could hardly avoid thinking of me. To pull off the conspiracy I had to take the game seriously and play along with whatever Max would devise as the pretext for introducing me to Blake. That night Max called me at home, saying he had an important opportunity for me, and told me to come to his office the following day wearing something demure.

In those days, I had two outfits for interviews—one was demure and one was slightly sexy. I had a joke with my mother: whenever I told her I had to get dressed for an interview, she would always ask, "Demure or slightly sexy?"

Looking quite demure, I arrived punctually at Mr. Arnow's office. With great ceremony he prepared me for my rendezvous with destiny by declaring, "You know, I have always believed in you and thought you had great potential. This may be your break." In fact, Max did believe in me, and his statement was sincere. When Columbia Pictures dissolved its talent department, Max was invited to join CMA, which later became ICM, and he signed me as one of his clients.

Max escorted me to Blake Edwards's office for the big moment. As I was still underage, Blake had to convince Max to leave us alone together, promising to keep the door to his office half-open for propriety's sake. Both Blake and I burst into stifled laughter, like two naughty kids in school.

Mom accompanied me to the screen test, and Lee Remick couldn't have been nicer, truly treating me as a younger sister. Lee and I would become great friends, and I had the pleasure of working with her again on the twelve-hour miniseries *Mistral's Daughter,* also starring Stacy Keach, which we filmed in France. Lee's accomplishments as an actress have always been underrated, but the excellence of her talent was only exceeded by her quality as a person. A long and painful struggle with cancer, which she battled like a champion, prematurely ended Lee's life. All of us who had the privilege of sharing her too-brief time are the better for having known her.

—∞∞∞—

THE ATMOSPHERE ON a Blake Edwards set was uniquely identifiable. I was too inexperienced to fully appreciate just how unusual the atmosphere was until after I had worked on many more sets. In keeping with his latent anarchism, Blake did not take kindly to the rantings of the studio production manager Jack Fears, who was notorious for his cloudbursts of expletives as a means of encouraging his directors to speed up their pace of filming. On one occasion, I had a slightly later call to work, since my scenes were scheduled for the afternoon. I arrived on the set only to find that the morning's work, a simple one-page scene in a karate school, was still not completed.

The tension was palpable as Blake and Mr. Fears (The "Fear of Fears," as he was nicknamed) emerged from a huddle in a corner of the soundstage. Jack Fears had worked his way up as chief studio hatchet man from meager beginnings around the same time young William Holden had entered those hallowed halls. Mr. Fears stormed off and the double doors of the soundstage hissed as they closed behind him. The crew, awaiting a verdict on the day's work, emitted an audible sigh of relief as they exhaled.

Instead of either carrying on to complete the already delayed morning schedule or scrap it and move on, Blake announced that we should all take a karate lesson. Charlie Parker was Blake's personal trainer and a household name among karate enthusiasts. Blake called to Charlie to put the class together, and he summoned me to participate. I have no doubt that karate class went down in the annals of excess as the most costly one of its kind.

Glenn Ford played the FBI man in the film, and Ross Martin played the asthmatic villain who kidnaps me in order to blackmail my sister into stealing money from the bank where she works as a teller. I should have been afraid of Ross Martin, but in life he was a sweetie and a wonderful actor. Glenn Ford was the one who intimidated me more than the villainous Ross. Glenn was not happy doing this picture, and he did not find that his character lived up to his screen image. Indeed, the film was the director's creation, with unusual angles, lighting, and editing.

Blake had brought innovative styling to television with his successful series *Peter Gunn* and *Mister Lucky,* and he was incorporating many of the same techniques in *Experiment in Terror.* Glenn felt he was more a part of the cast than the number one star, so his humor was not in top form. I had only one scene with Glenn, at a swimming pool—I was introduced to him on the set and then left to make small talk. The first thing he said to me, after a long pause, was, "Do you know your lines?"

Of course I did, but his question rattled me with the seriousness of its delivery. Later in life, I would come to know Glenn socially, and Bill would be his best man at one of his last marriages, in the presence of an all-star wedding party that included John Wayne, Frank Sinatra, and Jimmy Stewart.

Blake remained a mentor to me for many years, and I have had wonderful times with both him and Julie Andrews, his remarkable wife. My favorite memory of Blake involves a practical joke inspired by a chance meeting with Capucine and Blake's production manager at the Excelsior Hotel in Rome at the time they were filming *The Pink Panther.* I was with Mom in Rome as part of a public relations tour for the European release of *The Interns.*

People were always trying to surprise Blake by turning up at unlikely places and trying to get a reaction from him, which he never gave. It had become a huge inside joke among his crowd, and since it was far from likely that I should appear out of the blue in Rome, I got drafted. "Cappy" suggested we try to bust Blake by showing up together on the set completely out of context, and we made a date for the following day. We rode to Cinecittà together, giggling all the way at how Blake might react. When we walked on the set I said, "Hi, Blake," as I casually passed him. His only reaction was an equally casual "Hi, Stef," as if I'd been in Rome every day. To the best of my knowledge, no one has ever been able to catch Blake off guard.

To make matters even more coincidental, the other witnesses to my failure were Robert Wagner and David Niven, both of whom I would get to know better later on. But the greatest coincidence was staying with Capucine at the Excelsior Hotel under a complete veil of secrecy—none other than William Holden. His relationship with Capucine had to be discreet, as Bill's marriage to former actress Brenda Marshall was in its waning days; they filed for divorce in 1968, which, as a result of Swiss law, was final only in 1971.

Later, after Bill's death, Capucine and I became friends and saw each other quite often. When she came to L.A. looking for work, Robert Wagner and I were able to find her a guest-starring role in *Hart to Hart*, and I was also able to obtain a part for her in *Mistral's Daughter*. She was always gorgeous, with her aquiline features and sophisticated manner. Tragically, Cappy harbored hidden emotional demons. She fought as best she could until, in the end, she was overwhelmed by a feeling of life's futility and leaped to her death from her lovely penthouse apartment in Lausanne. Audrey Hepburn was one of her best friends, and she thoughtfully called me to explain what had happened.

Cappy and I had loved the same man, at very different times and under very different circumstances, but it never got in the way of our enjoying each other as friends. Jealousy is a poisonous malignancy and pointless in any context.

COLUMBIA PICTURES PUT me under a seven-year contract after *Experiment in Terror*, but it was not the usual term-contract deal. My agreement allowed for a guarantee of no fewer than two pictures a year and was exclusive to movies, with no allowance for television, which, at that time, was still considered to be the poor cousin at the wedding. As it turned out, I would do three films a year for five years.

My first film under the contract was *The Interns*, with an all-star cast headed by Cliff Robertson, James MacArthur, Inger Stevens, Nick Adams, Michael Callan, and me. It was made on a very small budget and did extremely well at the box office, elevating my status a bit at the studio. It was also my first in a long line of opportunities to work with Cliff, who had costarred with Bill in the movie *Picnic*.

Inger Stevens was a fine actress and a lovely person whose life was cut short by an accidental overdose of prescription drugs. Her untimely death cheated us all out of what would have been many wonderful performances. Nick Adams was one of a kind: funny, slightly wild, and a great friend of Natalie Wood and Robert Wagner, always appearing in movie magazine layouts in their company, splashing around in a pool. Nick had appeared as the paperboy in *Picnic*, making the world a very small place indeed. Unfortunately, Nick also had a dark side, and whether it was a combination of too much or too many, certainly it was accidental, but the result was fatal. Another bright light put out long before it shone its brightest.

My first "loan-out" was to Universal Studios. My contract allowed for Columbia to sell my services at whatever price they could get while still paying me my $400-a-week salary. I was to work on a film starring the then-hottest couple in Hollywood, Sandra Dee and Bobby Darin. Having just married after working together in *Come September*, which had been filmed in Rome, virginal Sandra Dee—everyone's teen idol—was the wife of nightclub superstar, "Mack the Knife," swinging-hotshot Bobby Darin. Today, crowd control would have been out of hand.

If a Man Answers was filmed with Ross Hunter's signature style, and Sandra and Bobby only had eyes for each other. With complete professionalism, we worked together, but I might well have been invisible. Ross was the quintessential purveyor of glamour on film and tried his best to maintain a standard while the studio system was collapsing around him. I remember his absolute insistence on elaborate wardrobe tests. All outfits would have every accessory dyed to match the carefully premeditated color schemes of the clothing, which would be complemented by those of the set. God bless him, Ross held the banner on the field of battle long after the war was lost.

My next loan-out was to Warner Brothers for its answer to the beach party movies. The film was called *Palm Springs Weekend* and it would depict the Easter-week school-break invasion of that desert community. Oddly enough, while in high school, I had participated in those yearly ritual migrations of free expression and general blowing off of overactive hormonal steam, much to the chagrin of the local inhabitants. Hollywood High School had social clubs with names in Greek letters, similar to those of college sororities—I was a Lambda and a Delta, having changed clubs in midstream. Our club would always rent a house for the week, and the girls' parents allowed them to do so only if there was an approved "house mother" to chaperone. Well, guess who won the vote by a landslide? My mother. She was so popular with my friends and all the strays who freeloaded at our "house" that she began to have her own collection of adopted sons and daughters I never knew about.

Starring in *Palm Springs Weekend* were Warner Brothers' hot teen idols Connie Stevens, Troy Donahue, Ty Hardin, and Robert Conrad. Jerry Van Dyke and I were the only non–Warner Bros. contract players in the cast. Our lack of status was quite obvious, because the others all had their very own personalized parking spaces—Ty Hardin had a hand-engraved wooden plaque fastened to the wall adjacent to his, with his name in

14-karat gold lettering. I, on the other hand, had to announce my name every day to the guard at the gate, who never ceased to regard me as some interloper. Daily, I was given a pink pass with my name misspelled, which I was instructed to lick and glue to the windscreen. I was then directed to the far end of the lot, where the unused sets were stored, to park my vehicle. I began to understand the true meaning of the word *schlepper.*

I felt so unwelcome in the commissary that I preferred to bring my lunch from home in a brown paper bag. It was the first time—during a moment of youthful introspection—that I realized I was not actually on the inside of Hollywood but more of an outsider. I worked in Hollywood, yet I had no social life or intercourse of any kind with my fellow actors. I was an outsider and quite comfortable on the outside looking in. I loved the work, I loved becoming someone else, but the fast life of some of those around me made me uncomfortable. Perhaps I was a late bloomer, but I avoided becoming involved with the young Hollywood set.

An invitation to join a film industry girls' softball team appealed to my tomboy sense of fun and seemed a benign activity within my comfort zone. Actors in New York had formed a softball league that had played in Central Park for many years, so when they migrated to the West Coast they brought softball with them. The boys' league had actors, agents, directors, producers, and writers on its roster, with team names such as the UJIs—the United Jews & Italians. We girls were mostly actresses at varying stages of development, and our coach was a rising young writer-producer by the name of Aaron Spelling.

Well into the future, it would be Aaron who made the phone call, with Tom Mankiewicz and Robert Wagner on the line, to talk about a pilot for a TV series to be called *Hart to Hart.*

I WAS LIVING at home, safely sheltered from the concerns of supporting myself, and I felt no real need or desire to jump into an independent lifestyle, as everyone else had. At that time, unlike today, most high school graduates left home for college, or found a roommate or two with whom they could afford to share an apartment, setting off on their own as soon as possible, even if it meant struggling to make ends meet. The rite of passage for most of my contemporaries was dependent on experiencing hard times through which life lessons were learned. The "school of hard knocks," as it was called, was very much a badge of honor for young actors who made their pilgrimage to New York to earn their stripes, following their idols Marlon Brando and James Dean to The Actors Studio.

I recall my first husband, actor Gary Lockwood, who considered himself a New York actor, proudly exhibiting an outward disdain for those of us who were safely sequestered in La-La Land. He would boastfully recount stories of having to count the slices of baloney in the refrigerator to be sure no one had stolen his food while he'd shared an apartment with four other young actors in Hell's Kitchen on New York's West Side. Today, Hell's Kitchen has been gentrified into a desirable neighborhood with many good ethnic restaurants and several off-Broadway theaters (one in which I performed). But then, in the late 1950s and early '60s, it was aptly named.

There truly were two camps of young actors in Hollywood, and the New York–trained ones not only looked down on us Hollywood types but also considered us frivolous and vacuous. My first boyfriend was the actor Peter Brown, who was then costarring in one of Warner Bros.' iconic TV series, *Lawman*. Peter was very handsome, and he had been around.

Somehow, Peter was attracted to me, in spite of my reluctance to leap into the fray of sexual liberation. In point of fact, I not only feared sexual confrontation but I also avoided it like the plague. Perhaps it was too much Sunday school. Perhaps it was the fear of conception. I think, most of all, I feared that engaging in sex brought with it the responsibilities of an automatic commitment that might trap me into a life I did not want. I was, therefore, quite emotionally underdeveloped, and it even showed in my work. Dear and long-suffering Peter tolerated my virginity until it became painfully ridiculous; fortunately, I had to go off on location for three months, which brought a tolerable end to his suffering.

While I was seeing Peter, I was introduced to Dean, Jeannie, and Dino Martin by my good friend Mark Nathanson. Soon I was playing tennis with them and enjoying the unpretentious hospitality of their house on Mountain Drive. Jeannie Martin, then as now, was an attractive, open-hearted, fun-loving woman, who was so youthful looking that you might have mistaken her for her children's older sister, not their mother. Dean would hold court behind the bar, which had been designed according to his specifications in an unusual fashion, providing him with the ability to have eye-level conversations with his guests, seated opposite him in armchairs, while he, on a lower level, was perched on a high stool.

The ubiquitous bar—a fashionable accessory and the hub of entertainment in most Hollywood homes—occupied an entire corner of the Martins' generous family-style den. That room and that house were the scene of wonderful gatherings. During one of their famous parties, Bobby Kennedy walked through the door. JFK was on his way to Palm Springs via Los Angeles, and it was unclear whether he was going to join Bobby at the Martins' that night. However, the air of excitement that Bobby's entrance created seemed to indicate this might be the case.

With the exception of Dino Martin, I was clearly the youngest person there. Like a heat-seeking missile, Bobby found me and asked me to dance. I don't remember how many dances we had that night, but I was the only one he danced with, and we talked incessantly. RFK was interested in what young people were thinking about, and while I was not an intellectual giant, I did have a thirst for knowledge and travel. As a result of my brother having attended school in Mexico City, I was learning Spanish and had an insatiable curiosity for other cultures and other countries. Bobby talked to me about our own country requiring the energy and participation of our youth and asked me to please get involved with the pressing issues concerning our nation.

We were locked in conversation for what seemed like hours, unaware that we were the party's principal object of attention the entire time. Eventually, a Secret Service agent interrupted us and whispered into Bobby's ear, causing RFK to turn to me, thank me for the dance, and, holding my hand, say that he hoped we would meet again. Then he left the party. JFK had changed his plans and flown directly to Palm Springs, precipitating Bobby's abrupt departure.

Nevertheless, I did see him again. In fact, I worked for RFK—Pierre Sallinger gave me a perfect job during the 1968 presidential campaign, attaching me to Charlie Evers (Medgar Evers's brother) and John Lewis with the NAACP. Together we worked the combined black and Latino constituencies up and down the West Coast. (By then, I could speak fluent Spanish.)

After Bobby left the party, I was immediately engulfed by everyone, wanting to know what we had been so passionately talking about. I remember Joan Collins inviting me to join her and Warren Beatty at their table.

That tiny moment marked a sea change in the company I was to keep. Even with my junior status, not yet having earned my membership into this club, I was generously included in evenings at house parties where great stars such as Danny Kaye might sing, accompanied by Sammy Cahn, while Johnny Green would display his piano virtuosity and Rosemary Clooney would serenade us with her velvet voice.

It might have been the last days of old Hollywood, but it was populated with personalities whose talents set the bar so high that we have never been able to touch it since.

I MUST HAVE had a guardian angel looking after me, because one day Max Arnow ordered me to go to Paramount Pictures for an interview at Batjac Productions. I loved Western movies, *The Searchers* being among my favorites, and if ever I dreamed about doing a Western, it would certainly have been a John Wayne Western. For those of us coming up in the industry, it was considered a prerequisite for us to know about everything and everyone who'd created the world we were inheriting. I couldn't have felt more stupid not to have done my homework sufficiently to know that Batjac was the production company created by John Wayne.

In spite of my negligence, I got the job, and what a job it was. I thought it was too good to be true. I would play John Wayne's and Maureen O'Hara's daughter in *McLintock!*—which was produced by Michael Wayne (eldest son), directed by Andy McLaglen (son of Victor), with Patrick Wayne (second-eldest son) as a love interest, and reuniting with Jerry Van Dyke as the dude. Yvonne De Carlo was also in the cast, as were Bruce Cabot and all of the signature John Ford extras. I was in heaven.

John Ford—aka The Admiral, Uncle Jack, and Pappy—was a consummate filmmaker. Although he was a sentimental man, he had little sense of humor. In fact, he was well known as a tough guy and a dour taskmaster. It was, and is, not uncommon for directors to surround themselves with familiar coworkers, but out of his production team John Ford created a family, assembling a loyal, if not battle-scarred, collection of cameramen, makeup artists, costumers, extras, stuntmen, and actors. This troupe was referred to as the John Ford Stock Company. He made so many movies in Kanab, Utah, and Monument Valley that the tribe of Native Americans consistently hired for those films became known as John Ford's Indians.

Having cast John Wayne in his 1939 film classic, *Stagecoach,* Ford considered it within his proprietary rights to claim responsibility for Wayne's career. Along with Wayne, other members of the Ford family of players—Victor McLaglen, Ward Bond, Maureen O'Hara—would be friends and employees over so many years that he saw the births of all their children and became the godfather to some.

In 1966, I was cast in the remake of *Stagecoach,* produced by Marty Rackin for 20th Century Fox. The costars were Ann-Margret, Bing

Crosby, Red Buttons, Mike Connors, Robert Cummings, Van Heflin, Slim Pickens, and Alex Cord. On the first day of filming, our director, Gordon Douglas, received a one-word telegram from John Ford. The telegram said, WHY?

McLintock! was very much an extension of the Ford tradition, employing many of his original, surviving crew. Bill Clothier, a veteran of seven John Ford movies, was our cameraman; almost all the stuntmen had some prior involvement with Ford; of course, his Indians were imported from Utah; and the sons of Wayne and McLaglen, who had grown up on Ford's movie sets, were running the show.

I was overwhelmed by the privilege of being embraced by this extended family and allowed entry into its fraternity. Even Mom was included, being invited by popular request to appear as an extra in one of the party scenes. When our movie company descended on Tombstone, Arizona, for a week of filming, it was as if there were no other reality but ours. We were the town, and it was difficult to delineate when the day's work ended and real life began. We were in our own dream world, and it lasted for twelve weeks. If, prior to *McLintock!*, my unfulfilled—or unfulfilling—romance with Peter Brown was dying a death, this lengthy location sealed its fate.

The filming sites chosen by the location department were stunning, none more spectacular than the Green Ranch outside Nogales. Situated on a high plateau, with an expansive view of big sky and golden grass, the Green Ranch house acted as a centerpiece for the pastoral grandeur of the unembellished landscape. In order to arrive on that high plain, we had to travel by caravan on a road fashioned from a riverbed, snaking through a gorge that eventually rose to the exploding view of the sweeping and seemingly infinite grasslands.

Never was it more obvious that local knowledge was essential to avoiding eating dust on our daily treks through the gorges. My driver was a local ranch hand, who taught me a trick that I have used ever since. Turning on the car's fan, he shifted the air-intake controls to recirculate, sealing the interior of the car from the chokingly fine powder of the dry riverbed. This handy tip has come to my rescue many times when I have found myself banging along some dirt track in Kenya, Mexico, or India.

After we'd been shooting at the Green Ranch for a while, Andy McLaglen became ill. I was not privy to what transpired in the executive suite, but the next day, when we reported for work, we were told to assemble on the set in full makeup and costumes. The assistant director announced that Mr. McLaglen would not be with us for a few days, that a substitute director was about to arrive from Los Angeles, and that we were to stand by.

No secret is kept for long on a film set. Our substitute director was to be none other than the great John Ford himself. His imminent arrival explained the anxious anticipation that permeated the set, especially coming from the direction of John Wayne and Maureen O'Hara.

Suddenly, there was a hush in the crowd—off in the distance, rising from the familiar river gorges, was a plume of dust heralding the Great Man's arrival. With bated breath, we watched the progress of the plume until the vehicle carrying its precious cargo popped up onto the plain in the distance and headed straight for us. Batjac had sent a car and driver to the Tucson airport to meet Mr. Ford, but in high dudgeon he had shunned the car and boarded a taxi. Because none of Mr. Ford's fledglings had solicited his advice or opinions prior to the start of filming *McLintock!*, he arrived in a cloud of extreme indignation . . . not to mention a cloud of dust.

Employing full dramatic license, Mr. Ford waited for the dust to settle. The taxi door slowly opened. First to emerge was a desert-booted foot, followed by a khaki-trousered leg, then the stained rim of his hat as he rose to full height wearing his soiled and well-worn signature safari jacket with red-knotted neckerchief. He pushed aside John Wayne, who was holding open the taxi door, passed by Maureen O'Hara without acknowledgment, strode up to the diminutive Bill Clothier, his trusty cameraman, and punctured the silence by declaring, "Bill, let's get to work."

With the exception of myself, everyone else in the above-the-titles or costarring cast had already worked for Mr. Ford. Fortunately, I was not prominently involved in any of the scenes scheduled to be filmed during the few days of his presence, and I was quite happy to be a blur in the background, not attracting either his attention or his wrath. But I will certainly never forget his remarkable entrance and the indelible effect it had on us all.

That occasion marked the last time John Ford would ever take his place alongside a motion-picture camera. We will never see his like again.

FOUR

Acting with Authority

—⊗⊗⊗—

Finally, the state of my protracted virginity had reached its due date and I did the deed of darkness. I was not in love, which I had thought was a prerequisite, but I obviously felt the person was appropriate for the task, and with far less fanfare than the event deserved, I was relieved to put it behind me. I do recall looking at myself in the mirror the next day and, seeing no detectable difference, I wondered what all the shouting was about.

Not that this single act opened the floodgates to the pursuit of rabid sexual activity, but I did discover that practice does make perfect. However, for me it is better when sex follows emotional attachment. For most of my life, I have been a serial monogamist. That notwithstanding, I can wholeheartedly join Julio Iglesias and Willie Nelson in saying thanks to all (although far, far less than they) the men I've loved before.

—⊗⊗⊗—

ONE MORNING, in the fall of 1963, I was about to leave my mother's house for the studio, having a late call to work. The phone rang. Mom answered it and called out to me to put on the television.

"They've shot the president," shouted one of the panicked bystanders during the chaos of the live reporting. Mom and I were paralyzed in front of the TV, not wanting to speak in case it might somehow contribute to the still-yet undetermined fate of our King Arthur. Live news reporting on TV was not yet as evolved, provocative, and self-serving as it would become. Reporters and the emergency service personnel were in such a state of shock and panic that the few available details of the incident were repeated over and over again while the world waited.

The New Interns was filming at the Columbia ranch. I did not have a telephone number for the set, or any other way to contact them. So, in the doldrums between the shooting in Dallas and the results from Parkland Hospital, leaving my mother with the gathering friends at our house, I drove to Burbank. They were filming a wild party scene at the time the news reached the cast and crew, and a TV was brought to the set. The balloons, confetti, and paper streamers all seemed to be frozen in time and space as all eyes were glued to the television reporting.

Much has been written about the dreamlike state of the following days, during which we as a nation, and the world as a united people, mourned the passing of the Man and the Hope. Little did we know how much more was to come. The rest of the decade would be turbulent, revolutionary, tragic, and extraordinary: the passage of the Civil Rights Bill; the escalation of America's "police action" in Vietnam; Haight-Ashbury and the hallucinogen-fueled counterculture; the antiwar demonstrations; the rise of the SDS and the Black Panthers; the shooting at Kent State; the riots at the Democratic National Convention in Chicago; the riots at the Sorbonne in Paris; Russia's invasion of Czechoslovakia, crushing the Prague Spring; Woodstock; the first landing on the Moon; and, of course, the assassinations of Martin Luther King . . . and Bobby.

I remember the moment I heard the screams on TV coming from the crowds at the Ambassador Hotel after Bobby delivered his acceptance speech. I had just finished a long day canvassing the city with my team. We were late, so one of the young men from the Justice Department who had been with us on the California campaign came to my house to shower and change before we left for the Ambassador in time to catch if not the speech then the after party. My husband Gary was not a supporter, but nevertheless he was watching the speech on TV. I remember having put one arm into my coat when the screams rang out from the television. I was frozen in my tracks.

The unthinkable had happened—again.

In some kind of fog we found our way to the hotel. Something compelled us to go there; it was impossible to stay away. We saw some of our team, but no one was able to speak, not that there was anything enlightening to say. The bullet had said it all.

In the following days and years, so many of us lost faith. In one short decade, every aspect of the Establishment was challenged, and we as a society even challenged ourselves, enhancing this challenge with sex, drugs, and rock 'n' roll.

BACK IN HOLLYWOOD, which was my real world, my contract with Columbia was in the doldrums. The studio continually passed me over, casting other actresses for roles in movies that I seemed right for, while offering me B-movie scripts just so I would turn them down and then be put on suspension. *Suspension* meant I was off-salary and could not work for anyone else for the duration of the film I had refused. Those weeks were then added to the length of my contract.

Cliff Robertson had gone on suspension so many times that his original seven-year contract had turned into ten years. *Love Has Many Faces* was to be the last picture on Cliff's extended contract, and he was most anxious to be gone from Columbia. The film starred Cliff, Lana Turner, Hugh O'Brien, and me in a love square, not a triangle, which should have given us a clue as to the impending disaster. At the very least, it will go down in the annals of the best bad movies ever made.

We were to film on the beach and in the high desert of Mexico. The legendary costume designer Edith Head was to dress both Lana and me. Miss Head chose to clothe me entirely in beige so that I blended nicely with the background. Lana, on the other hand, was resplendent in costumes of aquamarine, chiffon, sequins, and shocking pink. The director had come to Columbia after his much-applauded success with a black-and-white thriller called *Dark at the Top of the Stairs.* In our initial meetings, Alexander Singer told both Cliff and me that, as writer/director, he was about to do massive rewrites to our parts and our relationship in the film. As he had written it, Mr. Singer's script had literally out-soaped the soap operas.

Feeling much better about the role, I left for Mexico City to visit with family friends who were connected with the bullfight world. Through my darling adopted Mexican family, Paco Ross Oviedo, his daughter Marina, and wife Betty, I was introduced to the inside world of *tauromaquia.* I was fascinated by the traditions of breeding and raising bulls, and impressed by the long, hard struggle it took to become a matador, whose wounds of hunger were sometimes greater than those from the bulls.

The bullfighting world was filled with larger-than-life personalities, whose meticulous adherence to tradition kept alive this ancient ritual. I enjoyed quite a few platonic friendships with the bullfighters themselves, so while in Mexico City, before reporting to the location in Acapulco, I went with the "boys" to watch them train in Plaza Mexico, the world's largest bullring. As we were leaving after they had finished working out, we stopped just outside the bullring, where a street vendor was selling *tortas de lomo,* small, bite-sized sandwiches with a fatty cut of meat that made them *para chuparse los dedos*—finger-lickin' good. We gorged ourselves on *tortas,* and I went back to the house where I was staying to pack my bags and leave for the airport, catching the plane to Acapulco.

By the time I arrived in Acapulco, the *tortas* were doing the Aztec Two-Step in my stomach. There was no one to meet me at the airport, which I thought was odd, but it was even odder when there was no reservation in my name at El Presidente Hotel, where I had been instructed I would be staying. By now, the *tortas* were having a war council to determine which orifice they would attack first. I was willing to accept a broom closet at that point, and so the desk manager obliged. A broom closet was a perfect description of my room.

With luggage piled high into the ten-by-ten-foot space, I spent the night shifting between the bathroom toilet and the sink in the adjacent room. In the morning, with still no contact from the production office and no messages for me at the desk, I did the only thing I could in my weakened condition: I rang Uncle Teddy.

Teddy Stauffer was Mister Acapulco. His past was folklore. He had been the big band leader of the social set in Vienna before leaving Austria when Hitler came to power. Finding his way to Hollywood, he went through five wives, including Hedy Lamarr, and palled around with Errol Flynn. It was on one of Flynn's infamous cruises aboard his notorious yacht, the *Scirocco*, that Teddy found himself stranded in Acapulco. They had dropped anchor in Acapulco Bay and swum to shore at night in what must have been an inebriated state. Teddy awoke in the morning to find himself alone on the beach and the *Scirocco* long gone.

Somehow, he picked himself up and saw in Acapulco a great opportunity. One day, Ted was fascinated by young men who were diving off rocks in a narrow gorge, timing their dives to the incoming waves. "I wonder how high they could dive from," Teddy must have thought, because with encouragement, and by crossing their palms with silver, he created a world-renowned attraction. His restaurant, La Perla, overlooked what he billed as a traditional diving exhibition, and it brought fame and fortune to him and his divers.

Teddy was also the front man for Carl Renstrom, who financed the building of the Villa Vera, the most glamorous hotel in Acapulco, and the first ever to have submerged barstools at one end of the pool, serving swimmers fanciful drinks with miniature umbrellas in them. It was too wonderful. Teddy immediately sent a car for me, and soon I was in the protected bosom of his hospitality. I had left a forwarding address at El Presidente, but it took three days for a panicked production manager to find me. He gave me a call for the first day's filming and I dutifully arrived on the set to find an extremely disgruntled Cliff.

It is an old adage in the motion picture industry that when a director doesn't know what to shoot or how to shoot it, he asks for forty feet of dolly track to be laid, which will take a crew until lunchtime to accomplish. By then, the director might have figured out his shot. This was the case on our first day. Although Cliff and I had been promised rewrites, there were none in sight and none, apparently, to come. It would soon become obvious that the director was so overwhelmed by his budget, his cast, and, most of all, by filming in glorious Technicolor, that he concentrated more on what was going on in the background to fill the frame than on the contents of the scene and the performances of the actors in the foreground.

Cliff had had it. He convinced me that this film would only go from bad to worse, and he asked me how soon I could be packed and ready to leave. Without questioning his authority, I said, "Fifteen minutes." He said, "Okay, I'll pick you up in fifteen," and we left the set with the knowledge we would not be missed until after lunch. I had complete confidence in Cliff, who had always positioned himself as my Dutch uncle.

Aerolineas Mexicana was famous for its non-scheduled airline service between Acapulco and Mexico City. After we arrived at the airport, we were forced to wait in un-air-conditioned bliss for the next aircraft to arrive. All at once, like the posse after the bad guys, a phalanx of vehicles led by a siren-blaring police escort approached the airport in pursuit of us. With the guns of their threats a-blazin', we were persuaded to return to the set.

Things went from bad to worse. Dear Lana was a vulnerable beauty, and in her eyes I saw an unexpected childlike innocence. She was worried about everything, and so nervous that the silk of her dress would quiver from the tremor of her body. She was eager for me to become friends with her daughter Cheryl, and whenever I saw Lana in the years to come, she would always speak to me about Cheryl as if we had indeed grown up together. I liked Lana very much, and I couldn't help but feel concerned for the fragile state of her emotions. That fragile state would even cause us to shut down filming for ten days, during which Lana repaired and I took scuba diving lessons.

While in Mexico, I was sent a script from the studio for a movie called *Fanatic,* to be shot in England. I longed to return to England, which I had visited before, and this seemed a perfect opportunity. What's more, the script and the role were a huge step up from my current predicament. I didn't discover until later that I would be costarring with a legend in her own time: Miss Tallulah Bankhead.

⸺ ∞ ⸺

TALLULAH WAS ILLUSTRIOUS, notorious, provocative, and flirtatious. Over the years, she had become a caricature of herself. The persona of *Tallulah Darling* far surpassed and overwhelmed her talents as an actress, the one thing she took seriously. Her self-destructive streak reared its ugly head throughout her life and career, consequently providing her with such a checkered reputation that many producers would not touch her with a barge pole.

She was, however, a hugely talented actress with a rapierlike wit of such originality that one could clearly say they broke the mold after she was born.

She was born Tallulah Brockman Bankhead to a dynasty of politicians in the state of Alabama. Her mother died shortly after Tallulah's delivery, leaving her father so overwhelmed with grief at the loss of his young wife that his own sister and brother-in-law housed and raised the two Bankhead girls until their father resumed partial custody whenever he was not serving in the state legislature. Tallulah's elder sister, Eugenie, was quiet and sometimes sickly. From a very early age, Eugenie observed that her sister demonstrated "a boisterousness at odds with the codes of gentility."

Eugenie and Tallulah were actually raised within the gilded environment of a post-antebellum South that had never forgotten its glorious past. Their exaggerated pampering was overcompensation for the loss of their mother. Tallulah told me that she had taught herself how to cry at will as a means of garnering attention accompanied by histrionics that always elicited the desired response. Tallulah learned early in life how to manipulate her audience.

When the Barrymores toured the South with a repertoire of plays, the Bankheads lavishly entertained them, and young Tallulah attended every performance they gave, earning her the interest and friendship of Ethel Barrymore. Seeing some theatrical potential in Tallulah, Miss Barrymore offered to help her should she ever decide to come to New York to pursue the theater. That is exactly what Tallulah did.

Whatever Happened to Baby Jane?, starring Joan Crawford and Bette Davis, had been a tremendous hit at the box office, resurrecting the dormant careers of both women. Miss Davis was famous for being one of the first female stars to go public about the indignities that befell leading actresses over forty. She had a needlepoint pillow in her sitting room that read Old Age Ain't for Sissies.

Fanatic—titled *Die! Die! My Darling!* in the U.S.—was Columbia Pictures' answer to *Baby Jane,* although why anyone thought that required a response is beyond me.

Tallulah had not done a movie since *Lifeboat* twenty years earlier, directed by Alfred Hitchcock. She had received rave reviews for *Lifeboat* and had added to her notoriety by famously refusing to wear underpants, inevitably flashing members of the crew and the camera alike. This was a practice that remained constant throughout her life, even on the set of *Fanatic*, embarrassing the respectful British crew as she slouched in her director's chair, cross-legged in a skirt. "I'm a natural blonde, daahling," she would say, "and I'm here to prove it."

Silvio Narizzano, our director, had underestimated the eccentricities of Tallulah, so he was doubly shocked when Tallulah's unfortunate arrival in London precipitated her immediate physical collapse.

Tallulah told me the story of the turning point in her career, which happened to have occurred in London. She had been offered a starring role in a West End play, and on the eve of her departure from New York City she received a cable from her producer, telling her that he had to cancel the production. Ethel Barrymore was in Tallulah's apartment when the cable arrived. Miss Barrymore gave Tallulah this life-altering advice: "You never got the cable. You get on that boat and go to England."

Arriving in Southampton, Tallulah ordered a car to take her to the Ritz Hotel. It was the best hotel in London, and reservation or not, that was where she was going. She even charged the car to her fictional hotel room. "Whatever you do, it has to be done with authority," she told me. "Then everyone will believe you."

Her arrival in London did exactly what Ethel Barrymore had predicted. It forced the producer to do the play, Tallulah triumphed in the role, and it was the making of her career.

When Tallulah materialized in London for *Fanatic,* the Ritz, her hotel of choice, had momentarily fallen on hard times and was not in its customary pristine condition. Whether she tripped or there was a flaw in the brass-covered edging of the stairs at the entrance to the hotel, Tallulah fell over backward, landing on her derriere. Naturally, there happened to be a photographer who captured the entire event, and the following morning, plastered all over the front page of the number one rag sheet, was a photograph of Tallulah on her backside with the banner headline: "Tallulah's Triumphant Return!"

This charming tabloid reception sent Tallulah to her bed. While the rest of the cast filled the time with wardrobe fittings and hair-and-makeup tests, Tallulah was sequestered in her hotel room . . . with a case of "laryngitis." Finally, the day arrived for the start of rehearsals. This was a new practice for me, but it was not unusual for films in England to have a few days' rehearsal, reading through the script and, in some cases, blocking scenes. To this day, it is an efficient and productive means of saving time on the set, and it allows actors and directors to find values in the script that might otherwise go undiscovered due to the pressures of a filming schedule.

The cast included Yootha Joyce and Peter Vaughan, stalwart products of the British theatrical tradition, and Donald Sutherland in his first feature film. We all assembled around the rehearsal table and, having exchanged niceties, we awaited Madam's entrance. And what an entrance it was. Stepping out of her oversized Austin Princess limousine in trousers and an ankle-length mink coat, with her head bent over and her ash blond hair covering her face, she was escorted in, supported on either side by attractive young assistant directors who all but carried her into the room while we, respectably on our feet, stood by.

Tallulah was placed in a chair. Once comfortably situated, she flipped back her shock of hair and, in a weak and crackly but still famously identifiable voice, uttered, "Hello, daahlings. So sorry about my voice. You just carry on." So, carry on we did.

Through all the rehearsals and through the first week of filming, Tallulah was so nervous that her voice failed to improve. Silvio devised a perfect plan. Each day of that first week of production, Tallulah would be called to the set at a civilized hour of the morning, be escorted into hair-and-makeup and wardrobe, break for lunch, and be in the first shot after lunch; it was usually a long shot with no dialog, after which she would be dismissed to return to the Ritz.

On the fifth day, at lunchtime, we were all invited to look at the rushes (the previous four days of work) at a nearby film studio. Tallulah came along and had to endure watching everyone else's scenes, finally seeing herself far in the distance of four long shots. Whether it got her dander up or her professional integrity rose to the surface, Monday morning of the following week Tallulah was fully restored to perfect health and was ready to roll. She grew stronger and more confident daily, even to the point of insisting on doing her own stunt. It was the scene in which I was pushed down the stairs and knocked unconscious, and Tallulah was supposed to pull me under my arms down the final steps and through a door leading to the basement. I outweighed her by quite a bit, so appropriately a stuntman was called in to lift and drag me. When Tallulah saw the stuntman's stocking-covered legs, she bellowed in horror and insisted on doing the dragging herself. With Herculean strength, she reached under my arms, grabbing a handful of tit along the way, and pulled me down the stairs and in through the door, collapsing offscreen. But still, she did it, and she did it her way.

Tallulah's bisexuality had always been suspected, and I can attest to the fact that it was alive and well . . . and that she hadn't lost her touch.

In hindsight, it's hard for me to believe that she was only sixty-three at the time we worked together. The ravages of overindulgence had taken their toll, so you can imagine that it was not necessarily a pretty sight when Tallulah would pound on the wall between our dressing rooms, summoning me to her room, and upon entering I would find her naked on the toilet. Never mind, she was one of a kind, and I adored our brief but colorful friendship. I would always ring Tallulah whenever I was in New York, and her maid, sounding like Butterfly McQueen, would answer the phone. "Oh, hell-o-o-o, Missy Powers," she would say. "I'll get Missy Bankhead for you!"

There were strict hours to call Tallulah, because she religiously watched her soap operas and would not be disturbed. "Missy Bankhead, it's Stefanie Powers on the phone." Tallulah would answer the phone in her unforgettable voice: "Patricia, daahling," always calling me by the name of my character in the film. Fortunately for Tallulah, in her waning years she was surrounded by a covey of acolytes, all exchanging stories and gossip. Once, when I was visiting Tallulah, her entourage begged her to tell the tale of when her cousin had arrived unannounced at her door.

Tallulah had been dressed, jeweled, and perfumed, and about to leave for a dinner party on Park Avenue. There had been a political convention in town, and appearing at her door had been a rather toothy-looking cousin from Alabama. Not knowing what to do with him, she'd taken him with her to the dinner party. As the evening had been coming to a close, the hostess had realized she had not said good night to Tallulah. Looking for her, she'd come across Tallulah in the library of her sumptuous apartment, in the process of going down on her cousin. The hostess had interrupted her, saying, "Tallulah, what on earth are you doing?"

Flipping back her hair, Tallulah had retorted, "Anything, daahling, to get away from that face."

They do not make them like that anymore.

AT THE AGE of twelve, I was given a book on archaeology as a Christmas present, called *Gods, Graves and Scholars*. Since then, I have been besotted with all things Egyptian. I dreamed of visiting the magnificent ruins along the Nile. While still filming *Fanatic*, the London newspapers we were reading carried stories about how the inundation of the valley beyond the Aswan Dam would flood some of the precious temples and tombs of upper Egypt. International teams of archaeologists were racing the clock to relocate gargantuan edifices such as the tomb of Ramses II to higher ground or risk losing them forever under the water, and I wanted to see them.

I assessed my resources, calculated the total cost of a trip—including the credit produced by cashing in our first-class airline tickets in exchange for tourist class—and concocted a plan. Mom was acting as my companion during the filming of *Fanatic,* as provided for by my contract, along with airfares, accommodations, and per diem. In spite of the fact that I was living on a budget, I insisted that Mom allow me to cover all of her expenses.

England and Egypt had severed diplomatic relations, and the closest embassy was in Paris. I came up with the idea of contacting Columbia's man in Paris to inquire if there was anything I could do for the company in France. I was hoping they might provide us with a hotel room for at least part of the two-week waiting period required for visas to Egypt. Columbia's man in Paris was Jack Wiener—then called "Jacques." During my publicity tours on behalf of Columbia Pictures, we became great friends. Jacques understood completely what I was after and said I could leave it with him and he would come up with something.

Columbia had quite an elaborate office in Paris. After World War II and until the late 1970s, Europe and the United Kingdom had currency controls restricting repatriation of funds earned from the release of movies abroad. This created growing caches of frozen funds and required the film companies to establish offices in key cities abroad to oversee their interests. Jacques arranged for us to do one week's worth of publicity for the soon-to-be-released *Love Has Many Faces* along with the recently completed *Fanatic.* He put us up at the George V Hotel for the first week, and for the remaining one he found us a cheap but cheerful alternative. Bless him, we were on our way.

Mom was completely absorbed with acquiring guidebooks and information on Egypt, which we devoured over lunches and dinners. In order to travel light, we planned to send home from Paris all but the barest of wardrobe essentials after the week of publicity. As we would be spending most of our time crawling around the ruins, we decided to restrict ourselves to one "A" outfit along with whatever we would travel in. In those days, people dressed in travel attire.

After our luxurious week at the George V, and according to plan, we shipped our surplus luggage home and moved across town to the wrong side of the Faubourg St. Honoré and the France et Choiseaux, a charming if run-down establishment with toilet and shower down the hall. We had begun our adventure, so any inconvenience was overlooked. Soon after we had organized ourselves in our new abode, our floor was invaded by the first of many jovial and sociable crews from Air India, who brought with them all their necessary foodstuffs and cooking gear. The next week was an epicurean delight, filled with a series of banquets that were generously foisted upon us as a result of our sharing those close quarters. It was unavoidable under the circumstances, but fortunately the food was delicious and the company adorable.

Before we left Paris, Jacques took Mom and me to dinner and gave us the name and contact information for the Columbia man in Cairo—Mohammed Beltagui—in case we needed anything. Gratefully, I pocketed the note in my trench coat, and he wished us bon voyage.

In the mid-1960s, postwar turbojets were still in active passenger service and mass tourism as we know it was at least a decade away. Our plane must have been the last one scheduled to land in Cairo that night, because no sooner had we touched down than they turned off all the runway lights. We taxied to a corner of the tarmac, near the customs hall, and like a scene out of *Casablanca,* the *douane* was constructed out of an old army metal Quonset hut, with one overhanging light illuminating the sign.

We climbed backward down the ladder of steps from the rear of the fuselage and followed the other passengers around the plane toward Immigration & Customs. As we walked, a throng of photographers raced by us, giving the impression that someone of importance was about to descend from the front of the aircraft. Pushed forward through the narrow entry of the hut, we were immediately greeted by the sights, sounds, and smells of the crush of arriving passengers and baggage handlers, all shouting in incomprehensible Arabic.

As the cacophony continued to rise, I glanced behind me and was surprised to find that the horde of photographers had entered the room, accompanied by a man springing up above the crowd, calling out, "I am Mohammed! I am Mohammed!" Today, this declaration might worry some people, but back then, touching the note in my trench coat pocket, it dawned on me that the jumping man was indeed Mohammed: Mohammed Beltagui, the Columbia man in Cairo.

As it turned out, my arrival in Cairo marked the first time since Nasser had assumed power that an American actor's visit coincided with one of their films being shown there. All our best-laid plans dramatically changed, and our "A" outfits got a real workout, given that shops with suitable European-style clothes were nonexistent.

Mom and I made wonderful friends and traveled up the Nile in the privileged company of an expert escort from the National Museum. There were no hotel boats littering the waters of the Nile then; in fact, there were no tourists at all, as evidenced in our snapshot photos, walking through the Valley of Kings and Karnak.

We were allowed entry into the yet-to-be-conserved tomb of Queen Nefertari, and we crossed the Nile on graceful sailboats, called *feluccas*, filled with local people transporting livestock, fowl, and items for barter and trade, as they had done for thousands of years; we walked atop the unfinished obelisk in the rose-granite quarry, where workmen hand-cut monuments for the pharaohs; and we watched the building of the Aswan Dam while drinking pink gin on the veranda of the Victorian-style Old Cataract Hotel. What was to have been two weeks turned into four, and when we said good-bye to our generous hosts and our Columbia man, it was with great reluctance.

In my plan, I had calculated that we could get as far as New York City before running out of air tickets and funds. Once there, we took a page out of Tallulah's life, ordering the taxi to go to the Sherry-Netherland Hotel, where Columbia had put me up on many business trips to the city and where they might accommodate us without a reservation.

I heard the echo of Tallulah saying "always do everything with authority." And so I did. I convinced the desk manager at the Sherry-Netherland that I had sent a cable from Cairo requesting a suite, which he had obviously never gotten. May God not strike me down for lying.

Installing ourselves in our hotel rooms, I rang my friend Bruce Cooper, who was the booker for the *Tonight Show* with Johnny Carson, which still broadcast from New York. My darling Bruce booked me for the show, providing us with two return tickets to L.A. and a small fee just large enough to pay our expenses.

I was young enough to have no fear of living on the edge, and somehow my mother had such complete confidence in me that she never attempted to bail me out.

———

SOMETIME AFTER WE returned to California, I began thinking about buying my own house. The obligatory savings bonds, purchased with the money set aside from my salary as a minor in accordance with the Coogan Law, were maturing, and I had to decide what to do with them. The total revenue was $42,000, and that is what I paid for my first house in Beverly Hills.

My friend, actor George Furth, had just finished decorating his new home and was giving a housewarming party. Lots of people I knew would be attending, so I went to the party on my own. The house was on three levels. I was walking up a narrow staircase, trying to find George, when I rubbed shoulders with someone. As we turned to face each other, I was immediately struck by a sort of heat between us. He was good looking and he radiated sexuality. I recognized him as one of the Hollywood bad boys. We had both been included on that year's *Photoplay* magazine "Stars of the Future" list. Briefly under contract to Elia Kazan in New York, he had played the rapist in *Splendor in the Grass*, starring Natalie Wood and Warren Beatty, and had come to California to play the leading role in a TV series called *The Lieutenant*.

His name was Gary Lockwood.

From U.N.C.L.E. *to Peru*

—❦—

Most parents have hopes and dreams for their children, and they do the very best they can to protect them from taking a road that might not be ideal according to their own assessment of the situation. My mother assessed the situation from the moment Gary arrived to pick me up for our first date, and it was not good.

He did not come to the door; he tooted the horn, and I bounced out and jumped into his car. Not since high school, when a carload of my friends might casually pass by to pick me up, honking the horn to announce their arrival, had anyone collected me for anything remotely resembling a date without respecting the rules of common courtesy and etiquette by coming to the door. Mom had always enjoyed meeting whoever I was going out with of an evening, and we would always wind up having a good laugh before leaving the house. My mother highly disapproved of Gary's lack of manners and was a bit shocked that I was so accepting of his behavior.

I don't think I consciously intended to rebel against what others might have viewed as a sheltered upbringing . . . but I did. I had never known anyone like Gary, and there was something dangerously attractive about him. When the physical attraction moved to the next step, I found out what all the shouting was about. For the first time in my life, I was involved in an irresistible and compelling relationship that I mistakenly interpreted as love instead of lust.

We were dating officially and exclusively in spite of Mom's disapproval. When I closed escrow on my first house, as gently as possible I moved away from her home and influence. It had to happen sooner or later, and we both understood that, but it was my first break from the security of the familiar to the unknown of life on my own terms, and the break was tough on both of us. I was still a late bloomer.

Through my good friend actor Richard Deacon (Mel Cooley on the *Dick Van Dyke Show*), I met Rock Hudson. Rock loved to entertain at home, and it was always stylish and fun. Rock—or Roy to his intimates—invented a ritual Saturday night musical get-together with Richard, Portia Nelson at the piano, Marion Wagner (second wife of Robert), Roy's interior decorator Peter Shore, and a regular host of others—including me. We would all gather around the piano either before or after dinner and sing through entire scores of Broadway musicals. Sometimes we would do charades.

Peter Shore had decorated the homes of many Hollywood notables, including those of Robert Wagner during his marriages to Marion and Natalie. So, I was thrilled when he agreed to help me at a greatly reduced rate with my first house. In the process, Peter taught me the majority of what I know about interior design and created a little jewel of a house that I loved.

Most of the time when I saw Gary he came to my new house. His *bachelor pad* had seen far too much *service* for my taste. Suddenly, Gary had a major stroke of luck—he was cast in Stanley Kubrick's new film, which had the working title of *2001: A Space Odyssey*. We idolized Kubrick, as did most of our generation; he had directed *Paths of Glory, Spartacus,* and *Dr. Strangelove,* and to be cast in one of his films was a huge coup. The film *2001* was shot in England, where Stanley Kubrick lived. Gary left for London and sent for me a few weeks later. His agent, Dick Clayton, had managed to find a flat for Gary to rent during the filming. It belonged to another client of Dick's—Sean Connery and his actress wife, Diane Cilento.

The flat on the Bayswater Road was actually Diane's, and Sean lived there briefly when they were first married, before *007*. After James Bond made him a star, Sean and Diane moved to a large house in Acton and kept the flat as a rental property. Having just completed my education in interior decorating, I was surprised by the look of the flat. Royal blue carpets were complemented by a brown, modern *lounge suite*, a love seat and two chairs, while the white walls were contrasted with ceiling-to-floor draperies of cream background with large red cabbage roses.

When Gary was at the studio, I took the bull by the horns and attacked the offending color scheme. I had the curtains removed, cleaned, and carefully hung in the spare room; I went to the store Liberty on Regent Street, well known for its wonderful fabrics, and bought lengths of hand-dyed Indian cotton in blue and white with which to cover the brown furniture; I bought large pillows to sit on, as well as candles, plants, and incense sticks. It did the trick—a perfect '60s London flat.

The flat came equipped with a charwoman (or *char*, for short). Betty Galpin was a housekeeper who cleaned for a few hours three times a week, for the sumptuous sum of £3. It might have been an acceptable wage in those days, but to me it was slave labor, so on the side I would supplement Betty's take-home. When Gary finished the picture, Betty made sure the flat was immaculate, with its new look intact. However, Diane hated my redecorating and said we had damaged the place.

In retrospect I think Diane was more upset that I had stolen away Betty Galpin. Betty took a leap of faith and came to Beverly Hills to look after me; she stayed for eight years.

———— ✺ ————

BEFORE I'D LEFT L.A. for London, Gary had sent me the script of *2001* to read on the plane. I had never seen a script with so many blank pages. Indeed, much of what was to be shot was in the process of being invented inside the remarkable and innovative mind of Stanley Kubrick. The set of the spacecraft had been erected on the largest soundstage in England, located at MGM in Borehamwood.

The centrifuge wheel of the spaceship taking Gary and Keir Dullea to Jupiter was constructed as a vertical wheel; something like that in a hamster cage, as tall as the soundstage itself. The exterior was covered in plywood, with lights and 16mm projectors bolted to the frame. The projectors were strategically placed and threaded with a loop of film containing animated graphics that would project into the set through computer screens, giving the effect of digital readouts. At the time, pocket calculators did not exist, nothing digital existed, and the average computer took up an entire room. Stanley invented everything, and he hired young Douglas Trumbull to create animated designs simulating digital readouts yet to be conceived.

Gary and Keir worked inside the wheel. There was so little space inside the set that Kubrick directed from outside the wheel, using another of his innovations—a video camera attached to the viewfinder of a 35mm camera, both of which were operated by remote controls outside the set. That set was the most exciting place to be, and it magnetized growing numbers of international scientists from various space agencies, all fascinated by Stanley's inventiveness.

All the visitors would eventually wind up being invited to Stanley's and his talented artist-wife Christiana's dinner table. As those dinners became increasingly larger, so, too, grew the length of the table. I vividly recall sitting between two scientists who were arguing not the feasibility, which they had already accepted, but the methodology of blowing Mars into orbit with the Earth, when the Earth would inevitably become uninhabitable due to pollution and overpopulation. Remember: this was 1966.

I suppose I was technically the first voice of HAL, although my tenure was brief and only during rehearsals. I was immediately replaced by Nigel Davenport, with his mellifluous, deep baritone voice. He lasted a bit longer than me, before being replaced by the androgynous voice Stanley had wanted all along but had needed to compare before committing. One day, I saw Stanley wearing two watches—"Check and double-check?" I asked. Stanley smiled, all-knowing.

There was something else unusual about Stanley. He was able to accept and embrace an idea that bettered his own, no matter where it came from. In this light came the idea for the now-iconic moment that signals the film's intermission. It was late in the afternoon when Stanley began rehearsing with Keir and Gary the pivotal scene when HAL discovers that the two astronauts doubt his abilities. The scene was not going well, and Gary voiced his opinion. Stanley knew the scene was not up to standard, so he said to Gary, "Okay, Lockwood, you go home and come up with a better idea."

Gary returned from work in an intense mood, and I made myself scarce and spent the night at a girlfriend's house. The idea came to Gary around 3:00 a.m. He called Stanley, who sent a car for him, and what they worked out was the lipreading observed by HAL as Dave and Frank discuss disconnecting it. This was largely Gary's idea, although Stanley brought it to life.

There can never be enough said about *2001* and the extraordinary innovations of Stanley Kubrick. As we take for granted our life in the computer-enhanced age, it is important we not forget the time when artistic imagination was self-generated.

⎯⎯⎯∞⎯⎯⎯

WHILE I WAS swanning away in the world of science fiction, MGM was negotiating to buy out my contract from Columbia in order for me to play the title role in a TV series called *The Girl from U.N.C.L.E. The Man from U.N.C.L.E.* was a proven success and they wanted to complement the franchise with a female version. It would turn out to be the first hour-length U.S. television series starring a woman. I returned to L.A., excited by the new venture. At my suggestion, and with help from others, we were able to get Noel Harrison to play my sidekick. Noel was not only the son of Rex but also, on his own—then as now—a wonderful and original singer-composer who would make a great success singing the Michel Legrand/Bergmans title song for the Steve McQueen movie *The Thomas Crown Affair.* But "Windmills of Your Mind" was a couple of years away when we went to work on *U.N.C.L.E.*

The work was extremely demanding, the hours were long, and we were in every shot. The stories concocted for us were like pop art compared with the more "serious" approach of *The Man from U.N.C.L.E.* Nevertheless, we had great fun with the absurd plots of our show, and we had fabulous guest stars: Peggy Lee was a saloon-owning madam in the Old West in "The Furnace Flats Affair," Stan Freberg and I were popped out of a giant toaster in "The Carpathian Killer Affair," and Boris Karloff wore drag in "The Mother Muffin Affair."

The show attracted a rather eclectic audience, and the ratings were reasonably good. One day while we were filming on the MGM lot outside stage 21, where our permanent sets lived, Noel and I were standing on our marks getting ready to do a scene when we looked down the alley between the stages and watched, transfixed, as a woman with an undeniable demeanor walked straight up to us at full throttle. In her distinctive Yankee accent she said, "Spencer and I watch your program all the time." Staring into the face of Katharine Hepburn was so awe inspiring that we could only mumble an unintelligible response with which she turned on her heel and trotted off.

The halls of MGM still echoed with the footsteps of its great stars, whom you would sometimes see having lunch in the commissary—Greer Garson, Robert Taylor, Gene Kelly, Fred Astaire, and Cyd Charisse. Whenever we actually had the opportunity to go to lunch in the commissary, there was always someone notable there. Most of the time Noel and I were slogging away from morning to night at a pace that few television shows use today.

One season of television consisted of twenty-six hour-long shows, each episode of which we produced in five days.

While we were going over the top with story lines, NBC was not amused and thought we should take our jobs more seriously.

After four seasons of *The Man from U.N.C.L.E.* and twenty-nine episodes of *The Girl*, we were both canceled.

IN THE MEANTIME, Gary and I were having a not-too-successful telephone romance, with him still in London. Marriage had never been mentioned between us, so when he gave me the ultimatum that he was either staying on in Europe to travel around or coming home to get married, I found myself saying yes to the latter.

I thought it was the right thing to do, but it was not.

Reluctantly, Mom bought me my wedding dress and gave the family dinner for both sides, but she did not attend the ceremony. Neither did Gary's parents. "Doomed before we took the vows . . ." We took a bunch of friends on a chartered 110-foot yacht and sailed to the island of Catalina, where we married and had a party all weekend. Oddly enough, I still remember that as the ring went on I said to myself, "This is not forever."

Nearly eight years later, our marriage was over. But then it was over long before it ended. Finally, we had to agree it was useless to carry on such a charade. The day I chose to leave was a Sunday, and it just happened to be Mother's Day. Amazingly, all my clothing was able to fit into my car—something that certainly wouldn't happen today—so I put all the clothes in my car, the cat in a carrying cage, and left for my mother's house. My friend Roddy McDowall knew I was having a difficult time, and he had invited me to his Mother's Day party in case I was free. In a daze, I stopped by Roddy's house to find it full of friendly faces.

I discovered Roddy talking to two women on the sofa. He jumped to his feet as he saw me come across the room and asked if I was all right. I must have looked as if I was in a state. Then he turned to the two women he had been talking with and said, "Do you know each other?" I looked at them and, for some reason, burst into tears and said, "I'm getting divorced."

One of the women said, "So am I."

The other said, "It happens to all of us, honey, you look like you need a drink."

"So am I" was Elizabeth Taylor.

"You need a drink" was Ava Gardner.

Ava escorted me to the bar and poured me a water glass filled with vodka. We talked all night and became friends for life.

Ava even came out of semi-retirement to appear in the role of my sister-in-law in a TV pilot called *Maggie,* filmed in London, where she lived. It was my friend John Huston who came to my rescue to convince Ava to trust our cameraman and work again. Ava had had a dreadful experience during her previous time in front of the camera, guest-starring on *Falcon's Crest* in California—she was lit so badly that she never wanted to work again. However, our cameraman Tony Imi was, and is, a rare species who still knows how to light women beautifully, and he made Ava look wonderful.

Sadly, *Maggie* was the last piece of film Ava would appear on, and I am proud to say that she never looked better and was very pleased with the results. I often wondered, *What if the pilot had sold? What if we had been working? Would she have fallen ill, the last illness that led to her physical decline?* But it is always pointless to dwell on such things. There are many things I remember fondly about Ava: how she moved; how she extracted a cigarette from a pack and rolled it around before lighting it. I think she was the most naturally sensual person I have ever met. She was also a true girlfriend.

In spite of the emotional roller coaster that best describes the years of my marriage, those same years were not without their high points. I seemed to be constantly working, either in films or on TV, as Gary became increasingly selective about his work. I had to fuel our real estate and construction projects by accepting all the work I could manage. Some of the work was not bad, some of it I have long forgotten, and some of it was so ridiculous I can't help but remember.

ONE FILM, A Western called *Gone with the West* (aka *Bronco Busters,* aka *Little Moon and Jud McGraw*), stands out as one of the most colossal turkeys of that period: a gang of outlaws attacks the remote ranch of a young couple, killing their child, raping and killing the wife, and beating up the rancher. For some reason I cannot recall, the rancher winds up in prison, and when he is let out, he resolves to find and kill all the outlaws. During the years of the rancher's incarceration, the outlaws have taken over the entire town, which they supply with a full bar and a bevy of prostitutes. One day, an unwitting young Mexican-Indian woman arrives in town and she is immediately attacked, violated, stripped of her clothing, and publicly tormented, leading her to seek retribution equal to the revenge sought by the rancher. While riding through the Valley of Fire, the rancher comes across the Mexican-Indian woman bathing herself, her wounds, and her blemished pride. The two join forces, eventually killing everyone in town and burning it to the ground.

The cast featured James Caan as the rancher; Aldo Ray as Mimmo, the head outlaw; Robert Walker Jr. as the sheriff; and Sammy Davis Jr. in a cameo appearance as the pistol-packin', gun-twirlin' Kid Dandy. I, a freckle-faced redhead, was perfectly typecast as the Mexican-Indian. And some of the prostitutes played themselves.

We began filming the interiors at a studio that formerly housed American International Pictures, near downtown Los Angeles. The outlaws and the prostitutes were involved in most of the first two weeks of filming, so they were well established in the movie and with each other. My first day, I was called around noon and directed to the second floor of a building that housed all of the dressing rooms. As I ascended the two flights of stairs, the echo of my steps must have announced my arrival, because, stopping on the top landing, I saw naked bodies streaking across the hall from one bank of dressing rooms to another, and, entering my designated room, I found used towels everywhere. I had obviously interrupted business as usual.

It got worse.

After two weeks of work, I had not received a salary check, leaving me no alternative but to threaten the producer with not showing up the following day. That night, there was a knock at my door. Two men in black suits entered, one carrying a black leather bag, which he handed to me. Inside it was a lot of cash. In fact, it was the full sum of my guaranteed salary for the picture. This was a first for me, and also a last.

When we moved for exterior locations to Las Vegas, the entire company was housed downtown at the Mint Hotel. In those days, downtown Las Vegas was more down than town. The very first night after we arrived, the desert surrounding Las Vegas was hit by a ferocious windstorm, doing much damage to the environs and blowing down the set of our outlaw town. The shooting schedule was immediately revamped, causing the production to keep on hold and on salary all the outlaws, stuntmen, and prostitutes while they rebuilt the town and shot everything they could with James Caan and myself.

This pleased some of the cast enormously and allowed them to pick up a little extra needed change. We would meet them at 5:30 in the morning as we were leaving the hotel and they were coming home. Some of the girls would generously try to give me their "elixirs," lest I find myself in need of a 10:00 a.m. pick-me-up or a 9:00 p.m. downer. At their insistence, I would pocket the pills for later disposal down the toilet.

Early on in the production, I did the best acting of my life, attempting to convince our director that, except for a few sentences of expositional dialog, nothing that I had to say in the film was relevant to the story and could just as easily be said in Spanish, adding to the "authenticity" of my role, which had previously been aided only by the use of dark makeup and a long black wig. Miraculously, he agreed. I have no idea what medication he was on at the time.

After Jimmy Caan finds me bathing in the Valley of Fire, he gives me some of his clothes and a hat to wear. Throughout the movie, I seemed to be running after Jimmy spouting insignificant rantings in Spanish, like some sort of cross between the Little Tramp and Cantinflas. Periodically, after we completed a scene, Jimmy would look at me and say, "We will never work again after this movie comes out." Thank God he had a sense of humor. It got us both through the production.

One night after shooting, Jimmy asked me if I wanted to come with him to meet a friend of his who was appearing at Caesars Palace. We were to meet his friend in the Caesars Palace coffee shop between shows. As we arrived at the entrance to the restaurant, we heard the booming voice of Don Rickles shouting from a booth in the back, "Here they are! Big stars! James Caan and Stefanie Powers staying at the *Mint!*"

⊶⊷

DEAR BETTY GALPIN was always keeping the home fires burning, no matter how late I came home from work or how long I was away on location. Betty had been a young woman during the London blitz, and she told me endless stories about the war and the food shortages that had forced everyone to invent new ways of cooking such delicacies as eggless cake and meatless meat loaf. As a result, she could make the most wonderful surprise meals out of the barest essentials.

One of my girlfriends was also an excellent cook, but her specialty was brownies. Brandy's brownies were laced with either pot or hashish, and her technique was so perfected that there was no trace of aftertaste, and the experience was as delicious as the brownies. While I was at work one day, Brandy dropped off a freshly made batch, which she told Betty to put in the fridge. Sometime that afternoon, my mother stopped by my house to drop something off, and Betty, being a proper Englishwoman, offered Mom tea. Along with the tea, Betty decided to serve a few of the "lovely cakes" Brandy had brought that were "*ever* so nicely wrapped in foil."

God only knows how long their tea party lasted, but they went through about half of the stash. Later, I came home with some friends in tow, and while we were sitting in the living room, having drinks and talking, Betty Galpin, stepladder and bucket in hand, walked out of the kitchen, through the dining area, into the sitting room, set up the ladder, and began to wash the walls. Struck dumb by her performance, I broke the bemused silence by asking Betty what she was doing.

She responded by saying, "It's got to be done, dear. It's got to be done."

The next day, after speaking with Brandy, I put two and two together and immediately rang my mother, fearing for her life.

ME: How are you?

MOM: *Very* well.

ME: I understand you came to the house yesterday and had tea with Betty.

MOM: Yes, we had a *lovely* time.

ME: *Really*. What happened when you got home?

MOM: Funny you should ask. I don't know what came over me. I felt so sleepy, I lay down for a nap and didn't wake up until this morning!

I didn't tell either of them what they had eaten until sometime later, when they were at a safe enough distance to appreciate their trip into hipdom.

RECREATIONAL DRUGS WERE everywhere in the 1960s and early '70s. In Brazil, they were openly part of traditional life and religion. I was invited to attend a film festival in Rio de Janeiro, and it was a perfect pretext for a trip around South America. Rio was still relatively safe to walk around in, as was the beach in front of the Hotel Copacabana, where I stayed. I was eager to explore all the places I had seen in the movie *Black Orpheus*, which I had watched three or four times.

I became friendly with two young filmmakers whose upper-middle-class background perfectly positioned them to be revolutionaries. Revolution was in the air—Che Guevara had been captured and shot in Bolivia, and his associate Régis Debray was in Camiri prison, awaiting extradition to France. Young South American filmmakers were challenging the Establishment as their counterparts were doing in the U.S.A., so Julio and Neville appointed themselves my official tour guides. When I expressed an interest in Macumbo, a mixture of African voodoo and Christianity, they took me to a park on the outskirts of Rio where open-air ceremonies occurred in the midst of sacred trees and hallowed ground.

The air was permeated with the smoke of the cigars everyone was puffing on. Something about the aroma was different. In a flash, I got it. What passed as a joint of marijuana up north was rolled into a cigar down south, and all you had to do was inhale the secondhand smoke and you were away. The smoke was, in fact, part of a spiritual cleansing ritual. We came away from our visit cleaner than clean.

I went on to Buenos Aires to stay with a friend of mine who had worked for Columbia Pictures. Living up to its reputation, Buenos Aires was one of the most beautiful cities in all the Americas. It seemed to me that everyone on the street was impeccably dressed. Almost every man, except the workers repairing the roads, wore suits and ties.

Fernando Lamas had guest-starred in one of *The Girl from U.N.C.L.E.* episodes, and he had regaled me with stories about Argentina and the Argentine male, of his pride, exemplified by this expression: *Tocame algo, pero no jodas con mi ropa.* Roughly translated: "You can touch me, but don't fuck with my clothes." He also gave me his classic description of an Argentine: "An Argentine is an Italian who speaks Spanish but thinks he's English." Thank you, Fernando, for those unforgettable words of wisdom.

Unfortunately, I wasn't as yet playing polo, otherwise I would have stayed longer, but after a week of tango bars and wonderful hospitality I moved on to Bolivia to begin the expedition phase of my trip. I had longed to visit the ruins of Machu Picchu, and I also wanted to cross the highest navigable lake in the world, Lake Titicaca. The gateway to those delights was through Bolivia. Off I went with no regard for, and no medication against, the consequences of the altitude I was to encounter in La Paz.

At 12,008 feet above sea level, La Paz is the world's highest capital city. No sooner had we landed than I was struck by a horrendous headache. Fortunately, it took no time at all to clear customs and find a taxi to the hotel that had been recommended to me by a friend in Buenos Aires. I was sick as a dog for two days, until the manager of the hotel suggested I drink some tea called *maté de coca.* Throughout their history, the descendants of the Inca have chewed, drunk, smoked, and processed the leaves of the coca tree as both a sedative and a stimulant. I was told that some of the old families had "cooks" who passed from generation to generation the secrets of cooking the leaves for the desired effects. My desired effect was definitely achieved, and overnight I was acclimated. I looked at my carton of Marlboro cigarettes and decided we had to part company. The idea of anything interfering with my lungs' full capacity to assimilate all the oxygen available was out of the question.

There were very few tourists traveling the Andes in the late '60s. Most of my fellow travelers were Europeans with backpacks. One young German student attached himself to me on the bus to Lake Titicaca and was good company as we carried on across the lake, on the train to Cuzco, and up the narrow trek to Machu Picchu. The lake was, indeed, magical. At the turn of the twentieth century, twin steam-powered passenger boats were brought from England, carried overland to Bolivia, and reassembled on the lakeshore to begin service from the Bolivian side of the lake to the Peruvian, crossing each other nightly. For years, the boats saluted each other as they passed in the night with a short toot of their steam whistles; that lovely sound brought forth in all of us passengers a nostalgia for a bygone age.

These small vessels, perfectly maintained, were miniaturized versions of the grand ships of their day. The freshwater of the lake served to preserve the beautifully polished brass adornments and mechanisms, including the exquisite gas lamps that cast a period glow in the grand salon. The spectacle of the star-filled sky, and the sounds and smells of the environment, were so intoxicating that I spent the night wrapped in a blanket, sitting on the deck. There was a momentary suspension of time, and I wanted to absorb the entire experience.

In the morning, as we approached the Peruvian side of the lake, we observed one of the phenomena that Titicaca is famous for—the *water steps* that seem to defy explanation. How can there be a current in a lake? Perhaps it is the result of a magnetic field. Whatever the reason, there they were, steps in various locations, as if the water was cascading down a cement stair going nowhere.

A small-gauge steam-powered train awaited us in Puno. We disembarked and said good-bye to our divine watercraft, only to board yet another mode of transportation out of the last century for the twelve-hour ride to Cuzco. We were traversing the *alte plano* (high plains) at 14,000 feet, with regular stops along the way, during which Indians would appear out of nowhere, approaching the train with hot corn on the cob that had been barbecued on an open fire and, of course, *maté de coca*. Both were consumed with the relish of a five-star meal. I recommended this trip to some friends four or five years later. By that time, mass tourism had descended, sadly corrupting the beauty, simplicity, and authenticity of the people and their services.

Cuzco was very much as it must always have been, serving the area as the major center of commerce and trade for the highlands. The market square was a shopper's paradise, presenting colorful arrays of handicrafts, all with practical applications. I could not resist the brilliantly colored ponchos, intricately woven of llama wool, whose tight weave and natural oils made the fabric impervious to rain.

After our bus broke down, we were forced to climb the narrow track leading up to Machu Picchu. The mist was just burning off, exposing ruins that took our breath away. It was said that special recipes for coca leaves were employed to stimulate the construction of this magnificent, religious city in the clouds, and its mystical vibrations were still very much intact. The tiny hotel at the entrance to the ruins was fully booked, so my German friend and I, along with two others who had joined us, spent the night in the ruins with pillows and blankets loaned to us by the hotel, which was more like a hostel. Fortified by bread, cheese, and wine purchased on the way to Machu Picchu, which seemed like a feast in the cold night air, we tucked ourselves into the corners of the remaining walls in the sacred city and, with the light of a full moon, attempted to sleep in spite of the exciting surroundings.

In the morning, I was awakened by the soft puffing of sniffing breath around my face. I opened my eyes to find a herd of llamas, attracted by bread crumbs, acting as my wake-up call. I was in heaven. It is always a difficult adjustment to return to the blaring sounds, frenetic activity, and human aggression intrinsic to the cities of the developed world. I was still wearing my beloved poncho when I arrived in Los Angeles and was regarded with suspicion by Immigration and Customs, who tore apart my luggage in the hope of finding something incriminating. Disappointed, they brushed me aside, leaving me to attempt the reassembly of my strewn possessions into their previous neatly packed inventory, which had been perfectly accommodated in my suitcases. Of course, it was impossible to do this.

Once again, I *schlepped* my belongings to a taxi, forever undaunted by the indignities of travel.

EACH TIME I returned from Europe, whenever possible I chose to sail on one of the last remaining luxury liners, which made those crossings a gentle alternative to air travel. Beautiful and graceful, ships such as the *Queen Elizabeth* and the *France* were relics of a time when the enjoyment of life was elevated to a fine art. Even if the harsh reality of landing in New York City was a jarring experience, the pleasures of the previous five days made it well worth the price.

I crossed four times on the *France,* giving me an opportunity to meet both captains while enjoying the privileges of regular visits to the bridge and their private quarters. My special status was due to the success in France of the TV series they called *Annie Agente Secret . . . The Girl from U.N.C.L.E.*

My voracious appetite for travel began in Mexico, where I first learned a language and a culture. Columbia Pictures expanded my horizons by sending Mom and me to Japan and several times to Europe to publicize the release of films. We always managed to fit in side trips, further exposing us to languages and the customs of other cultures. I was the happy inheritor of a talent descended from my grandmother, whose name, Zofja, I also inherited. *Baci* ("grandmother" in Polish), at one time in her life, learned fourteen languages due to her diplomat father having been posted around Middle Europe and the Balkans. Blindly fearless and naively positive, I thought that by total immersion and some sort of osmosis I might be able to learn other languages. This was partially true, but I also needed and received tremendous help through books and supportive friends.

What resulted is a passing knowledge of seven languages: Polish was before English; Spanish, which I speak almost daily; French, which was enhanced by marriage; Italian, which became a necessity; Kiswahili, the Arabic-based trade language that united the tribes of East Africa; and Mandarin Chinese.

But that is another story. . . .

My Silvano

———— ∞∞∞ ————

Although it certainly wasn't my motivation for marrying Gary, after the fact it occurred to me that might now be in a position to resolve my feelings of commitment to Silvano and my four-year attempt to help him either through adoption or by fostering. The road to Silvano was one of the most unusual journeys of my life, and it began while I was in high school, when an unexpected encounter was triggered by an unlikely source.

Just prior to auditioning for *West Side Story,* one of my "big brothers" completed his obligatory military service and came to stay a few days with us. Mom was a surrogate mother to a collection of my brother's friends, who from time to time took it upon themselves to act as my protectors. It proved embarrassing more than once when some of them would show up at a party I was attending and simply take me home if they didn't approve of my date. Ernie Baltzel had been a star football player in high school, and the army had filled out his physique even more. The only time he felt comfortable showing his gentler side was when he would come to see Mom, and he felt similarly open with me.

Ernie was big, and although he had a heart of gold there was also an extremely aggressive side that had put him in trouble more than once. One day, he told me a story he had kept secret from everyone else: over a period of time, and at different locations, total strangers, seemingly unconnected to one another, had approached Ernie, saying they had a message for him while giving him a piece of paper with an address on it. Out of curiosity, after the third or fourth time, he decided to go to the address and investigate. The address took Ernie to a house in Watts, a black neighborhood that would become prominently associated with the 1965 race riots in L.A. In the 1960s it was neither a common occurrence nor a particularly safe one for a white person to appear in that part of town.

It was evening when Ernie arrived. The light above the door of the house cast a greenish glow; the door was partially open, so he walked in. The parlor of the house had been converted to a meeting room with a lectern at one end. The guests appeared to be more of a congregation than an assembly as they began to sing gospel songs from a hymnal. The leader of the group was an ample, joyful woman wearing a choir robe. She smiled at Ernie, welcoming him in, and as the congregation finished its song she came over to him, introduced herself as Willie Mae Flowers, and, putting her hand gently on his shoulder, said to him that he should not waste his time with all his anger. It would do him no good at all.

At this, Ernie broke into tears and felt a great heat engulf him with a feeling of love. He did, in fact, struggle with his violent side, so it was unbelievable that this total stranger to whom he had been directed should know so much about him. Ernie wanted to see Willie Mae Flowers again, but he was not anxious to go alone, so he asked me to go with him. The circumstances were exactly as he described them to me: we drove to Watts and saw the green glow of the light over the door, and as we entered, the assembly of people were singing gospel hymns along with Willie Mae herself.

We sat in the back of the room. Willie Mae finished singing, looked up from her hymnal, and focused on someone in the audience. She looked at a man sitting in the front row as if there had been no one else in the room and walked over to him to say something I couldn't hear. I was the next person she looked at. As she did, I felt my eyes fill with tears, and a great heat came over me. Willie Mae walked up to me and said, "Oh, child, don't be worrying about what you're gonna do, it's nothing like what you think you're gonna do . . . you got lots of studying to do, but they're not books, they're bigger than books and they have soft covers." Then she turned away and that's all she said.

The people who had been spoken to by Willie Mae began to leave, so we took that as our cue and also made our exit. I never thought about that night again until almost two years later, when I walked back to my chair on the set of *The Interns* and picked up my script. As I did, I heard Willie Mae saying, "They're bigger than books and they have soft covers." A *script*. She was describing a script. How could that have been? I was overwhelmed by the epiphany. I had to see her again.

Somehow, I found my way back to Watts. There was the house with the green glow coming from the light over the door. The scene was exactly as I remembered it, gospel songs and all. After putting down her hymnal, Willie Mae spoke with a few people, and then she turned and looked straight at me with her intense focus, as if there had been no others in the room. As she approached me, I felt the same heat and my eyes filled with tears. She told me that she saw me with a boy-child; we were walking hand in hand; he was not mine but he would be like mine.

A YEAR LATER, Mom and I were touring Europe, publicizing the opening of *The Interns*. We began our tour in Paris, then went to five cities in Germany, then Vienna, and finally Rome. Throughout the trip, I did endless obligatory starlet-type photo shoots, posing in front of all the major monuments. By the time we got to Rome, I was desperate to find another way to accommodate the journalists and their photographers. When I asked the Columbia PR woman, Maude Muller, if she could help me in this respect, she left the room and came back with a newspaper.

That morning, the Vatican had given out its annual honorable mentions and medals to people in Rome who had performed acts of kindness and goodwill. One man stood out from all the rest as the potential object of a publicity opportunity that might satisfy the photographers *and* me while doing something worthwhile. His name was Marecello André Azzena, and he and his wife had a simple house in the poor suburbs of Rome where they sheltered abused and abandoned children. There were twenty-seven children in the home, varying in ages from three to thirteen.

Maude organized gift bags with shoes and sweaters, candy and toys, for each child, and a large basket of food supplies for the home. We packed ourselves and all of the items into several cars and, followed by an army of journalists and photographers, we arrived at the home of Marecello and Signora Azzena. All the children had been forewarned, and the entire household awaited our arrival with great excitement. The dwelling was clean but sparse; perfectly swept dirt floors ran throughout the house; the dormitories consisted mostly of mattresses on the floor; there was no hot running water; and electricity was rationed. Still, everyone did their best to keep everything spotless, and their pride shone in their smiles and in the sheer happiness of the atmosphere created by the Azzena family.

All at once, I locked eyes with a nine-year-old boy. Maybe it was the excitement of the moment; maybe it was his recurring dream he told me he had years later of a woman whose language he did not understand but who he knew was more important to him than his mother. The boy rushed into my arms, gave me a big hug, and wouldn't let go of my hand. The pictures I have from that day are as close as possible to the scene Willie Mae Flowers had described to me years before. Mom and I were determined to do something to help the children, the Azzenas, and the boy called Silvano.

I began to speak with everyone I met in Rome on that trip and started collecting donations, which I matched, and so did Mom. I carried on collecting funds in the States, and eventually we were able to provide the home with cement floors, hot water, a proper electrical supply, and—their pride and joy—a washing machine. I was corresponding with Silvano the whole time while trying to figure out how we could help him. Mom and I had already visited the appropriate embassies to enquire how we might adopt Silvano, but with me under twenty-one and unmarried, Uncle Jack no longer in the picture, and Mom a divorcée, there was no way the Italian government would approve us to adopt. The U.S. government had a quota system that was so full the waiting list was years long. To single out Silvano for help over and above all the other children would also be impossible. Boarding school was ruled out because he would have to go home during vacations and the only home Silvano could go to was very different from those of his schoolmates. We were advised that boarding school could have disastrous emotional consequences. Everything we thought of turned into a dead end.

Each year, I would visit Silvano, and our relationship grew. In helping the entire home, I was indirectly helping Silvano. So, until another arrangement could be made, all was working reasonably well. Chuck Painter, a publicist I knew from MGM, moved to Rome, and I was able to get him involved in my cause. Chuck grew very fond of Silvano and would invite him out from time to time, becoming Uncle Chuck. By the time I was able to introduce Gary to Silvano, the boy was thirteen and considered an adult by the U.S. embassy. I had hoped Gary might take to the idea of us adopting Silvano but having him live with my mother, but sadly, he never did.

One of the great disappointments of my marriage and probably the biggest nail in its coffin had to do with Gary's rejection of Silvano.

Over the years, Silvano and I stayed in touch and saw each other whenever possible. Meanwhile, I would send Chuck funds to buy Silvano clothes, books, and other necessities. In 1979, Silvano was finally able to come to the United States, on a student's visa. I was just beginning to work on *Hart to Hart*, and living between Beverly Hills and Palm Springs with

Bill Holden. Bill was very touched by the saga of Silvano's and my relationship; he even bought Silvano a motorcycle as a means of transport and independence. We found odd jobs for Silvano while he went to school to study English.

My good friend Tom Mankiewicz introduced Silvano to Cubby Broccoli, who was looking for someone to work around his house. The Italian connection was made. "Don Broccoli" was not only Bill's former agent but he had also become a very successful independent film producer, creating the 007 franchise that is carried on today by his daughter, my dear friend Barbara, and his stepson. More important than all his credits put together, Cubby Broccoli and his wonderful wife, Dana, were warm, caring, generous people. Cubby loved the fact that Silvano knew how to make homemade pasta, and they would have cooking sessions late into the night alone in the kitchen.

One famous night, they were having a midnight snack, and Silvano, anxious to find a way to remain in the States, broached a rather delicate subject with his boss. As it was recounted to me, the conversation went something like this:

SILVANO: Signore Broccoli . . .

CUBBY: Yes, Silvano?

SILVANO: Signorina Barbara [Cubby's daughter], she's a *wonderful* girl.

CUBBY: Yes, she is, Silvano.

SILVANO: I think she like me!

CUBBY: Yes, Silvano, we *all* like you.

SILVANO: *Ma,* Signore Broccoli, what if I could marry Signorina Barbara? Then I could become American citizen!

CUBBY: Yes, Silvano, that's true . . . But why would you want to become a *dead* American citizen?

In the end, Silvano returned to Italy, where the system was easier for him to negotiate. It turned out to be for the best. Silvano opened his own business and with a bit of help has worked his way up to a modest but comfortable lifestyle, which now includes a wife, three children, dogs, and an exotic bird. We still consider each other family, and whatever fate put us together, we are completely grateful for the good fortune.

SOMETIME AFTER MY divorce from Gary, I was subletting a small house off Benedict Canyon from a high school friend. One of my neighbors invited me to a dinner party at their home. As I walked in the door, the hostess said to me that they had hired a clairvoyant for the night, and if I wanted to have a reading before dinner I could go down the hall to the guest room, where the woman was waiting.

I entered the guest room and saw a pleasant-looking black woman, who looked at me, smiled, and said she had a message for me from Willie Mae. I was stunned. I had not thought of Willie Mae Flowers in years. The woman went on to say that Willie Mae was on the Other Side and wanted me to know she was doing fine and feeling happy.

I told the woman to give Willie Mae my regards, and I hope she got them.

SEVEN

"Hi, Bill Holden"

———— ◆◆◆ ————

D ivorce left me with a sobering personal inventory: I was without a place to live; everything I had earned over nearly fifteen years of work was invested in half-finished construction projects; and our two-and-a-half-acre lot in Malibu, fronted by a private beach, was tied up in litigation. It was 1972, the Golden State was involved in a mortgage crunch, and, on top of that, restrictions on the development of all properties within the mist off the ocean were being imposed by the newly formed Coastal Commission, fueled by Proposition 21. All our real estate investments were near, or on, the beaches of Southern California.

We were paralyzed, unable to liquidate any of our holdings, and we had no choice but to continue supporting them, putting a great strain on my finances, which had been reduced to very few digits. Since I was, at that point, the main source of all cash flow, I had no choice but to roll up my sleeves and, like Scarlett O'Hara, embark on reconstructing my life and my net worth. I looked up to the sky and vowed, "They're not going to lick me. I'm going to live through this, and when it's all over, as God is my witness, I'll never be hungry again."

———— ◆◆◆ ————

GRADUATION FROM HIGH school had marked the end of my formal education. Now, years later, I found myself embarrassed by my lack of knowledge and ignorant of the books people referred to. Someone to whom I'm eternally grateful gave me a very simple solution: I was told that the average English course at university required reading roughly two hundred books for a bachelor's degree. All I had to do as a California resident and taxpayer was call the English Department at UCLA and ask for the reading list. For the better part of the next two years, I spent every moment of my free time devouring not only the two hundred books but also the complete works of almost every author on the list. I made up my mind I did not want to be a victim.

So many women, then and even now, followed an odd traditional thinking passed down for generations that assumed "a woman's place is in the home," and that anything as weighty as the most rudimentary understanding of financial matters was far too heavy for us to bear. This emotional blackmail and brainwashing conditioned many women to leave the subject of money in the hands of their husbands, only to become disoriented, dismayed, and sometimes dispossessed when their husbands died or left them.

But at the end of the day, it is not how we are regarded by others that counts but how we regard ourselves. So, with determination, I set a new course. My trustworthy and conscientious business manager was a woman called Mini McGuire. I was blessed to have her in my corner. I always had the impression that if I telephoned Mini in the middle of the night, waking her from a deep sleep, she could rattle off my bank balance. I told Mini I wanted to learn everything I could about money management. I wanted to learn every aspect of investing, the pitfalls of real estate, how to assess risk, and how to domino investments in order to rebuild my crumbled house of cards. Mini gave me the foundation of a fundamental understanding. Building on that, with homework and guidance from many advisers and qualified friends, I began to absorb information like a sponge.

⚬⚬⚬⚬

IN 1973, MY high school friend Doug Grant was about to follow his heart and the sunset to Hawaii, and he wanted to sublet his cottage-style house off Benedict Canyon. Yoakum Drive was a perfect place to hang my hat. The houses were so small and so close together, and the neighbors so friendly, that we could—and did, frequently—call out to announce that we were serving breakfast, coffee, or drinks, and if any one of us wanted company we would soon have a houseful. The atmosphere was like a village: an artists' colony with musicians, composers, actors, writers, and comedians. The added advantage was that the neighborhood seemed to attract the newly unwed, all of whom were starting over. It was a perfect place for me.

Charitable events have often been called a euphemism for social life; that notwithstanding, they have also raised an enormous amount of money for good causes. Since the days of the Hollywood Canteen, actors have always made themselves available when called upon to help. In the 1970s, pro celebrity tennis tournaments were very popular as fund-raisers. Seriously good players participated in these tournaments, and they were great fun.

I *loved* playing tennis, but in the beginning I was not on the A-list. Charlton Heston took the game very seriously, Clint Eastwood looked great on the court and was a good competitor, and Abby Dalton was the best of all the actresses. My game eventually improved with practice, and after a while, with coaching from Debbie Irwin, I was not too bad. So I became one of the regular players on the circuit. The La Costa resort near San Diego played host to several of the tournaments, and one of them in particular would change my life.

The first time I saw William Holden in the flesh was at a New Year's Eve party given by Dominick Dunne and his wife, Lennie. The Dunnes gave their party every other year, and it was *the* New Year's Eve party to go to. Dominick and Lennie created such a comfortable atmosphere that literally behind every potted palm was a recognizable face.

Every so often, my friend Moss Mabry, a costume designer, would call to invite me out, first asking, "Are you involved with a man, dear?" I would say, "No, Moss, are *you*?" We would laugh and then go to some fabulous party he wanted to attend. New Year's Eve found us at the Dunnes'. Moss had gone for drinks, and I was standing alone. As I turned, the man behind me also turned, and I was face-to-face with William Holden. I blushed. He smiled. He said, "Hi, Bill Holden." I somehow made a sound that resembled speaking and said my name. Moss returned, Bill lifted his glass, said, "Happy New Year," and moved on. His smile always lit up the room, and when he walked away the temperature of the air seemed to drop.

A few years later, I was browsing the shelves at Hunters' bookshop on the corner of Rodeo Drive and Santa Monica Boulevard in Beverly Hills. I began looking at photographic books on Africa, relishing the shots of animals and landscapes, when an unmistakable voice behind me said, "Try this one." I turned to see that face and smile. "Hello, again," I said. "We met at the Dunnes' a few years ago."

I felt stupid the minute those words left my mouth. How could he possibly have remembered that brief meeting? Still, graciously he said, "Oh, yes, how nice to see you again. Are you interested in Africa?"

"Yes," I replied, "I've been to Egypt but never farther south."

"Well, if you ever get to Kenya, look me up," he said, and he was gone.

Look him up? Oh, sure, I thought.

As they say in the movies, fade out, fade in.

Much water had gone under both our bridges when we met again at La Costa. Merv Adelson was one of the owners of the La Costa resort; he was also a principal partner in Lorimar Productions, which produced a mini-series called *The Blue Knight,* starring William Holden and Lee Remick. Merv gave a cocktail party for everyone involved in the tennis tournament, and since Bill was staying at the La Costa Spa for a week, Merv invited him to the party.

I don't know why Bill decided to attend, as he was normally a loner, but happily he did. We met again, and by now, while he might very well not have remembered our previous meetings, he had seen some of my work, so he did not regard me as a stranger. As the cocktail hour was coming to an end but our conversation was not, he asked me to join him for dinner, and I accepted. Having filed for divorce, I was a free agent, so there was no reason not to be seen out with someone, even *this* someone. Ever discreet, Bill chose a quiet local restaurant. Our attraction was undeniable, but Bill was from the old school and maintained a certain formality, even when he invited me to his house in Palm Springs the following weekend.

My aunt and uncle owned a house in that desert community, and my grandmother wintered with them every year. In keeping with Bill's decorum, I thanked him but said that I had already planned to be in Palm Springs the following weekend to see my grandmother and would be staying with my aunt and uncle. "Then come for lunch on Saturday," he said.

Mom and I drove to Palm Springs together to have our little family reunion. We always drove everywhere together because she was a *terrible* driver. She loved her 1957 T-Bird, which was her pride and joy, but it lived mostly in the garage.

While having our little family reunion, I slipped away to lunch with Bill. His house was filled with the treasures from his travels. He had a great eye for art, and his collection represented his life in the Far East, as well as his love of Africa. It was truly a reflection of him. There was also a great story associated with every piece in the house.

Bill had a curiosity about the world and had begun to travel extensively in Korea, Japan, Singapore, Hong Kong, and East Africa in the 1950s, when very few Americans ever left the familiar environs of home. It was a special time to be traveling to those parts of the world, with Japan recovering from the war, Korea in the midst of conflict, and most of the region to the south in transition. Bill began to cross paths with new and exciting people who were influential and eclectic.

On one occasion, he was flying on Garuda Airlines from Jakarta to Singapore; the plane accommodated about thirty people in one cabin, the first two rows of which faced each other with a table in between. As the aircraft hit turbulence, the plane began to bounce around, at one point doing a barrel roll, at which point Bill looked behind him to see a woman sitting with her dachshund strapped to the seat next to her, both throwing up, she into her cup and the dachshund into the cup she held for him. Turning back, Bill saw the man opposite him pull from his jacket a flask. Indonesia being a dry state, and Garuda serving no liquor, the man had brought his own. He offered Bill a drink and they shared the flask. Soon, the man recognized Bill. I think the man's name was Johnson—for the sake of this story, we will call him that.

Mr. Johnson introduced himself as the number two at the U.S. embassy in Singapore. In those days, that position generally meant he was a member of the CIA. It was a Sunday morning; they would arrive in Singapore early that afternoon. Johnson said he always had an American-style barbecue on Sunday evenings and asked Bill if he would care to attend. He also said there would be some people there whom Bill might enjoy meeting. The world was a small place back then, particularly in the circles which Bill traveled.

That night, Bill met two exceptional people. Malcolm MacDonald (son of the former British prime minister Ramsay MacDonald), who was called the "Lamplighter of the British Empire," helping newly independent countries transition from colonies. He had closed down India, was in the process of closing down Malaya, and would go on to do the same in Kenya. MacDonald invited Bill to his headquarters for lunch and a briefing on the Southeast Asian situation. The other person of interest at the barbecue was a handsome Eurasian woman called Han Suyin. She had just completed the third book on her life, in this case the story of her great love, an American journalist she met in Hong Kong who was killed on assignment. The book was called *A Many-Splendored Thing*, and she gave Bill a copy.

Bill read the book that night, transfixed by the story. In the morning, he cabled Paramount to say they should buy the book for him and Audrey Hepburn. A few days later, Bill received a cable back from Paramount, indicating that they had loaned him to 20th Century Fox for a movie with Jennifer Jones called *Love Is a Many-Splendored Thing*, based on the galleys of a book by Han Suyin.

That film was the beginning of Bill's fascination with, and attachment to, Hong Kong.

BACK IN L.A., my agent had obtained some work for me on TV and in the theater. Mini and I agreed that, with some of the income, I might be able to begin my investment recovery plan. I found a house for sale not too far from where I was living. The house was rented and the renters wanted to stay. I calculated the asking price, taxes, insurance, and the cost of the mortgage based on a 20 percent down payment and an 80 percent loan. With a small adjustment in price I would make a small profit. So, crossing the fingers of both hands, I dove into my plan.

When Bill started filming *The Towering Inferno*, also starring Robert Wagner, we would meet for early dinners at the restaurant in his hotel. During this time, I received an invitation to play tennis in a charity event in Hong Kong. Bill made the suggestion that I go to Hong Kong a few days before the tournament and let him show me *his* Hong Kong. But first, he had to finish his film and I had to go to Austin, Texas, to do a play.

Mom said she would keep me company on the trip to Texas and we could have some fun driving from L.A. to Austin. A few years before, I had purchased a Chevy Blazer from Chris Mancini, son of Henry. A Chevrolet dealer had customized the Blazer for Henry Mancini in the hope it would put his dealership on the map. There were very few luxury SUVs on the road at that time, and none so smart as this one. So, when Henry gave it to Chris and Chris wanted a different car, I bought the Blazer off him and called the car "Ralph."

Ralphy came equipped with a CB radio, but I had no idea how to use it. As we set off on our six-hundred-mile marathon drive, the government had just imposed the fifty-five-mile-per-hour speed limit, so it was going to be a *very* long trip. Mom, Mischa (the Yorkshire terrier given to me by my ballet teacher), and I piled into Ralph and hit the road. No sooner had we cleared the California border and entered the Arizona desert than our air-conditioning broke down. Since no one had the parts to fix it, we wisely decided to do most of our driving at night.

The road across Texas was dead straight. We stopped at a small roadside truck stop to eat and fill thermoses with black coffee. All the truck drivers were talking to each other, swapping stories about the road and complaining about the fifty-five-mile-per-hour restriction. One gregarious fellow walked over to our table and started a conversation:

TRUCKER: Y'got that California four-wheeler out there?

ME: Oh, you mean the Blazer? Why yes, that's us.

TRUCKER: Where ya goin' in that fancy rig?

ME: We're driving to Austin.

TRUCKER: Well, ah tell ya whatcha kin do. You kin turn that CB onta nineteen. Come on up behin' me, nice 'n' close, and I'll take ya on in ta Austin. I'm goin' on East but I'll getcha to the ramp.

What a charming offer! Mom and I could hardly refuse, and we did exactly as he said. For the first time, I turned on the CB radio, dialed it to 19, adjusted the static, and pulled up behind the biggest truck and trailer I had ever seen. Off we went.

We began cruising at just around seventy miles per hour. Catching the slipstream behind his trailer made me feel as if we were sailing. Soon, I heard a voice come across the CB—this was well before *Smokey and the Bandit,* so the jargon was new and unknown to me.

TRUCKER: Breaker, breaker, this is the Arkansas Sweet P'tater callin' the California four-wheeler. You got any ears on that thang?

ME: [spotting his Arkansas license plate and realizing it was our friend] Ah . . . Hello . . . Yes, it's me!

TRUCKER: We gotta big rig on up ahead goin' west. I'm jes' gonna talk t'him, so stay on . . . Breaker, breaker, this is the Arkansas Sweet P'tater. I gotta California four-wheeler behin' me and we're goin' east . . . You seen any smokies on up ahead?

TRUCKER #2: *Oh yeah!* There's one 'bout ten miles up the road and he's takin' pictures.

TRUCKER: Well, I tell ya what we're gonna do. We're gonna put on a clean white T-shirt and smile at him as we go by!

The dialog was fabulous, and the truckers were a breed unto themselves. They looked out for us all the way to Austin and all the way back home. It was the highlight of our trip.

The play went well, and Lady Bird Johnson came to see us, coming backstage to say hello. She was genuinely warm and friendly, and invited us to her home if we had the time, which sadly we never did. I was eager to return to L.A. and go on to Hong Kong with the most wonderful guide in the world.

HONG KONG IN 1972 was a far cry from Hong Kong today. While high-rise apartment blocks and office buildings were daily changing the skyline, the original streets and some of the original buildings of the early colonial period were still in existence. It was apparent and easy to identify the various cultures and social strata that have now been obliterated into one seemingly homogenized mass. The character of the people and city were very much alive when we landed precariously at the old airport of Kai Tak. Bill had made reservations for us at the Mandarin Hotel on the Hong Kong side of the colony, and as Bill was one of their valued guests, they sent their Rolls-Royce to collect us after landing.

The sounds and smells of Hong Kong were a sensual overload. From the humid air, with its sour dampness, to the pristine sweetness of the immaculately starched and pressed white cotton slip covers protecting the English leather of the Rolls, it was a spectrum of exotic delights that enveloped me in its splendor. I was to spend the first week as Bill's guest, afterward moving into the home of a dear friend, Elaine Forsgate, whose family was a well-known part of the fabric of Hong Kong. The tennis tournament was ten days off.

Although we had never discussed the sleeping arrangements, Bill, in his stylish way, reserved two rooms side by side but not connecting. Later, he would say that he never wanted me to feel I was pressured or obligated in any way. After a long and luxurious sleep in the deliciously scented linens of the Mandarin Hotel bed, I joined Bill for breakfast and we began to make the rounds of his regular haunts. We had coffee with his friend Gregory, a Greek money changer/importer, and visited Bill's tailor to order some of his impeccable suits that were instantly made; we lunched at Jimmy's Kitchen, a favorite local watering hole; and had dinner with friends of his on the Kowloon side, catching the last ferry back to Hong Kong.

The night was magical, the air fragrant and balmy. The ferryboat was almost empty as we walked to the bow to take in the glittering view of the city. I was consumed with emotion. When he covered my hand that was holding the rail with his, I turned to him and he kissed me so gently, yet with such profound feeling, that I was transported.

The rest of the week was a gossamer blur of high romance, interrupted only by the awkwardness of having to dodge the four room-boys stationed in the hallway, when one or the other of us attempted to discreetly return to our room. Those attendants could break all speed records when responding to a "call" button igniting the green light above a guest room door. So much for unconnected rooms.

I was in love. This time it was a grown-up feeling, not just lust, although that did have its place.

As the week came to a reluctant end, I was notified that the promoter of the tennis tournament had to cancel. Bill had his plans to go to Bangkok to look at art and then on to Kenya, where he also lived; I decided to stay on a few days with Elaine and her family.

Bill and I made no formal plans, but it was clear that we would reconnect in L.A.

I was so in love that the night before Bill left, I wrote the first—and only—poem of my life. I put it in his hand luggage and told him to read it on the plane. Its lack of erudition notwithstanding, it came from my heart:

A whisper speaks
As clouds descend on Asian peaks
You're everywhere

Making round my square
You've softened the edge that once was there

Elaine and I followed Bill to the airport; we had a brief farewell scene and parted. Elaine's family house was atop Kowloon Peak, and from the veranda we overlooked Kai Tak Airport's runway.

Elaine popped a bottle of champagne and we toasted Bill's plane as it took off, gliding over Hong Kong harbor and disappearing into the west, taking my heart with it.

EIGHT

"Luv—Bill"

———— ∞∞∞ ————

A ddiction in the 1940s and '50s, long before it became a rite of passage in the Celebrity Hall of Fame, was a word never spoken, certainly not in the context of anyone we knew or were related to.

Films of those decades attest to the fact that all sorts of indulgences were commonplace and unquestioned. Take, for example, the *Thin Man* series of films starring Myrna Loy and William Powell, in which they were either drinking or offering a drink in almost every line of dialog. And everyone smoked! It was the perfect punctuation for a scene in a movie, sometimes even found in the stage directions of a script . . .

"He reaches for a cigarette . . . Lighting it, he says . . ."

And . . . it was *sexy*. Lauren Bacall showed us that, as did Paul Henreid when he lit two cigarettes, passing one to Bette Davis in *Now, Voyager*. Smoke was everywhere. The only place where there was no smoking, funnily enough, was in movie houses, although I do recall going to the cinema in London in the 1960s, where I could hardly see the screen for all the smoke.

In the '50s, prescription drugs were everywhere in the form of pep pills and tranquilizers, frequently found in some of the best suburban homes. While Dad was away at work, the little woman, relieved of the drudgeries of housework by new time-saving machines, was free to indulge in Tupper-ware parties: Valium. But most of all, alcohol was the drug of choice, whether for social or business reasons. Drinking became a ritual in the form of the two-martini lunch and cocktails before dinner. Everyone knew someone in their circle who was called a "heavy drinker." They were the objects of humor, not criticism, and they were colorful . . . "Good old Al! Boy, was he *bombed* last night; he took a bath with his clothes on!"

Among some of the world-class drinkers were those who appeared on the silver screen and those who trod the theatrical boards. They were leg-endary for their exploits. W. C. Fields was famous for his films, his tomb-stone epitaph "On the whole, I'd rather be living in Philadelphia," and his ingenious method of concealing gin in the most unexpected places all over the studios where he worked. John Barrymore, great-grandfather of Drew and product of America's leading theatrical family, took drinking to new ar-tistic heights, creating a loyal band of young followers who helped prop him up and who, when he died, stole his body from the funeral home to have it witness their own final night of indulgence with him. Barrymore, known as the Great Profile, was a handsome leading man whose looks declined along with his career as the ravages of alcohol became conspicuous.

Similarly, Errol Flynn, a Barrymore acolyte who, in fact, engineered that final night of debauchery with his idol's corpse, concocted groundbreak-ing combinations of alcohol and drugs. He lost *his* beauty as well, which is clearly evident in one of his last films, *The Sun Also Rises,* in which he appeared alongside some other two-fisted drinkers, and which was based on a book by Ernest Hemingway, another legendary drinker. And Spencer Tracy, who brought to the screen some of the finest performances ever filmed, was known to disappear from time to time, only to be discovered in some obscure hotel, having consumed vast amounts of drink.

The remarkableness of all these people was their ability, despite their drinking, to be astonishingly productive on a very high level of accomplishment. Their incredible powers of physical recovery proved they had constitutions of steel, and they became role models for a new generation.

Enter William Holden.

WILLIAM FRANKLIN BEEDLE Jr. was the eldest of three boys born in O'Fallon, Illinois, to a schoolteacher mother and a chemist father. When the Beedles moved west, they settled in South Pasadena, adjacent to the Pasadena of Rose Bowl fame. Father Beedle opened his own laboratory and was working hard to support his growing family when he was misdiagnosed with a heart disease that was determined to be so grave that it would shorten his life. Wanting to ensure the future of his family, Father Beedle worked day and night, giving his wife full responsibility for the raising of his boys. Playing around the house was not tolerated, because the noise might awaken their father, who needed his rest.

Young Bill sought adventure, and being a bit of a daredevil, he was always up for a bet or a challenge. On one occasion, he was dared to walk the full length of a bridge in Pasadena, on his hands, using the railings. The viaduct was nicknamed the "Suicide Bridge" after the many leaps to their death by those who had lost everything in the Great Depression. Bill took the bet and won, becoming legendary among his peers and setting the stage for what was to come.

Many years later, after his death, I was asked to represent Bill on the occasion of the christening of the two newly refurbished final-dubbing theaters at Sony Pictures. The first project of the two theaters—each housing 150 seats and state-of-the-art mixing consoles that look like Mission Control—was to remix the digitally enhanced version of *Picnic,* starring Bill and Kim Novak. So they decided to name the theaters in their honor.

Kim came down to L.A. from her home in Oregon for the evening and we were both asked to speak. First to be inaugurated was the William

Holden Theatre. I spoke and told a story Bill had recounted to me years earlier.

It was a Sunday. Bill was meeting with the director Joshua Logan in his top-floor hotel suite somewhere in Kansas, on location for *Picnic*. It was warm, the hotel was not air-conditioned, and Bill had the windows of his rooms open. He was trying to convince Logan that he could do his last shot in the picture in one setup without a cut. The scene involved Bill backing away from Kim with a freight train passing behind him, which he would run to catch. Then he'd climb up the outside ladder to the roof of the boxcar and wave good-bye. Bill wanted to do the stunt himself, but the director and the studio were adamant that it was far too dangerous. In order to prove he was physically up to the task, he jumped out the window of the five-story hotel and hung himself outside, holding on to the ledge of the window until the apoplectic director relented and allowed him the stunt.

Given Bill's history of athleticism and daring, walking across that bridge in Pasadena, I would not be surprised if he enjoyed every minute of Logan's discomfort.

Kim never knew this side of the story. When it was her turn to speak, she told us all that on that Sunday, she was walking back to the hotel from church and saw a crowd gathered opposite the hotel, looking up. When she followed their gaze, she saw Bill hanging from the windowsill. In those days, Kim was a young contract player and she certainly didn't feel comfortable asking the star of the movie what had caused his display. So it was not until that night, all those years later, that she was able to fill in the pieces of the puzzle and was delighted to learn the other side of the story.

For someone who never belonged to a gym, Bill's natural athletic ability and sheer physical prowess were remarkable throughout his life.

Even at the end.

PASADENA, CALIFORNIA, was not only the home of the Rose Bowl; it was also the home of the Pasadena Playhouse. Built in 1925, the Playhouse quickly forged its reputation with the world premieres of works by F. Scott Fitzgerald, Eugene O'Neill, Noel Coward, William Saroyan, and Tennessee Williams, while its school of theater arts coached actors ranging from Victor Mature and Raymond Burr to Charles Bronson and Dustin Hoffman. Accordingly, the "Star Factory," as the Playhouse came to be known, served as a magnet for talent scouts from the Hollywood studios.

Bill found a different sort of freedom from the restrictions at home when he acted in his first play in high school and was encouraged to audition for a part at the Pasadena Playhouse. Suddenly, he found a new means of escape into the roles he was asked to play, which were generally character parts behind a beard or under a hat. He could hide in plain sight, and the game intrigued him.

His mother, Mary Beedle, was not enthusiastic about Bill's extracurricular acting activities, but she allowed them as long as he did his schoolwork. Mother Beedle had the discipline and nature of a schoolmarm, or perhaps she assumed that countenance with the weight of raising three sons and having a husband with a fatal condition. In actual fact, Father Beedle lived to the age of seventy-six and saw his eldest son become a world-famous film star; his youngest son become an ace pilot in World War II, tragically dying in a crash in the South Pacific; and his middle son take over the family business. Mary Beedle died in her early nineties, proving that Bill came from hearty stock.

It was always assumed that Bill would follow his father into the family business, where he had worked during school vacations and after school, more out of obligation than desire. Paramount Pictures came to the rescue in the form of a talent scout who approached Bill at the Pasadena Playhouse, inviting him to come to the studio. It was Father Beedle who gave his permission for nineteen-year-old Bill to accept the invitation. Bill boarded his motorcycle and took the long drive to Paramount Pictures in Hollywood, in the same location it occupies to this day.

Bill spent every day on the lot. Famous at Paramount was the line of star dressing rooms located on the ground floor of the makeup building, which stretched the length of a city block. The "street" had a facade of bungalows with individual entrances to elaborate dressing rooms and a proper sidewalk in front, where many of Paramount's top stars would hang out, sitting on the curb, telling stories, and filling Bill's head with actors' shop talk. The stories always included fabled incidents concerning either theatrical or film actors who managed to perform in varying states of inebriation. Some of these stories were told by actors who were themselves imbibers on an Olympian scale, all of them larger-than-life characters.

Bill approached his work and his life with an intensity born of a need to prove himself, not only to his mother and father and the Pasadena crowd he was a part of (but not of) but also to himself.

Brian Donlevy had come from the theater to Hollywood, and he had the bearing and the voice to prove it. He was also a dapper and immaculate man whose Irish heritage provided a weakness for "bending his elbow." He called it "fortification," and Bill found that to be the case when he felt that his insecurities might get the better of him. A shot of something now and then couldn't hurt, right? In fact, it made great sense; after all, didn't some people use it as a tonic?

Soon, Bill was swept up by work and by the studio system grooming him, changing his name, and selling half his contract to Columbia Pictures, where he would make some of his best films. But it was at Paramount that Bill met Billy Wilder, who was himself a contract player—his theater of play was the writers pool. Every studio had one, and out of those pools came some of the best dialog and stories ever put to paper. Everyone was young, and ambitious, and the future seemed bright. When Bill met a beautiful contract player at Warner Brothers named Brenda Marshall, he fell in love with her looks and her sharp wit. They were married in 1941, and at once Bill became a husband and a father to her one-year-old daughter, Virginia.

Shortly after Pearl Harbor, Bill joined the army, and when he returned to civilian life he was faced with a motion picture business that had moved on while he'd been away. There were many actors competing for the same jobs, and with a growing family Bill did everything available to him, including radio soap operas, plays, and commercials. Slowly rebuilding his career, Bill became one of Hollywood's solid citizens. When Ronald Reagan, then a Democrat, was elected president of the Screen Actors Guild, Bill became his vice president. Their friendship led to Bill's serving first as best man when Reagan married Nancy Davis, and then as godfather to their daughter Patti.

In the course of making *Sunset Boulevard, Stalag 17,* and *Sabrina,* Bill became extremely close with Billy Wilder, who always encouraged Bill to travel in Europe, which he began to do more and more. When Bill moved his family to Switzerland, Wilder remarked, "I said *travel,* not *move!*"

Switzerland offered an opportunity for Bill to give his children an international education; it was also slightly advantageous tax-wise when films such as *Bridge on the River Kwai* catapulted him into the dubiously enviable position of being the first actor to receive a salary of $1 million. In 1957, the Eisenhower administration established a 91 percent tax bracket for income exceeding $400,000. Being domiciled in Switzerland brought a small relief to that punishing but compulsory contribution. *He* might have seen advantages to his decision, but influential Hollywood gossip columnist Hedda Hopper did not, and she began a campaign in her syndicated column vilifying Bill for being a traitor and a tax evader. Fortunately, it did not affect his value at the box office and his career marched on.

Around the same time, Bill went back to Hong Kong to make *The World of Suzie Wong.* After the making of *Love Is a Many-Splendored Thing,* he had purchased a penthouse apartment on Robinson Road in a building designed by his good friend Al Alvarez. Al was one of the first of Bill's friends I would meet in Hong Kong, along with two others—George and Jessie Ho—all of whom would become like family to me. George started Hong Kong Commercial Radio in 1959, and Bill was one of his first investors.

A year earlier, Bill and two other friends, a Swiss banker and an American oilman, went to East Africa on a hunting safari and wound up buying a hotel. This impetuous purchase opened the doors to adventure in a way nothing had before. In 1960, the hotel was reopened as the Mount Kenya Safari Club, and Bill's celebrity put it on the map. It became *the* destination in East Africa. Kenya was just about to receive its independence, and everyone in the fashionable jet set wanted to visit the country. In fact, the Gold Book of the Club looks like a who's who of that era.

In 1966, when the two thousand acres surrounding the Safari Club became available for purchase, Bill's good friend, professional hunter extraordinaire Julian McKeand, introduced him to a gregarious American wildlife expert, Don Hunt, and the three of them became a perfect marriage of motives, combining know-how and enthusiasm in the creation of a game ranch. It was the first of its kind in East Africa, and it began a conservation effort long before the word *conservation* was in the public's mind or vocabulary.

William Holden was anything but a typical Hollywood actor. While he was conscientious about his work, he created a life that extended beyond Hollywood films.

How fortunate for me that I became a part of his world.

———— ❧ ————

A FEW DAYS after Bill left Hong Kong, I received a phone call from my agent in Hollywood, telling me I had a solid offer for a movie in Canada, costarring with Anthony Newley, a friend, and singer Isaac Hayes. The money was good and so was the part. My agent recommended that I cut my trip short and immediately go to Toronto. The only contact I had for Bill was a telex number: SAF CLUB KENYA. I wrote him . . .

LEAVING HK FOR JOB TORONTO . . . WILL FORWARD DETAILS—STEF

When I left Hong Kong for L.A. I made a stopover, during which I broke even my own record for unpacking and repacking, and left for Toronto to begin filming *It Seemed Like a Good Idea at the Time.* All the while, I was concerned that I might miss Bill's attempts to get in touch. I sent another telex to Kenya, giving my contact information, but two weeks went by before, *eureka,* I received a cable saying, IF IT'S TUESDAY, IT MUST BE TORONTO.

Did this mean he was coming to Toronto the following Tuesday? I waited, but crestfallen—no Bill. A week later, flowers arrived with a card, "Luv—Bill," followed by a call. He was just back from his trip and wanted to see me, but he needed time to organize himself, and then he would call with a plan.

It was early December, bitter cold with snow on the ground, when Bill arrived for the weekend. We stayed indoors the whole time with room service and lots of champagne. We both drank a great deal that weekend, but we were also drunk with each other. With Christmas on its way, the film was going to shut down for a week. Bill and I made plans for me to fly to Palm Springs and spend the holidays with him. My mother would be in the desert with my aunt, uncle, and grandmother, so it was a perfect idea.

I caught a flight from Toronto to Chicago, then directly to Palm Springs, landing in the delicious warmth of the sun. My heart was racing at the thought of our reunion. Walking across the tarmac and into the small airport, I looked around, but no Bill. He had said he would meet me at the gate. I scanned the reception area and walked out to where the cars would drop off or pick up passengers. There I saw Bill standing next to his Mercedes-Benz with a motorcycle cop talking to him. It did not look like a social conversation.

I arrived at the car and Bill greeted me in a way that clearly indicated he was in his cups and in no condition to be driving. The police officer was very nice, and I convinced him that I would drive the car home. Relieved, the policeman said he was not going to press charges, that Bill was a valuable member of the community, and that he was satisfied if I promised to get behind the wheel.

I had certainly seen people over-served before, and my generation openly indulged in grass and other adventurous assortments of stimulants, so I was not shocked, but I *was* disappointed. This was not how I envisioned our romantic reunion.

After we arrived at his house, Bill had nothing further to drink. Instead, he said he needed to take a nap and retired to his bedroom. Bill had given the help a few days off so that we could have privacy. Well into the evening, Bill had not stirred from his nap. I went to the bedroom to see if he was awake and found him convulsing. I put a pencil in his mouth to make sure he wouldn't swallow his tongue and began pounding on his chest to keep his heart going. Fortunately, the housekeeper returned to drop off some groceries, and I shouted to her to get help. She ran across the street to Dr. Supple, who came immediately. We called 911 and were taken to the Desert Hospital, where they worked to stabilize Bill.

It was a toxic reaction to alcohol that had caused him to convulse.

Dr. Supple was not Bill's regular physician, so in order for him to be admitted to the hospital, next of kin was required. Fortunately, Bill's sons were in the desert, staying with their mother. They were located and asked to come to the hospital. When we met, I was distraught and they were cold. One of them turned to me and said, "Don't think *you're* going to get him to stop drinking. Better people than you have tried and failed."

Once Bill was stabilized, Dr. Supple insisted on taking me home to get some rest. I didn't rest. I went to see my mother, aunt, and uncle and explained what had happened. Uncle Howard took me aside for a conversation that cast a new and completely different light on his life and our relationship. I never knew Uncle Howard was a recovering alcoholic, or a *dry alcoholic,* as he referred to himself. He had not touched a drink in thirty years, but he was, nevertheless, an alcoholic.

With great courage, as someone who loved me, he recommended that I leave Bill. He said he did not want me to go through the pain of being with a man who was an alcoholic. But he also said that if I decided to stay with Bill, I would learn more about being a human being than I could ever imagine.

I would discover how right he was.

NINE

The Mawingu

⟨⟨⟨⟩⟩⟩

I t is a daunting experience, in the early stages of romantic love, to be dramatically confronted by intimate and private details of the person who is the object of your love but who is, in fact, still a stranger.

In the "getting to know you" phase of all relationships, when clarity is blurred by the rosy glow of passionate love, we all tend to focus on mutuality rather than practicality. All the things we have in common are the icing on the cake, supported by that overwhelming phenomenon called chemistry! Bill and I certainly had both; it was an embarrassment of riches, as the chemistry was undeniable and the communality was as well. Despite the difference in our ages, we seemed to be on the same wavelength in so many ways and on so many occasions.

At the time it didn't seem at all unusual that I was attracted to Bill. Of course I had seen his films and loved him in them, but I was carried away by the man, not the movie star. He came from a world in which people just seemed to be more interesting, more tasteful, more sophisticated, more fun, more . . . more everything! And let us not forget talented! At that time all the icons of film, theater, music, and art were either recently dead or still very much alive and productive. Even though I was a *Photoplay* magazine "star of tomorrow," I had not yet earned my stripes to qualify entry to that exclusive club. I could at least enjoy the idea that I was eligible for it, and that was worth working for. Of course all great artists came with baggage—so did Bill and so did I—but I was to discover that his was seriously over-weight luggage.

While Bill was recuperating at the Desert Hospital, I stayed with my aunt and uncle, taking refuge from the harsh reality contained in the comments made by Bill's sons. My uncle's words also resounded in my brain. His own experience with AA had kept him dry, but not without effort and support from my aunt. Could I be like her? Was I that strong? I don't know if I was capable of making a rational decision at that time or whether it was simply that I am a stubborn Polack, I opted to stay the course.

Bill's release from the hospital left me with only twenty-four hours before I had to return to Toronto to complete the movie, so there was no time really to open the Pandora's box of his affliction. I took Bill's avoidance of any discussion on what had transpired, not to mention an apology for what he had put me through, as his way of dealing with a completely embarrassing episode. The eve of my departure was clearly not the appropriate time for an in-depth retrospective, and I thought it best for me to comfort rather than confront. Perhaps that was "enabling," but at the time I was doing the best I could to feel my way around this new landscape.

After completing the film I returned to my little cottage in "Yoakum Valley," as we referred to Yoakum Drive, shared with my friend Dougie, who was living partly in Hawaii. My financial ship of state was still a very leaky craft. Hoping one day to sell the tiny armada of properties that represented both my ex-husband's and my own net worth, as well as to avoid insolvency, a great portion of everything I was making went to maintain the properties, which were still not sellable. I was taking all the work I could get and not being very discriminating about what I was doing, making my agents very happy with the regular commissions but not doing my career any good. I was inching my way back from the financial abyss and learning a great deal on the way, dispelling the perception that women should leave all financial matters to their husbands. I was going to pay back every cent Gary had borrowed from my mother, and I was beginning to do my own investing with the domino principle I'd heard my stepfather talk about.

When Bill would come to town he would stay at the Beverly Hill Crest Hotel. The Yoakum Valley house had become far too small for my own needs, let alone for the both of us. On weekends I would drive to his house in the desert, on Driftwood Drive, which was becoming my home away from home. Bill would read scripts, looking for something interesting, and I would read scripts studying for the next job, which was always coming on the heels of the one I was finishing. Bill was amazed at my resilience but said that one day the jobs would not come so frequently, so I should be a bit more selective.

He was right of course, but at the time I had no options.

———— ∞ ————

IT WAS DURING this period that three first-time events happened. First, Bill decided to go ahead with his plans to build on the three lots he owned in Southridge. Southridge was the first gated residential development to be built in Palm Springs. It was located high on a narrow ridge overlooking the whole of the Coachella Valley. Bob and Dolores Hope, Steve and Neile McQueen, David Janssen, and other prominent personalities had also invested in property on the ridge, and the Hopes' house was well under way.

The second event was significant for both of us: Bill experienced his first "intervention."

The third event, which was really a first, was Bill's initial AA meeting.

Both Bill and I loved the desert and had a great deal of history there. It had been a playground not only for the Hollywood crowd of the 1940s and '50s but for my generation as well. We both had friends in the community who fortunately knew each other. On one occasion Bill and I were driving up to L.A. from Palm Springs on the freeway and we heard a car horn tooting at us; we looked over, and who was next to us, waving as they passed, but Robert Wagner and Natalie Wood. After their second marriage to each other, they lived in the desert.

Bill loved his motorcycle, and on the weekends we would go for long rides with me on the back. More and more we would ride up the Southridge incline to the raw land that comprised the site of Bill's dream house, "our house" as he called it. He would speak of lovely ideas as we took in the exquisite view of the desert below. Bill seemed to need a project he could sink his teeth into, and giving up his residential status in Switzerland to put down roots in the country he'd once called home was beginning to sound as if it was the ideal project.

When I was around, Bill seemed to control his drinking. At least it was restricted to a few beers. I was not drinking at all, but we both smoked like chimneys. When I was not there, however, it was different, and frequently I could hear booze in his voice on the phone when we said goodnight. I felt as if I could smell it on his breath through the phone.

At the time, Bill had a business manager who gave me the creeps. I never said anything about it to Bill, but I felt that there was something odd about their relationship. Frank Schappe was a former IRS man who went to work for Bill's accountant. When Bill's accountant retired, Frank suggested that he take over managing Bill's books and taxes. Frank not only became Bill's business manager but he also managed the affairs of Bill's ex-wife and the trust funds for all the children. Frank's entire practice revolved around the Holden enterprise, and I think he had a fixation on the family that was unhealthy. Making himself instantly on call was another way for Frank to ingratiate himself as a confidant and loyal servant.

What I did not know was that Bill kept an apartment that Frank would use when he came to the desert, and it was there that he established himself as Bill's drinking buddy and enabler. Each time Frank would leave the desert, Bill would be drinking. When I returned to L.A. after being away in San Francisco on location, I couldn't get Bill on the phone. After two more days I finally got his housekeeper, and she said that she thought he had gone to the apartment where Frank stayed. Indiscreetly she told me that he was a bit "tipsy," and I knew he was on a binge.

I didn't know what to do, but clearly I needed help. I had met Bill's lawyer, his great friend Deane Johnson, with whom Bill had enjoyed wonderful times in Europe and in Africa, where Deane had a share in the Game Ranch. Marty Rackin was a producer who had grown up in the business with Bill. I had worked for Marty in *Stagecoach*. I called them both, describing what had happened. We met at Marty's house and planned an intervention. I had never heard the word, but both Deane and Marty had had experience with the AA technique. The idea was for us to break in on his isolation and expose him to his drinking and his disease in a way that might help him see his illness before it was too late. Of course they had witnessed Bill's drinking, but they both held hopes that his love for me might change his life and his addiction. They were willing to make the effort, so we all drove to Palm Springs and banged on the door of the apartment where Bill was locked away.

It worked. He was not only shocked but he broke down as well, overwhelmed by the demonstration of how much we cared. This was the turning point. If he was ever to have a chance, it would be now.

One of Bill's motorcycle riding pals was in AA (let's call him "R"). R came by after the intervention at my request because I knew that Bill respected him. What I did not know was that he was in AA and he was the key to the next step. Like some guardian angel, R took the lead and he never left Bill alone, taking him to meetings and constantly talking with him.

AA was a new approach for Bill, nothing like the silk-sheeted treatment clinics he had known in Europe. AA was hard-core, and something inside him clicked. Bill would recount everything that happened at his meetings, which was not really allowed, but he was so enthusiastic that I just let him go. He even agreed to attend a seminar with me conducted by a philosopher who had helped me at one time in my life.

Bill was beginning to open his mind to other ways of thinking.

It was the 1970s, and people were searching their minds and their spirits even without the aid of substances, and he was voraciously absorbing everything, as if he had just discovered air.

For the next five years, Bill worked hard to maintain his sobriety. What resulted were five of the most glorious years of our life together. He rediscovered his curiosities about the world, and if it was because he was seeing it all again through my eyes, all the better, because I was not only the object of his love but I was also his best student. Bill had hoped to pass on his legacy to his children, but sadly they turned away from him. With me, everything he wanted to teach, I wanted to learn.

⸺ ∞ ⸺

BILL ALWAYS SAID that the true test of compatibility was going on safari. Indeed, I heard many stories from him and others about the rude awakenings when two people confront what can sometimes be compromising conditions under canvas.

Travel to faraway places with strange-sounding names was not a new experience for me. I was already well seasoned to life off the beaten track when I met Bill, so it was no effort at all to be able to hit the road at the drop of a hat. Bill enjoyed planning trips, but he also enjoyed the spur-of-the-moment decisions that would take us off to Death Valley, the Colorado River, or just riding motorcycles for days. Wanderlust was such a shared passion that it brought out the best in both of us and in our life together.

My baptism of fire was to come in the form of initiation into Bill's other life, the one he cared most about, the one that, in many ways, he was proudest of. His life in Kenya.

howing my assets. *(Personal collection of tefanie Powers)*

My first pair of toe shoes, I seemed destined to dance. *(Personal collection of Stefanie Powers)*

Jeff and me with the original Kitty and Tiger. *(Personal collection of Stefanie Powers)*

Our famous ballet class. Natalie on the left, Jill with hair bows, and me, the short one, on the right. *(Personal collection of Stefanie Powers)*

Playing the Duke's daughter. *(Copyright © 1963, United Artists. All rights reserved)*

Palm Springs Weekend with Troy, Ty, Connie, and Bob. *(Personal collection of Stefanie Powers)*

On the set of *2001: A Space Odyssey* with Gary. *(Personal collection of Stefanie Powers)*

Terrorized by Tallulah in *Die! Die! My Darling! (Copyright © 1965, Columbia Pictures. All rights reserved)*

Herbie Rides Again with Helen Hayes, who taught me to needlepoint. *(Copyright © Walt Disney Productions. World rights reserved)*

Maureen Stapleton
and Melissa Gilbert in
Family Secrets, my first
writer/producer credit.
*(Personal collection of
Stefanie Powers)*

On the set of *Maggie* with Ava,
what a beauty. *(Personal collection
of Stefanie Powers)*

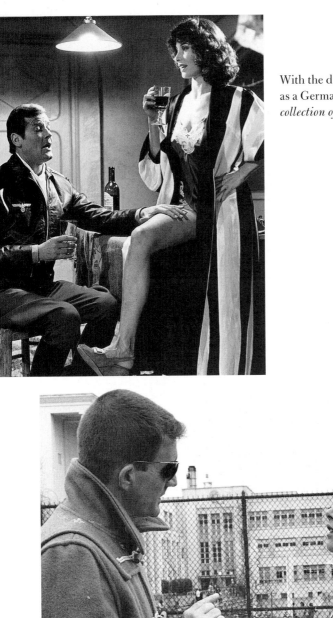

With the divine Roger Moore as a German officer. *(Personal collection of Stefanie Powers)*

Taking direction from Blake Edwards, who is wearing my sunglasses. *(Photograph by Bill Crespinel)*

With RJ and Lionel while filming in Greece. *(Personal collection of Stefanie Powers)*

As the Girl from U.N.C.L.E. with Leo G. Carroll and Robert Vaughan. *(Personal collection of Stefanie Powers)*

With Barbara Stanwyck, who loved Bill and RJ. *(Personal collection of Stefanie Powers)*

With RJ and Martina Navratilova, who made a guest appearance and began supporting the William Holden Wildlife Foundation. *(Personal collection of Stefanie Powers)*

RJ in drag , what great legs. *(Personal collection of Stefanie Powers)*

With RJ in *Love Letters*. *(Personal collection of Stefanie Powers)*

With Mr. Kissinger and President
Ford for lunch.

Bill as best man for Glenn Ford with John Wayne, Fran
and Barbara Sinatra, and Jimmy and Gloria Stewart in
the background. *(Photograph by World Wide Photos)*

With Placido. *(Photograph by Olympia)*

On the *Calypso* with Ted Turner. *(Personal collection of Stefanie Powers)*

Speaking Polish to Pope John Paul II. *(Personal collection of Stefanie Powers)*

The second time I met the Queen Mum. *(Photograph by Pic Photos, London)*

At the White House with you know who. *(Official White House photograph, 1986)*

With Mrs. Thatcher when she came to California and Johnny Grant emceed the dinner. *(Copyright © Alex Berliner, Berliner Studio)*

President and Mme Chirac and Guy Laroche at his Legion d'honour. A wardrobe faux pas. *(Photograph by Mesnildrey, Ville de Paris)*

With Mom in Lech Walesa's office in Gdansk the day his new government was legalized. *(Personal collection of Stefanie Powers)*

Left to right: Ani, Richard, me, a large friend from PNG, Bill, Gail, and Chuck, the night of the Feingarten Gallery show. *(Personal collection of Stefanie Powers)*

Stanley Sheinbaum, Mom, me, and my friends when they visited L.A. *(Photograph by Barry E. Levine, Inc. © 1995)*

Feeding a friend's black rhino at Lewa Downs. *(Personal collection of Stefanie Powers)*

atching reticulated Giraffe in Kenya, Bill
n the bumper, me on the hood, Don on
he ground. *(Personal collection of Stefanie
owers)*

With Mary at Iris's orphanage. *(Personal collection of Stefanie Powers)*

In Kenya, on the ranch with friends. *(Personal collection of Stefanie Powers)*

With Ani on the Great Wall of China. We were the only foreigners there. *(Personal collection of Stefanie Powers)*

The first time I met Silvano, he never let go of my hand or my heart. *(Personal collection of Stefanie Powers)*

Bill trying to teach Papuga the Col. Bogie march from *Bridge on the River Kwai*. She never learned.

My favorite picture of wild Bill. *(Personal collection of Stefanie Powers)*

Poolside with Bill in Palm Springs. *(Personal collection of Stefanie Powers)*

Leading the Pulaski Day parade with Mom. *(Personal collection of Stefanie Powers)*

With Tom on the high slopes of Mount Kenya for a day of fishing. *(Personal collection of Stefanie Powers)*

My favorite picture with Bill, taken when the house was under construction.

In 1958, while establishing his new residence in Switzerland, Bill joined two friends, Ray Ryan and Carl Hirschmann, on his very first safari to Kenya. Ray was an oil man, a wildcatter who also owned the famously glamorous El Mirador Hotel in Palm Springs, along with a resort casino in the Caribbean. Carl was a Swiss banker from Zurich whose family created the Handels Credit Bank.

It was a questionable time to be traveling to Kenya, largely due to the independence movement, whose guerilla fighters, called the Mau Mau, were hiding in forest encampments all over the country, from which they staged their raids. There was a generally nervous atmosphere, and a fully armed population, when Bill and his pals arrived in Nairobi. No one left the house without a weapon; even ladies carried small revolvers in their evening bags, and no one was driving up-country or out into the bush if they could help it. Even the farmers felt unsafe on their farms.

Tourism as we now know it began only as recently as the 1970s, so when Bill ventured forth to the Far East, Southeast Asia, and East Africa, most Americans were still staying close to home.

There was also the question of cost. When Bill and his pals arrived in Kenya for their big safari, all out to get the "Big Five" (elephant, rhino, lion, leopard, and buffalo), it required elaborate preparations, a professional hunter/outfitter, and a huge commitment of time and money.

The game department in Nairobi had organized the hunting areas by numbered grid squares called "hunting blocks." Surveys of animal populations were regularly updated by game wardens in the field, and hunters were not allowed to shoot more than a specific quota of animals from each hunting block. To comply with the Game Department's management of wildlife, it was necessary for the safari camp to move to a new location from time to time, even to a new hunting block. Serving three clients in the bush in the style that was established by the British required a large staff, all of whom were guaranteed fresh meat every day as part of their employment contract. Shooting for "the pot" added to the volume of animals to be shot and the cost of permits to shoot them.

All in all, a safari of this magnitude was certainly not in everyone's budget.

When it was necessary to move the camp, the process would generally take a few days, so it was recognized protocol for the clients to go off to repair themselves at some local watering hole in the form of an up-country inn. The closest and most suitable establishment in the area where Bill's safari was operating was the Mawingu ("clouds" in Swahili). The Mawingu was a beautiful house that began life as a private home, a love nest, built on the slopes of Mount Kenya with a magnificent view of the permanently glacier-covered peaks of this, the world's only ice-covered mountain on the equator.

The saga of the Mawingu has all the ingredients of an epic novel: Rhoda Lewinsohn and Gabriel Prudhomme were part of the small but infamous social set whose playground would come to be known as Happy Valley, and whose scandalous behavior would elicit the saying "Are you married? Or do you live in Kenya?" Rhoda Lewinsohn's financier husband successfully survived the depression to emerge as a millionaire known for his business acumen and philanthropy. Although in her fifties, Rhoda was a famously stunning beauty with an equally famous joie de vivre, and she joined some English friends on safari in Kenya. Gabriel Prudhomme was a dashing French hunter who enhanced his dash by piloting his own airplane.

Prudhomme made himself indispensably available. Soon Rhoda renounced her husband in New York, as well as her U.S. citizenship. Gabriel and Rhoda married in Paris and returned to Kenya to take up residency and build their dream house. Wasting no time, and with fortune on their side, the Prudhommes were able to obtain their slice of paradise in an enchanted expanse of forest near the small outpost town of Nanyuki, in a landscape sparsely dotted with farms. The style of the house, markedly grander in size and design than the up-country farmers', was finished in record time due to Rhoda's ability to hire extra labor.

Sadly, the house had only been occupied for one year when World War II began in Europe, causing Rhoda to return to the United States and Gabriel to join the Free French fighting in Algeria. When they reunited, the bloom was off the rose, and in the clear light of the realities of the day, their affection all but faded away. The house was eventually sold to the Block family, who owned two hotels in Nairobi and were growing their business. The Mawingu operated successfully as a weekend and holiday spot for locals coming up-country to escape the hot weather in Nairobi, but in the late 1950s, the Mawingu fell on hard times when its clients were put off by the insecurity of the Mau Mau emergency. The Blocks made it very clear that the Mawingu was up for sale.

Enter our three intrepid pals on safari.

The story Bill told me was that when they first stayed at the Mawingu, it was virtually empty, with the exception of one guest, a writer named Robert Rourke. Rourke was in the process of writing a book and was quite happy in the solitude of those idyllic surroundings. His books, like himself, would become legendary: *Something of Value, Uhuru,* and *The Reds and the Blacks.* The veranda of the house overlooked the forest and the mountain peak beyond and was a perfect site for watching the sun set, accompanied by the ritual assortment of drinks in keeping with the tradition of sundowners: the lower the sun, the more numerous the drinks and the greater the speculation on what could be done if someone—namely they— bought the place. It was common knowledge that the Mawingu was available at a good price. The end of the discussion was Rourke saying, "Put up or shut up." So when Ray returned alone to the Mawingu to recover from a gash above his eyebrow delivered by the scope of his rifle, he did just that. He put up his share and guaranteed that Bill and Carl would do their part. It was never mentioned how many drinks Ray had had that night.

As they transformed the Mawingu into the Mount Kenya Safari Club, Kenya received its independence, the jet set rose to prominence, and with Bill's celebrity, the club became *the* destination in East Africa.

Bill explained his transition from hunter to protector of wildlife through this story. Shortly after they bought the Mawingu, Bill was on safari and found an antelope in his crosshairs. He dispatched the animal with one shot. As he walked over to the animal, with its long, slender neck and its large eyes, he lifted the head and exclaimed, "Oh my God. I've just shot Audrey Hepburn." That was the last time Bill shot an animal for sport.

When the two thousand acres of land surrounding the Safari Club became available, he and two other friends bought it in partnership to create a game ranch, the first of its kind in East Africa to farm and preserve East African wildlife. They called it the Mount Kenya Game Ranch.

I WAS PREDISPOSED to fall in love with Kenya. So much of my life had prepared me to easily embrace and thoroughly enjoy life in a safari camp and on a game ranch. Having looked after so many animals both domestic and wild, having grown up playing childhood games on the Circle JR and riding fences on El Rancho Cola in the summertime in Ojai, California, and being a bit of a tomboy, it would not be too much of a stretch to adapt to life in the bush.

I always loved adventure, and I was *in* love with Bill.

TEN

Travels with Bill: The South Pacific

———⟨∞∞∞⟩———

One of the greatest affinities Bill and I shared was our love of travel, a pursuit neither one of us indulged in frivolously. *Vacations* held no interest for either one of us. Traveling with a purpose, with some interest in mind, preferably on an expedition, was far more attractive to us. Traveling with Bill was an entirely new experience. In anticipation of a trip, we would spend endless hours and days researching our destination and heightening our expectations. When we revisited Bill's old haunts, he took great pains to explain the cast of characters we would meet and what roles they played in his life.

Every place we went eventually played some part in my future. Little did I realize how much of a base Bill was helping me create. A new world that would restructure my life and, in some cases, change the course of my focus and priorities. Along the way I also fell deeper in love with Bill.

Our first magical mystery tour was to the South Pacific.

———⟨∞∞∞⟩———

IN 1972, JAMES Michener, Jean-Michel Cousteau, and William Holden (a rather stylish trio) were seduced by an Australian entrepreneur to join him in creating what today might be called a World Heritage Site out of a bite-sized piece of Melanesian paradise called the island of Wuvulu. Even the notion of this idea, let alone the name of the island, triggered a response in each of the protagonists that galvanized them to rise to the occasion of this enterprise.

Wuvulu Island, located just off the western coastline of the island of Papua New Guinea, is part of the Bismarck Archipelago, a name that reflects nineteenth-century German colonial ambitions. Names such as New Guinea, Guadalcanal, Lea, and Madang recalled for me the war in the Pacific so valiantly fought and so brilliantly recorded for the benefit of my generation by the iconic television series *Victory at Sea*. When I was a child, each week our household, along with every other family in the United States, was riveted to our television set, watching the images of the war our parents had fought, accompanied by that famously heroic musical score written by Richard Rodgers. In my mind, the names of the places I saw watching *Victory at Sea* epitomized exotic locations. Never did I imagine that one day I would stand on that ground.

For James Michener, the lure of Wuvulu was the ethnology of its inhabitants. When the great anthropologist Margaret Meade conducted her seminal work among the more than seven hundred tribes who spoke more than one thousand different languages on the island of Papua New Guinea, she called it the "Garden of Humanity." The resident ethnic group on the tiny island of Wuvulu, so close to its big sister, Papua New Guinea, would have been expected to contain elements of some of those seven hundred tribes. But amazingly enough, the people were not only unrelated to the main island tribes but also seemed to be unrelated to any of the inhabitants of the other small islands in their archipelago.

Jean-Michel Cousteau was drooling over the description he received of the uncompromised coral reef surrounding the island, formed as a result of its volcanic origins, with a maximum height of three meters above sea level. The reef was purported to be in an optimum and pristine condition, teeming with marine life.

And for Bill, ever driven by his curiosity, the reports of unusual subspecies of flora and fauna desperately in need of conservation were an irresistible magnet. The island had recently experienced an increase in human population due to traveling missionary doctors, and there were signs indicating that human predation on the island's fragile ecosystem would eventually render it so overexploited that it would be uninhabitable. It was fertile ground for education programs that would offer alternatives to habitat destruction, and Bill saw this as a marvelous opportunity.

In spite of General McArthur's conviction that the islands of the Bismarck Archipelago were crucial to his recapture of the Philippines during WWII, Wuvulu remained untouched, undefiled by either Japanese occupation or Allied liberation. It was a tropical Arcadia in need of assistance. Enraptured, the three men met in Sydney and embarked upon a mission of discovery. What they found did not disappoint them, and they formulated plans for a collective strategy to protect and preserve this invaluable human and environmental resource.

On his initial visit, before leaving Port Moresby on his way back to Sydney, Bill decided to spend a few days looking around. At the National Museum, still very much in its infancy, Bill began to acquaint himself with the fabled tribal art of Papua New Guinea, considered the finest of all Oceanian art forms. Soon he was directed to a place where he could purchase a few pieces. These works of art were to form the foundation of an extensive collection that was to come.

The object of our trip to Papua New Guinea was not to visit Wuvulu but also to travel up the Sepic River from Wewak (site of the Japanese surrender in the Pacific) to search for art. Bill was elated at the chance to explore the river areas, meet the tribes famous for their sculptures, and open a new territory for his, and now our, adventures.

Bill's interest in acquiring a collection of Oceanic art to accompany his already notable African and Southeast Asian collections was fed by his vision to display them in a gallery that would occupy a basement, the entire width and breadth of the new house. Bill was champing at the bit to express his considerably talented artistic "eye," and he saw the new house as a background for an art collection he was in the process of creating. Arranging these pieces was in effect *his* work of art. Today some of his collection can be seen on display in the William Holden Gallery at the Desert Museum in Palm Springs.

On the way across the Pacific from Los Angeles, loaded with mosquito repellent, first aid kits, and other essentials for jungle travel, we stopped off in Tahiti. I had kept in touch with a lovely wardrobe man with whom I had worked at MGM while doing *The Girl from U.N.C.L.E.* Jimmy was Marlon Brando's dresser when MGM filmed *Mutiny on the Bounty* in Tahiti. While they were on location, both Jimmy and his star met and married Tahitian women. Jimmy now lived full time in Papeete, and I wrote to him saying we would be staying a few days in his "town" before and after going to Bora-Bora. At the time, Tahiti was still a sleepy destination for all but the French, and it was clearly a small world where news traveled fast. I suspect everyone knew everyone else's business, because shortly after we checked into our hotel in Papeete, the telephone in the room rang. Bill answered the phone, and there was a long silence as the person on the other end was speaking. Finally Bill said, "Okay, Marlon, maybe on the way back before we leave."

Bill made a date with Marlon Brando to meet at our hotel on our return from Bora-Bora.

Tahiti's many islands were connected by a small charter airplane service. Landing on a man-made coral landing strip—emphasis on the *strip*—

was an exercise of nerve. A stretch of sandbar, packed with coral that was periodically washed away by the sea, constituted our terrestrial port of call in the middle of the incandescent, turquoise-colored South Pacific. Our expert bush pilot perfectly negotiated our landing to an ovation from his grateful passengers. We were met by a European, tanned to a mahogany hue, who greeted Bill as a long-lost friend and took us in his speedboat to our hotel. I have always found that most of the people who settle in out-of-the-way parts of the world have personal stories far better than any fiction could conjure, as was the case of the man who was our reception committee.

While in his late twenties and working in a factory in the dead of winter in northern Germany, he went to see a movie called *The World of Suzie Wong*. In the film, Bill played an American who left the States and a reasonably secure life to pursue his dream of becoming a painter. Bill's character settles in Hong Kong in one of the least salubrious districts called Wan Chai, which at the time was known for its open markets, fish restaurants, and brothels. The aspiring painter finds a modest apartment above a brothel, where he encounters the enchantingly beautiful Suzie Wong, played by Nancy Kwan.

The story became a paradigm for the young German: "If that guy can do it, so can I." He signed onto a tramp steamer and worked his way to the South Pacific, where he jumped ship in Tahiti, settled in Bora-Bora, and wound up owning the monopoly on all boat services for the island, which included meeting airplanes. Oh, and yes, he found his Suzie Wong in the person of a beautiful Tahitian/Chinese woman, with whom he produced four breathtakingly attractive children.

OUR BUNGALOW AT the original Bora-Bora hotel (then the only hotel on the island other than the ClubMed), was built on stilts over the ocean, where giant manta rays swam under our veranda in an endless ballet of loop-the-loops as they scooped plankton from the sea. Eventually we swam with these gentle giants, diving off our veranda into heaven. It was the closest thing I ever came to a honeymoon.

All too soon we were back in Papeete with the Marlon Brando rendezvous imminent. Brando had chosen to sail the thirty-six miles from his island, Tetiara. When he arrived, he looked like every nautical mile. He was the Marlon Brando post–*Last Tango in Paris* but pre-*Godfather,* still recognizable, with traces of the beauty of his youth. I was about to say that we had met before, having been introduced to him by my "uncle" Luther Adler, brother of Stella Adler, Brando's acting coach and mentor, but I thought better, and his greeting clearly indicated that my presence was not required. So I excused myself and found my way to the hotel pool.

After getting settled in a lounge chair, I looked up and was surprised to see Bill scouring the circumference of the pool looking for me. Obviously the meeting had adjourned in record time. Mystified, Bill explained what had happened. While filming *Mutiny on the Bounty,* Brando not only fell in love with a woman; he fell in love with an island, where he established himself and his growing extended family. In an effort to keep his island nation financially afloat, he constructed thirteen bungalows for well-paying guests, all of whom, no doubt, had expectations of, at the very least, getting a glimpse of their host.

Knowing that Bill was an owner of the Mount Kenya Safari Club, which had a constant stream of guests, Brando had sailed thirty-six miles to ask how Bill managed to avoid the guests. "How do you do it?" he'd asked. In fact, Bill didn't avoid the guests but had a strategy in order not to get trapped by anyone. Bill had a way of walking through the bar or the dining room at just enough of a pace not to get stopped, while smiling at people with a little wave of the hand when necessary. That seemed to satisfy them sufficiently, so the guests generally left him to his privacy in bungalow 12.

At this explanation, Brando had dropped his head into his hands, shaking it for the longest moment, then abruptly gotten up, embraced Bill . . . and left. Just like that.

Apparently, Brando heard what he came to hear, not necessarily what he wanted to hear, and that was that.

We said good-bye to Jimmy and Tahiti and pressed on across the Pacific to Australia. Since there was no flight directly to Port Moresby, the capital of Papua New Guinea, we were obliged to go all the way to Sydney, spend the night, and catch a flight that took us backtracking north, the width of Australia, to our destination. We arrived in Sydney in the late afternoon. In the 1970s, Sydney was still quite a provincial town, not yet emerged from its chrysalis to become the beautiful butterfly it is today. With its reputation as the last true frontier, Australia had a far rougher exterior at the time. Restrictive drinking laws required pubs to close early, encouraging their clients to drink as fast and as much as humanly possible before the doors were locked, leading to the quaint expression that Australian architecture was anything you could *hose* out.

<hr />

Post–World War II Papua New Guinea was under the rule of the Australian Trust, yet, at the time, few Australians traveled to those parts. Not so today, when international flights land directly in the capital and entrepreneurs from all over the world exploit the many resources hidden in the rain forests and mountain highlands, which are now being decimated by a gold rush. But in the 1970s, the Australian entrepreneur who had beguiled Michener, Cousteau, and Holden also saw a potential for himself on the island of Wuvulu. Even as we dined with him in Sydney the night we arrived, relations were strained. It was becoming apparent that behind his pretension to benevolence was his plan for a full-blown island resort, capitalizing on the three celebrated names as a front for his venture. Once the unholy nature of the proposed alliance was revealed, its doom was sealed. The only positive action to emerge from this failed enterprise was taken up by Jean-Michel Cousteau. Once Jean-Michel experienced the coral reef of Wuvulu Island, he began leading groups of students from Pepperdine University to study the rare and exquisite reef, eventually returning with his father and the *Calypso* to film the precious waters of the island. Through Jean-Michel's efforts, world awareness has led to greater protection for Wuvulu's glorious natural resources.

Undaunted by the collapse of the Wuvulu partnership, neither Bill nor I lost enthusiasm for our trip, and so with great anticipation we left for Port Moresby the following morning. Upon landing, the door to the plane opened and we were immediately inundated by overwhelming humidity, giving way to an extremely bad hair day for me. We were met by two friends of Bill's, Paul and Patty, who had recently severed their relationship with the Australian entrepreneur but who were still interested in the island of Wuvulu. That magical island did indeed live up to all my expectations.

Our time on the island was brief, living in fly tents on the sand, swimming in the delicious sea in lieu of a morning shower, and listening to the fables about the dolphins who came into the shallows to take the old ones on their backs out to sea, never to return. We were assured by many of the locals that this was more fact than fable, having been witnessed by more than one of the people we met.

We left our island paradise for the Sepic River, one of the most primitive places on earth, with reputedly more bugs per square inch than any other rain forest, all of which seemed to be fascinated by my insect repellent, leading to a less-than-attractive display of bites in various stages of inflammation on all my body parts. The river and its many tribes were relatively unspoiled by the modern world, save for the missionaries and the traders, who trafficked in crocodile hides exchanged for hard goods. We discovered an intoxicating variety of magnificent carvings, all traditionally produced to express emotional and spiritual life, as different from village to village as from tribe to tribe.

Once back in the capital, we met Michael Sumari, the designated first president of the newly independent Papua New Guinea. He was a young man who had done great work pacifying unrest among his people. President Sumari was interested in speaking with Bill about Kenya's early days of independence. We went to a party given by the newly appointed government, who were all young men and women, and it was like attending a college beer bust with kegs of beer and old rock 'n' roll music playing on a cassette boom box. They were filled with hope and dreams, and they loved Bill for his enthusiasm and admiration for their art forms, many of which were now in crates bound for Palm Springs. Leaving Papua New Guinea, we were obliged to return to Sydney to make our onward connection to another island paradise, Bali.

The first fully operational runways for long-haul aircraft had just opened at Denpasar's airport, mass tourism not yet having descended upon them. Kuta Beach was a string of shacks, and Ubud was unsullied. The sound of wind chimes always stay with me for weeks after I leave Bali, which was then and still remains a magically beautiful place.

Our next stop was Singapore.

WHEN BILL FIRST began traveling around Southeast Asia, there were three doyennes of the Asian art world—Helen Ling in Singapore, Connie Mangskau in Bangkok, and Charlotte Horstman in Hong Kong. Helen Ling had a magnificent gallery in Singapore, and Bill was looking for something special to add to his collection, which she unfortunately did not have. But it was fascinating for me to meet the woman in whose weekend house Jim Thompson disappeared.

In the 1950s, Jim Thompson, an American, brought brightly colored

Thai silk to *Vogue* magazine, where it became a fashion statement in clothing and interior design and created a cottage industry out of a handicraft, changing the economy of villages around Bangkok. He became a national hero in Thailand. Thompson was also great friends with Bangkok's premier art dealer, Connie Mangskau, and together they found the beautiful Thai Village houses that comprise the Jim Thompson Museum, still a must on every tourist's itinerary. Thompson and Connie traveled together to the highlands of Malaysia to spend that fateful weekend as houseguests of Helen Ling and her husband.

After lunch, Thompson was seen to take a walk to the far end of the garden on a path leading to the surrounding forest. He was never seen again. Many books have been written on his mysterious disappearance, and it remains part of Southeast Asian mythology.

Helen invited us to spend a weekend at that fabled house, but we had made plans to drive up the east coast of Malaysia to Quantan to see the sea turtles spawn. We all dined together the night before we left at a long table, Bill and I sitting at opposite ends. I recall looking at him admiringly, down the length of the table, as he conducted an animated conversation, and I felt so thrilled to be with him, so proud that he was mine.

That night, the hotel air-conditioning went off and there was no way to open any windows in the modern skyscraper hotel, so we simply fell asleep in pools of perspiration, only to find in the morning that sometime during the night the air-conditioning had come back on in full force; I awoke with my head rooted to my shoulder, frozen in a cramp that made it impossible for me to lift it from a horizontal position. It was pretty funny through breakfast, but when the desk called to say that our rental car had arrived, I realized that I was going to have to make the entire trip looking at Malaysia from a decided list to the left. I wrapped my neck with a towel in a sort of ersatz neck brace and tried to be inconspicuous as I walked through the lobby, but it didn't work.

The drive to our destination was four hours of absolute agony on a two-lane highway. It was well before the modern superhighway was built, so we had to dodge potholes and enormous logging trucks speeding in the opposite direction with the trunks of giant trees held down by thin strips of chain, promising to crush us at any mishap. Finally we arrived in Quantan, but sadly the turtles didn't. We sat on the beach, my head on my and Bill's shoulder, after I'd taken every conceivable painkiller and muscle-relaxing elixir, none of which had had any effect whatsoever.

WITHOUT THE TURTLES to keep us in place, we decided to move on to our next destination. We were to cross the highlands of Malaysia to Kuala Lumpur, turn north to Ipo and Butterworth, where we would catch the ferry across the Strait of Malacca to the island of Penang. Our hotel in Quantan had kindly packed us a delicious picnic lunch, which we happily consumed at a lovely spot just off the main road crossing the north-south mountain range that runs the length of the Malaysian peninsula. As we sat on the grass enjoying the view, we were serenaded by the calls of gibbon apes ringing across the forest of the valley below. Suddenly the gibbons' song was interrupted by the sound of automatic weapons, reverberating against the mountains, from which direction we could not tell.

Bill knew very well what that sound meant. In the early 1960s, Bill made a film in Malaysia called *The Seventh Dawn,* inspired by a book Bill had read. It told the story of the guerilla war fought by Communist-backed insurgents, which began after World War II ended and was still going on, the same guerilla movement that was suspected to have kidnapped Jim Thompson.

We jumped into the car and headed for the main road. Miraculously, coming up the road was a military-escorted convoy accompanying a line of private cars attempting to make the journey across the highlands to Kuala

Lumpur. Gratefully we joined the fleet, and in Kuala Lumpur we picked up our route by following the signs indicating north. Somewhere along the way, our rental car had lost its air-conditioning, but with the windows down it was not too bad, as long as we kept moving. Finally we arrived at the ferry dock, luckily just in time to be the first car on the ferry.

Behind us the ferry filled up with commuters traveling home at rush hour. We shut the engine off and got out of the car to enjoy the spectacle of the golden sun setting into the waters of the Strait of Malacca. It was like a postcard. As we came close to the dock, we returned to the car. Bill put the key in the ignition and turned it over. Nothing. Not even the sound of the starter attempting to ignite the engine. Behind us was the entire population of Butterworth on their way home from work and not at all happy for the delay.

After many tries it was apparent that the car was frozen and the only thing we could do was to try and push it up the ramp and out on to the dock so that the horde of passengers could disembark. As we pushed, me still with my stiff neck, it was obvious we were not going to make it. Coming to our rescue was a carload of Malays, one of whom had a few words of English. They took over pushing the car up the ramp and onto the side of the dock so the impatient commuters could speed home. These more than kind people not only helped us off the ferry, they also insisted on taking us to our hotel.

Fortunately their tiny compact car had a sunroof. I sat on Bill's lap with my head half out the roof while eight of us squeezed into the car. Our luggage was stuffed into a pedicab, who was instructed to follow us. We drove to the far side of Penang, stopping on the way to call the hotel to say that we were arriving.

As we pulled up to the grand hotel, we must have been quite a sight. The manager of the hotel and his staff had formed a reception committee awaiting our arrival. Disgorging the passengers from the tiny car made for a rather inglorious entrance: I backed out rear end first, not to mention the condition of my hair, but Bill, ever gracious, managed to exit the car looking exactly like a movie star, somehow compensating for my farcical deportment. There was no way we could have thanked our saviors enough, and they refused any form of recompense—even a drink—so we said our grateful good-bye. I will always carry with me an abiding affection for the Malaysian people.

I was totally unprepared for the hustle and bustle of Bangkok, whose once graceful serenity was irreversibly altered by the Vietnam War when it became the location of R&R for the U.S. military. Connie Mangskau's gallery was located in the Erewan hotel and was a treasure trove of beautiful objects. Clearly Bill and Connie were dear friends, and it didn't take long to learn what a remarkable woman she was. How fortunate for me that Connie would also become a dear and treasured friend of mine, as would her daughter and her grandchildren. While going through room after room of magnificent art looking for the piece Bill had described, I found a sculpture I instantly fell in love with. It was a torso, probably a depiction of the Buddha; Connie said it was Khmer from Cambodia and most likely late ninth or early tenth century. I had never owned, if anyone ever really owns, a piece of such age, and it was a daunting idea and a bit more than I could afford.

Bill called me over to see a piece he was interested in. It was also Cambodian and also a depiction of the Buddha, but much more complete a sculpture than my torso. By the glint in his eye I knew he had found what he was looking for. Surprisingly he did not purchase it.

"I want to want it more," he said, and we agreed to "sleep on it."

In the morning over breakfast both of us were still lusting over our choices, and he made a deal with me. He wanted me to buy "my torso," and he would bet that either I would shortly get a job that would render the price of the piece irrelevant, or he would reimburse me.

"Sometimes you have to bet on yourself," he said.

No one had ever given me that kind of confidence. His believing in me as much as he did at that moment made me believe in myself. In the end, I did get a job that made the purchase, while not irrelevant, at least not painful. That sculpture, under Bill's tutelage, opened a door for me, leading to my appreciation of Southeast Asian art and history that will ever be my life's companion.

BY THE TIME we arrived in Hong Kong, our relationship was maturing. Like wine, the bouquet of shared emotions was becoming full and rich. Hong Kong rekindled the beginning of our romance with one most important caveat: it was not clouded by alcohol. I knew that Bill had rituals when he would arrive in a place as familiar to him as Hong Kong. Having a drink was not only a ritual; it punctuated his life, as did cigarettes, an addiction we shared. My drug of choice bore the red and white iconic label of Marlboro, while Bill chose Salem menthol. Cigarettes always seemed a natural accompaniment to a drink, so it must have been agony for him, but he never touched a drop the whole time we were in Hong Kong, despite the usual round of social activities that were typical of life there.

Between his friends and mine, all of whom knew each other, we navigated the rounds of events that constituted the intercourse of the unusual society attracted to the "Fragrant Harbor." One of those whose family had prospered in Hong Kong was Elaine Forsgate. I met Elaine while she was visiting Hollywood, and we immediately connected and have become lifelong friends. Her family embraced me as one of their own. All of Bill's friends knew the Forsgates, but Bill did not, and I was happy they all got along.

We lingered in Hong Kong as long as we could until the call of work summoned us home.

Work was always interfering with our wanderlust.

ELEVEN

Travels with Bill: Africa

From the day we met, we talked about going to Africa, and I could hardly contain myself when finally the time was right for my first safari.

Safari is a Swahili word meaning "trip." Swahili is a language that evolved as a means of communication for the traders who sailed down the east coast of Africa from the Arabian Peninsula in their graceful vessels called dows. Eventually Swahili found its way from the coast through what we now know as Kenya, Tanzania, and around Lake Victoria. When the colonials began to travel to that part of the world, they were not only looking to colonize but they were also drawn to hunt the exceptional species that populated those parts. Thus "safari" became synonymous with hunting, and later, when shooting cameras became more popular than shooting guns, "photographic safaris" replaced hunting for the new form of traveler . . . the tourist.

WHEN I FINALLY got a break from work, we took off, stopping first in New York City for the launch of Peter Beard's book *Longing for Darkness*. Peter spent a good deal of time in Kenya on his way to becoming a renowned artist, author, and colorful eccentric. Peter was an original, wild in every way . . . wildly talented, wildly eccentric, and wildly wild. New York engulfed us for the long weekend, and we were swept up by the typical round of lunches, dinners, and plays.

Knowing that I admired her, Bill arranged for us to lunch with another great friend of his, the writer Lillian Hellman. The two had not seen each other for some time. Naturally I held no real interest for her, so I played the part of fly on the wall and learned the lesson that sometimes it is best to admire legends from afar.

We dined after the theater with Lauren Bacall, whose friends call her Betty, and that was much more rewarding, since I did know her. Candy Bergen stopped by the table to say hello and talk about Africa, where she had been for the first time the previous year and was full of enthusiasm. Jack Nicholson paid his respects to Bill. The restaurant, Elaine's, was and is one of the most popular spots for running into people in the arts, and everyone wanted to say hello to Bill.

Our last day in New York was occupied with shopping, not the least of which was at the magic store, where Bill would stock up on tricks such as flash paper and pop-up flowers, all to amuse and delight the tribal children we would meet in the bush. We were more than ready to leave when we boarded our Pan Am flight that would take us across the Atlantic, stopping first in Liberia, next in Nigeria, and finally in Nairobi twenty-two hours after leaving New York.

We were met by the smiling faces of Don Hunt and Iris Bridenbend, who would become two of my best friends in life. Don, a gregarious, red-haired Irish Catholic from Michigan, and Iris, a well-bred, naturally blond German with a wicked sense of humor, who had grown up in the Middle East, met each other in Nairobi. A more perfect and complementary pair it would be hard, if not impossible, to find. They were Bill's partners, who, along with their good pal Julian McKeand, founded the Mount Kenya Game Ranch.

After a hectic day shopping for essentials in the bustling city of Nairobi, we drove in Don's heavily laden Land Rover over a partially paved roadway north to the slopes of Mount Kenya, where the Mount Kenya Safari Club and the comforts of a shower and a bed awaited us.

I don't recall having taken a sleeping pill, but then I don't recall much after the shower, because the trip and the altitude of seven thousand feet above sea level had combined to produce the most delicious sleep in memory. That much I do remember. Cottage 12, Bill's private abode, was located at the end of a line of cottages all discreetly hidden from one another's view by lovely plantings. In full view was the magnificence of the second-tallest mountain on the African continent, Mount Kenya. Kirinyaga, the Kikuyu name for Kenya, holds myths and legends, and exudes all within its majesty.

The "Club," as the locals called the Mount Kenya Safari Club, lived up to its reputation. The exceptional position of the property was indeed worthy of all the folklore surrounding its development within the context of two great love affairs. In fact the place seemed to have an exceptional attraction for lovers, which was personified by Durie, the woman occupying the cottage next to us. She was an Eastern Seaboard patrician. She had the style and easy manner portrayed by Grace Kelly on the screen. When she was eighteen years old, she and the young John F. Kennedy were the golden couple at the exclusive Newport Beach Club in Rhode Island. It was rumored that they had eloped that summer but their marriage had been annulled and the story buried by the powerful political machinery of Ambassador Kennedy, the patriarch. Durie had come to Kenya to spread her second husband's ashes on Mount Kenya. If the Kennedy marriage was true, they would have been her third husband's ashes.

Both Durie and her husband Tommy held similar pedigrees that effused the aroma of very old money, which they wore lightly and without pretension. For years they would come to the club, take cottage 11 for two months, and use it as the base for their activities.

The club offered services for their regular clients that included storing their safari clothes and gear in specially made trunks, perfectly looked after until their next visit. In some cases, clients left furniture, paintings, and stereo sets, everything to make their cottage feel like home. When the guests were due to arrive, all their belongings would be installed in their bungalow, their clothes would be taken from their trunks, pressed and hung in the closet just as they requested, the ice would be in the bucket, and the fireplace lit. Those were the good old days.

Durie was my friend until the day she died, and she generously became my passport to Palm Beach and Newport society when I began fund-raising for the William Holden Wildlife Foundation after Bill's death.

The Mount Kenya Game Ranch was established as a conservation effort, and Don's capture unit was the finest live capture operation in East Africa. He received orders for animals from zoos and zoological parks all over the world, providing only reputable organizations with wildlife for their collections. Being adept at the lasso, Bill would join him on many of the captures. On some occasions, the government, in the form of the Game Department, would ask for help in areas where species were being poached. My first safari was to be in pursuit of Grevy's zebras, at the request of the government.

Don and Iris had established a camp far into the northern frontier, where the Grevy were on the brink of extinction. This was a long-term project that entailed the capturing and translocation of large numbers of these zebras to the safety of a national park in the south called Tsavo. The Grevy is a subspecies of zebra found only in Kenya, and it is defined by its large size, its many fine stripes, and its rounded Mickey Mouse ears. The effort was in its second season when we arrived.

Don and Iris's organization of the camp and the capture unit was so flawlessly done that they made it seem effortless. It did not occur to me until years later how difficult it was to accomplish. After having lived in Kenya for nearly thirty years now, I still marvel at how well done those camps were and how inventive the cook was in order to produce wonderful meals over a campfire, with freshly baked bread and all the trimmings, served in a mess tent with cloth linens that were washed and pressed daily. A hot shower was never more than a few minutes away, after calling for it with the first Swahili phrase I was taught: *"Maji moto, tafadali!"*

EACH MORNING WE were awakened before dawn with hot tea and biscuits. We climbed out of our cozy beds and into our gear, then loaded onto the vehicles and went off for the chase. It was essential to arrive on the open plains, where it was flat enough to pursue an animal at first light, while it was still cool.

The scenario would go like this; Don was the driver of the capture car, a short-wheelbase Land Rover the size of a military Jeep specially modified for the job with a platform where the passenger seat should be and a large rubber tire fastened to the roll bars that formed a crossed support in case they overturned. Bill stood on the platform and inside the tire, which was meant to cushion him as he maneuvered a lasso attached to a long bamboo pole, with which he could lasso either zebra or giraffe. He was very good at his job. It might have been due to all the Western movies he did that made Bill amazingly accurate and fast. Once the chase began and Don maneuvered the animal into ever decreasing circles, the capture had to be done within minutes or there would be too much stress on the creature.

In all the years I was involved in those captures, no matter what the animal, I saw only one that had to be destroyed. That was due to its foot having previously been wrapped up in a poacher's snare, causing it to break its ankle.

Iris drove the backup vehicle with the crates for the animals, and on many occasions she acted as the side flank to drive the animals in a specific direction. The minute a zebra was caught, Don, Bill, and the three men in the backseat of the catching car would jump out. Then it was a rodeo to slowly bring the animal in close to the vehicle, where they could press it against the side of the catching car and administer injections, first an anti-stress vitamin complex to boost its metabolism and not allow it to go into shock, and then a full-spectrum antibiotic to minimize the intestinal parasites that might multiply with the stress of capture. They were so good they made it all look easy. In the beginning I rode with Iris and took pictures, as did she, although hers were much better than mine. Eventually I graduated to the capture car and to giving injections.

Each day three or four zebras were captured and the corrals began to fill up. Bomas, as they call paddocks or corrals, were carefully constructed and surrounded by a curtain of bamboo matting to shield the animals from view. This made them more likely to calm down and feed on the cut grass and water placed inside the confinement. If an animal did not drink within twenty-four hours, it would be released. All precautions were taken to ensure the safety of the animals over all other considerations.

After the first week, we began to see a white zebra with beige stripes grazing on a hillside we passed, going out each morning and coming home each night. The zebra never seemed to be stressed with our presence and calmly watched us on our way to and fro. At lunch one day, Don and Bill decided to capture the white zebra; not only was it rare but someone might also get the idea that it was more valuable as a carpet.

Bill passed on to me a famous old hunter's tale that had been told to him on safari. It was about approaching animals in a herd. Once they smelled or caught sight of you and began to panic, you had to choose your quarry carefully and home in on it. After you made your choice, all the other animals seemed to know it was not them, and they stopped running and watched. Likewise, the white zebra stood still, watching us as the capture car turned toward him. After so many days of our passing him by, he obviously thought he wasn't wanted, so he stood there for the longest time, staring at us in disbelief until we got so close it was hardly a chase at all. This young male was destined to return to the game ranch, where he lived a long and productive life, but it took five years before his "white" gene pool showed up.

One day a baby zebra was born that was an odd shade of dark brown. As it grew, it began to lighten up in the same way a gray horse does. Today the game ranch has the only herd of albinized Burchell's zebras in the world, and now they are born white with beige stripes, proving that the mutant color gene has established itself successfully enough to call them a true subspecies. The "white" zebras have been such prolific breeders that Don decided to release some into the national park forest adjacent to the ranch. One day they will be known as the famous white zebras of Mount Kenya, and no one will remember where they really came from.

WE RETURNED TO the club after catching the quota, and after a few days to collect ourselves, we took off on the next leg of the safari.

Dougie Aldrige was Bill's bush pilot of choice. He and Bill had worked out an itinerary by plane that would take us north again, this time to Lake Rudolph, whose primordial landscape makes you think of the beginnings of mankind. The Leakey family, who discovered the oldest hominid remains, in the Olduvai Gorge in Tanzania, had a dig at the lake and were discovering more remnants of early man, which seemed appropriate in that atmosphere.

The most interesting accommodation on the lake had been closed, but we flew over it and saw the picturesque Robinson Caruso arrangement. We landed on the west bank at Loingalani, where there was a small outpost with a missionary school and a considerably less-romantic-looking guesthouse, whose manager drank endless bottles of champagne while lounging near the half-filled excuse for a swimming pool.

Bill had filmed a documentary at Lake Rudolph, now renamed Lake Turkana. During his time at the lake, Bill had met the El Molo tribe, who were few in number and on the verge of extinction, suffering from protein starvation. With only fish to eat and no complex carbohydrates, the El Molo were literally wasting away from too much protein. In an effort to help, Bill had arranged for regular shipments of cornmeal to augment their diet. The tribe was rebounding from the brink, and they were extremely happy to see Bill. After Bill's death I visited them whenever I could, each time bringing what I was able to get into my plane, and they were always happy and loving.

Now they have intermarried with other tribes, and some have gone away, so the El Molo will soon be only a memory, but once, with full stomachs, they played with the balloons Bill inflated for them along the shores of Lake Rudolph and time stopped.

Next we went to the coast, to the picturesque town of Lamu, once a major port for the dow traders. The Arab influence dominated the architecture and lifestyle, and the call to prayer at the mosque punctuated the day. Don and Iris joined us at a favorite coastal inn called Pepone, run by a family everyone seemed to know. Lamu had not yet been "discovered," so it was still intimate. I had a private joke with Bill that involved my Polish heritage: it was uncanny that almost everywhere we would go, I would find someone Polish. We were all sitting at the bar at the Pepone when I heard someone speaking Polish. I whispered to Bill that there were Polish people here. He said, "Now I'm going to get you. I know everyone here, and there are no Polish people."

"Oh, yes, there are," I said.

"Oh, no, there aren't," he said.

Finally, Don got involved.

"Are there Polish people in Kenya?" I asked.

Don looked over to a table and called out, "Hey, Stash, how are you?"

It was Stanislaw Sapia, a Polish aristocrat who had lived for so many years in Kenya that Bill had forgotten he was Polish. LOL.

Lamu was filled with wonderful artisans who crafted wood into beautiful doors and furniture. Every once in a while, a rare Lamu chest would appear for sale that was authentically from dow: the captains of the dows traditionally would keep their valuables in a large wooden chest made of a wood called banda coffee, which was impervious to the sea air and spray. If the chest had some age, there would be elaborate brass designs hammered into it on all sides, signifying each trip the vessel had made. Bill was after a chest, so we scoured the back alleys and came up with two beauties, or rather, once the muck was off them they would be beauties. He bought one for me and one for himself and, with fingers crossed, arranged to have them shipped. I think it took the better part of a year to receive them, but they did finally arrive in California, along with a magnificent door that wound up at the entrance to his office in the new house.

We left Lamu for Mombasa, checking in to the Nyali Beach Hotel. Bill was looking forward to a nice shower, but just as he turned on the faucets and soaped up, the water reduced itself to a trickle and died. The hotel was completely out of water. I managed to get a few large bottles of drinking water downstairs and Bill was able to rinse off most of the soap, but he was not amused. Don, Iris, Dougie, and I were, of course, and opted for a swim in the sea and a hose off by the pool.

The next day we landed on the famed spice island of Zanzibar. I never for a moment questioned any of the arrangements—I just assumed everyone knew what they were doing and I was along for a glorious ride. In actual fact, we had landed without permission in another country, with no visas and no invitation, both of which were necessary at the time. To make matters worse, our pilot was wearing shorts, not acceptable garb according to the Muslim rules. Finally, as it was getting dark and we had argued until the time had passed for us to take off, the authorities relented and we were allowed to go to their only hotel, provided our pilot wore a sarong wrapped around his shorts.

Zanzibar was a part of Tanzania, which at the time had a Communist government that was simultaneously courting both the Russians and the Chinese. We found a taxi and rode down the beautiful, tree-lined, perfectly asphalted avenue that led from the airport to the hotel. Quite typical of the Soviet aid packages of that era, there was one road and one hotel whose architecture was reminiscent of a cement bunker. As we looked down the adjoining streets, they were a shamble of broken tarmac and rubble. A few years earlier, the prosperous Asian community of Zanzibar had suffered annihilation by racial cleansing, and the pockmarks of the gun shells were still in evidence on the walls of the buildings in the old town. All the shops were closed and the place was a ghost town. Our hotel, on the other hand, was a beehive of activity—mostly guests from the USSR and China. The atmosphere was reminiscent of a black-and-white spy movie starring Peter Lorre and Sydney Greenstreet.

Finally we could no longer avoid going to our rooms. It was the sort of place where you wanted to sleep in your clothes to avoid touching the sheets. Bill was determined to shower, but there was no shower, so he had to try a bath. I left him in the tub and went downstairs to the bar to get a bottle of water for a sponge bath. I met Don and Iris there, and all of a sudden the lights went out in the entire hotel. All I could think of was Bill half submerged in the dark. At least the water worked. Kerosene lamps came out and Bill appeared, not amused, which only made us laugh even more, since we were already giddy with fatigue.

In the clear light of dawn things looked different. They looked worse. So we said a fond farewell to Zanzibar and left it to the Reds.

We flew into the crater at Ngorongoro, stopped for lunch at Fort Incoma, the last stronghold of the Germans, and stopped for the night at Tita Hills Lodge, run by the former manager of the Safari Club. The next day we arrived home to the club and crashed. We still had a lot of geography to cover.

I had obviously passed muster with Bill's friends, and in his eyes I fit in. It made me glow when I heard him praise my ability to adapt to even the most uncomfortable surroundings and in the next moment be able to put on an evening gown. I had no doubt that in saying good-bye to Kenya, it was only au revoir.

———

WE SPENT THREE days in Addis Ababa, mainly to look up some of Bill's friends who had survived the Ethiopian revolution and the change of regimes. The pall over the once vibrant city was palpable. Still, one of the surviving friends made our stay as jolly as he could.

My most memorable souvenir of Ethiopia was our visit to a famous whorehouse in Addis, where it was said the food was the best in town. The only thing you had to be prepared for was to be fed by the hand of a complete stranger, and I mean by *her hand.*

Wat and ngera is the national dish, and it consists of a large, yeast-filled doughy sheet that is draped over a table like a cloth, then all sorts of meats and vegetables are put onto the center of the round sheet. Your "server" rips off a piece of dough with her fingers and grabs a bit of this and that from the center, then pops it into your mouth. There was no way to anticipate the taste, or the combustible results of the dinner. Thus giving way to the nickname of the dish . . . *wait and endure.* The local brew was an interesting honey liquor that seemed innocent enough until you attempted to stand. My first trip to Ethiopia was not as fascinating as subsequent trips would be, but at least I got my feet wet.

We were on our way to the film festival in Tehran, where Bill had agreed to head the jury. It was also a pretext to see his son, who was living and working there. First we had to spend the night in Athens, where it was very cold and snowing. Tehran had also been snowed upon, but it was in the process of melting and the skies were clear. Alexis Smith and Craig Stevens, two dear friends of Bill's, were also at the festival, and we became inseparable. Our hosts were part of the royal family. The minister of culture was married to the eldest sister of the shah of Iran, and officially he was the organizer of the festival. They were very generous to us and provided us with wonderful trips to the legendary cities of Isfahan, Persepolis, and Shiraz.

Finally, after our lovely sightseeing, duty called, and Bill had to see some movies. On the day of the night we were to meet the Shah Pahlavi and the Empress Farah, Bill recommended that I go see the famed crown jewels while he was occupied at the festival. We had a translator assigned to us, and she agreed to accompany me to the oldest section of town, in the center of Tehran, to the vaults where the jewels were exhibited, which was quite a distance from our hotel. The opulence of the collection of gemstones on display defied description. The size and number of stones, all arranged in baskets and mounted in separate displays according to the type of jewel, were jaw dropping.

Perhaps I lingered too long, or perhaps it had taken us too long to fight the traffic to get to this part of town, but when I finished my adoration of the jewels we found ourselves in the middle of rush hour. As we inched our way back to the Hilton Hotel, the translator said something to the driver of the taxi and handed him some money. She then asked me if I wouldn't mind excusing her, because if she had to go with me to the hotel then return to her house to dress and accompany us to the palace, she would never make it in time. She said she had paid the driver and instructed him where to go, and with great emphasis, she said, "Under no circumstances get out of the car."

I didn't feel threatened, so I happily agreed, and off she went. Rush hour is as filled with tension in Tehran as it is in any capital city. Still, we were moving slowly but in a forward path, until out of the blue we entered an intersection that merged the traffic from six directions. It seemed more like a rugby scrum, only with cars, all trying to move against the flow, if there was a flow.

Farsi is not one of the six languages I'm able to get along in, nor is it in any way similar to anything I could relate to, but my driver's frustration was expressed in a universal language, and I nodded in agreement. Moving perpendicular to the bow of the taxi was a car driven by a man who seemed oblivious to the fact that both his car and ours were made of metal, not a substance that easily gives way. Without so much as a sideward glance, the car began to plow into the front of the taxi. By this time everyone in every other car was screaming at each other, shouting expletives that I later discovered cast aspersions on the moral character of their sainted mothers. My taxi driver was in full voice directing all his insults at the offending driver, who, at a certain point, changed the expression on his face so dramatically that I, even as uninitiated as I was, could tell that my driver had crossed the line. Suddenly all sorts of hard items and garbage were thrown at the driver's window. In response, my taxi driver reached under his seat and extracted the largest ball-peen hammer I have ever seen. Calmly he rolled down his window and climbed out, walking across his car to the hood of the car belonging to the instigator, and proceeded to bash in the windscreen and the roof of the car.

After a suitable amount of time, quite satisfied with his work, the taxi driver climbed back into the taxi through the window. Traffic began to dislodge itself from the coagulated mess it had become, and without even a glance at each other, both adversaries moved on toward their destinations.

I was very happy to see the Hilton Hotel, and when, a few years later, during the revolution against the shah, we saw on TV men marching in the streets of Tehran, whipping themselves with chains in a demonstration of solidarity, I didn't recognize any of the faces, but I certainly recognized the emotion.

Our way back to the States included a stop in Geneva, where Bill was in the last stages of closing his apartment and giving up his Swiss resident status.

We took a lovely drive along Lake Geneva to the village of Mourge, where we turned off the main road, following a small route that gave access to the houses, or rather estates that lined the lake, one of which was called Beau Jardin. The house was aptly named. The beautiful garden that surrounded the house and sloped down to the water's edge to the boat dock made it a dream property. Sadly it was no longer in the family, having been sold after Bill's divorce.

According to the Swiss laws at the time, all residents who filed for divorce were subject to Swiss jurisprudence, regardless of their nationality. Whereas California divorces required a 50/50 split of all assets, generally regarded as highly punitive, Swiss law demanded separate maintenance for a term of three years, during which time one of the spouses, depending on who had the larger income, was obliged to maintain the other in the manner he or she had become accustomed to. The definition of the lifestyle to be supported was rather loose, which gave way to rampant abuse of monthly expenses and shopping sprees that sometimes had to be stopped by a court order.

One day an old friend of the Holdens sat me down, unsolicited by me, on the pretext of telling me how good I was for Bill. She gave me a blow-by-blow description of his relationship with his wife—from her point of view, of course, which included all the gory details of the acrimonious divorce. I was raised to believe that there are always two sides to every story, so suffice it to say that I am sure they must have had some lovely times together at Beau Jardin; at least it was an ideal setting for a beautiful life.

⊸⧉⊶

WE RETURNED TO L.A. in time to usher in the new year at the home of the award-winning producer Sam Spiegel. Spiegel was the producer of *Bridge on the River Kwai.* The party was a command performance for whoever was in Hollywood at the time. Behind every potted palm was a recognizable face.

Historically, distinctive faces were the criteria for casting films. There was an old Hollywood saying that described the five stages of an actor's career:

- "Who's Ava Gardner?"
- "Get me Ava Gardner!"
- "Get me an Ava Gardner type!"
- "Get me a young Ava Gardner!"
- "Who's Ava Gardner?"

Young actors of today are not so cultivated for their uniqueness as for their similarities, and many of them are instantly replaced by a crop of younger look-alikes.

I feel very sorry for the new generation, who find themselves has-beens at twenty-eight.

TWELVE

Travels with Bill: China

———— ⊷⊶ ————

Bill was in New York City filming *Network,* and I was working in L.A. He asked me to bring him some items from his wardrobe and his mail, so I drove to the desert and picked up what he wanted, finding a letter addressed to both of us sent from Papua New Guinea. The letter contained a proposition from President Michael Sumari regarding the sale and promotion of Papua New Guinea art. I read the letter to Bill over the phone, and I knew that it ignited his sense of adventure, as it did mine. He was fascinated with the idea, and he was looking forward to ruminating over it with me when I arrived.

I had a close girlfriend in New York who was a Ford model married to an up-and-coming young lawyer. Bill loved Ani and grew to like Richard, whom he vetted as if Ani had been his own daughter. The first night we all had dinner in New York, Bill and I were filled with enthusiasm over the proposal we had received. The president of Papua New Guinea, in an effort to help establish a viable economy for the diverse people of his island, wanted to create cottage industries for those who still lived in a traditional manner and represented a majority of the population. Because there was a moratorium on crocodile hunting, traders were not going upriver to bring and trade essentials. Seeking employment, villagers were migrating to urban areas, where there was no work for people unskilled in modern methods. Unemployed, the villagers had nothing to do but chew betel nut all day and loiter on street corners, becoming a serious social problem.

President Sumari offered to pay for the production of tribal art as a means to attract villagers home. He knew of Bill's admiration for the art of the local people, and he offered us the exclusive right to represent Papua New Guinea art for the world! It was a grandiose idea but far too all-encompassing. It did, however, appeal to our pipe dream of using Bill's great taste and understanding of primitive art to make collections we could put on exhibit and sell, which would be the pretext and financing for further adventures to unusual places.

As the four of us indulged in the fantasy of an art business, Richard came up with an idea: Bloomingdale's department store was at the height of its popularity, and the home furnishings floor was a magnet for clients who perused the displays in the beautifully decorated model rooms. What if we could interest Bloomingdale's in taking a collection of art to accent the decor of the rooms?

Before I knew it, Richard had made an appointment for us with the manager of the home furnishings department, who, coincidentally, was the brother of my first agent. Carl Levine was very interested in our idea, but he wanted to see some of the pieces in Bill's collection.

Filled with more enthusiasm than sense, I flew back to Palm Springs, took lots of Polaroid pictures of Bill's collection, and returned to New York. The appointment was set, and I met with Richard to give him a tutorial on the country and the art. On my way to Richard's office I stopped at Rizzoli's bookshop and picked up a large book on the art of Oceania. Armed with the book and thirteen Polaroid pictures, Richard and I set off for our meeting.

As we were ushered into the giant boardroom of Bloomingdale's, adorned with an extensive mahogany table overlooked by the mammoth portraits of the department store magnates leering down at us, the atmosphere was decidedly more serious than it had been at our prior meeting in Carl's office.

When all the players had assembled, Carl entered and began the introductions. I was given the floor, and with no experience, never having made a presentation of a business kind, I began.

Flying by the seat of my pants, I sounded like a dissertation on the anthropology of the South Pacific: "Let me first locate Papua New Guinea for you. Papua New Guinea is the largest island in Melanesia, with a population consisting of seven hundred tribes speaking over one thousand different languages among slightly over two million people . . ."

On and on I went, intermittently sliding the book and the thirteen Polaroid pictures around the table, hoping to cover our complete lack of experience in the ways of the retail world. The faces of those at the table reflected a sort of mesmerized shock at my unconventional presentation.

When I sat down Carl took over, and it became instantly apparent that he had already made the decision to commit to this venture. Carl outlined the parameters of the deal, and it came at us with the speed of a Gatling gun: three hundred pieces FOB NYC for $100,000 retail value, including a 120 percent markup. It was all an alien language to me, and we left the meeting in a bit of a daze.

It took us two blocks to realize that we had done it! We jumped up and down in the middle of the rush hour traffic on the corner of Lexington and 62nd Street.

That night, we had a celebratory dinner and came up with a name for our little company: W.A. Stefrick Imports Ltd. The W was for William, the A for Ani, and Stef and Rick because we were going to do most of the work. It was then and there that we began thinking of China and how our venture might give us access to the PRC, as it was called—the People's Republic of China.

WHILE BILL WAS finishing the movie, I was doing all the groundwork for our return to Papua New Guinea, as well as taking a fast course on the rules and costs of shipping and import handling. I also devised my own *Polish version* of bookkeeping; I had to calculate the retail price of a given item and go backward, giving us a 100 percent markup, costs of shipping, FOB (freight on board), and then the wholesale price, or what we could afford to pay for a piece. I was getting on-the-job training for retail sales that would come in very handy in the future.

Michael Sumari's letter had indicated that he was organizing strategically located cultural centers as repositories for traditional artworks collected from the villages in each area. The criteria was that the art must have tribal significance or must have been used practically; it couldn't be an "airport art" version of the real thing. We received glowing cables (prior to faxes or internet) encouraging us that all would be in order for our arrival. We took off filled with excited anticipation.

Our friends from the Wuvulu project, Paul and Patty, met us in Port Moresby, after our long trip across the Pacific and up from Sydney. The National Museum agreed to create a seal of authenticity that could be clipped to each piece with the use of a wire and a pressed bit of lead. We paid a call on President Sumari, who assured us that we would have complete cooperation. With all our ducks supposedly in a row, we left the capital for Wewak, where we would base ourselves in the Sepic district.

Our first foray into the bush, to where we were told a cultural center filled with art awaited us, was a major disappointment. In fact it was a complete bust. Yes, there was a building, and yes, there were a few pieces on display, but there was no organization, no representative of the Department of Cultural Affairs to show us around. It was our rude awakening to the fact that nothing that had been promised was going to appear. With the best of intentions, the person in charge was attempting to obtain art, but it was difficult for the villagers to understand the concept of consignment. When it was apparent we would have to pay cash for everything, Bill arranged a letter of credit to a local bank and underwrote the entire project. Finances having been organized, there was still the problem of inventory. Where were we going to find the three hundred pieces Bloomingdale's had ordered?

When we returned to Wewak we were introduced to a larger-than-life character named Kevin Truman. Kevin was an Australian entrepreneur whose size was as large as his imagination. His business was a bit of this and that while he cruised the waters of the Sepic River, trading for copra, croc hides, and artifacts. His warehouse was a potpourri of all his adventures. He agreed to take us to some villages where we might be able to find some good "stuff," as he called it. So, we boarded Kevin's version of the *African Queen* and chugged our way into the interior of the jungle. We stopped at many villages and, in pidgin English, negotiated for the purchase of some very attractive pieces. With Kevin as our agent, the villagers agreed to spread the word on the jungle telegraph and meet us in Wewak with the art they wanted to sell.

Living in the jungle and sleeping in hammocks with mosquito nets that had seen better days left us vulnerable to lots of flying critters. One of the swarm of "mozzies" that circumnavigated my hammock each night must have carried the dreaded dengue fever, because when we returned to Wewak and ended up in Kevin's warehouse office, I found myself one minute standing and the next minute on my knees. The massive Australian looked down at me over his desk and said, "Aye, looks loike yea gat a tach a the dayngi." He pulled out an ancient bottle of something, blew off the dust, poured me a handful of pills, gave me a small, half-consumed bottle of whiskey, and said, "Tike 'em." I woke up three days later feeling much better. Bill located a local missionary nurse, who looked in on me and assured him that I would be fine. In the meantime, while I was under the weather, the villagers were massing at the cultural center and negotiations began. Bill picked out some lovely pieces, then left me to bargin. By then I had picked up a smattering of the language and was enjoying the game. One woman had come with three small masks that were absolutely beautiful, but she wanted a lot for them and was decidedly unwilling to settle for a lower price. She stuck her heels in and, with a scowl on her face, would not budge, try as I did. After most of the people had gone, I returned to where the woman was and paid her the price she asked for.

Bill said that her husband had probably given her a price, and if she'd returned with less he would have beaten her, so I felt relieved that I had saved her from that fate. In spite of the fact that during the entire transaction the woman had remained sullen, the next day, while I was walking down the street in Wewak, I heard her call out to me. I looked across the street, and there she was with a big smile on her face, smoking a cigar. "Happy noon, madame," she shouted, then she turned and continued to saunter proudly down the street, very pleased with herself indeed. Whether or not she thought the pieces weren't worth what I paid for them, all three masks are, to this day, in my own collection, as is the memory of that woman.

Word of our shopping trip went all the way up the river, so with each sortie our results improved. When we returned to Port Moresby to await the arrival of our art, we were introduced to a member of the government by the colorful name of Ebia Olewale.

Ebia came from a tribe called the Gogodala, who lived in the Fly River area not far from where young Michael Rockefeller perished after swimming to shore from his becalmed sailboat. The Gogodala people were renowned for their tribal art and for their longhouses. The longhouses were the size of airplane hangars and housed the entire village.

The carvings the Gogodala produced were reminiscent of some modern sculpture, using the same primary colors employed by the artist Alexander

Calder. We chartered a plane to fly us two hours across the Papuan Gulf to the west, Ebia insisting all the way that his people's art was the most beautiful of all.

We landed in the rain, transported by another miraculous bush pilot. Rain in fact fell nonstop on this part of the island and was the principal reason the longhouses were so long. Since we'd come all this way with one of their own, the Gogodala were determined to formally receive us, which entailed rituals that would normally require days to perform. Our bush pilot nervously looked at his watch, remarking that there was a limit to the miracles he could perform. Because the Port Moresby airport was not equipped with landing lights, the deadline for all planes was sunset. Risking a break with protocol, Ebia cut short the dances and got straight to commerce. Sculptures were brought out for us to choose from, and they were indeed remarkable and completely unusual. Bill fell in love with an eighteen-foot snake consuming a ritual clan figure. Since the sculptures were made of a light wood similar to balsa, weight was not as much a concern as size. I agreed to straddle the snake in the back of the plane. It took so much time to load the plane and go through the politeness of farewell that the pilot was increasingly worried about not arriving at Port Moresby before sundown.

As we made our way across the Papuan Gulf the sun was fading fast, and the pilot began to look for viable alternatives in case we were unlucky in making the deadline. There was a small abandoned field on a tiny island that seemed to be the safest choice. As the clock ticked, we all said a silent prayer while our options reduced. Ebia had no idea of the precariousness of our flight and was happily enjoying the view, chatting away about how wonderful it all was. As a last resort, the pilot was able to contact some pals in Port Moresby who were willing to bring friends with cars to light up the landing strip. The airport officials agreed to leave the lights on in the terminal so the pilot could judge the depth of field of the strip. We all breathed a sigh of relief that our pilot's fast thinking saved us from spending the night on a deserted island. I don't know how many of our nine lives were used up that night.

In a few days, our shipments from the Sepic arrived in Port Moresby. We had to number and photograph each piece before it was crated, for insurance purposes. This was easier said than done. Thanks to Paul and Patty we managed. Did I mention that the heat and humidity never abated, and it was always scorching and drenching?

Bill rolled up his sleeves, or, rather, opened the front of his shirt and pitched in, helping us all keep our sense of humor. The seals of authenticity we were intending to wire to each piece was never forthcoming from the National Museum, so we would have to make up one of our own in the States. At least we had permission to do so. Finally, we had no choice but to leave our precious cargo in the hands of the forwarders, who guaranteed us they would carefully wrap each piece, crate, and ship them on the first vessel bound for the States. The only thing we failed to think of was fumigation. Considering the fact that all the pieces were made of wood originating from a humid, insect-infested rain forest, someone might have suggested we fumigate the shipment—and do so sooner rather than later. Sadly, no one did. Taking a deep breath and with fingers crossed, we packed up and headed onward.

There was only one way to fly out of Port Moresby in a forwardly direction, avoiding a long backtrack to Sydney, and that was to fly to Manila. In fact, other than Brisbane and Sydney, Manila was the only other international destination available to travelers, and it was worth a try because it offered us a connecting flight to Bangkok.

THE ORIENTAL HOTEL was a favorite watering hole of Somerset Maugham, and a wonderful place to repair ourselves from the jungle. We dined with Bill's friends, who were quickly becoming mine. We bought lovely Thai silk clothes from Jim Thompson's shop, which cooled our skin in the hot air, and we indulged in blissful, air-conditioned sleep under the soft sheets of the Oriental. While we recovered and reviewed the events of the previous weeks, it was clear that our adventure had enhanced the increasing sense of partnership in our love affair.

Bill had a date with a production company in Munich to film a TV movie about the dreadful events of the Munich Olympics, so we left Bangkok and arrived in Geneva, where the temperatures were decidedly colder. Bill had a wardrobe in his apartment filled with lovely cashmere sweaters, which I purloined gratefully. With Duno Caspar, the former houseman whom Bill financed in his own chauffeur business, we drove to Munich. Duno had been a valued member of the Holden household and was always at Bill's disposal whenever Bill was in Geneva. We had a few days to settle in Munich before Bill was to begin filming, and they nicely coincided with the visit of Don and Iris from Kenya, who were in Germany to see Iris's relatives. It was fun for the four of us to be together again in such completely different surroundings.

When Bill began shooting I left for New York, principally to meet with Bloomingdale's and our "partners" Richard and Ani.

My stay in New York was very productive. Richard and I were able to price the entire inventory from the numbered photos we had taken of the 465 pieces acquired in Papua New Guinea. Since we were contractually bound to produce three hundred works of art for the show, we arranged to store the excess in Los Angeles. Bloomingdale's gave us a check with which we could begin to reimburse Bill. I was also able to turn in the story I was commissioned to write for *Vogue* magazine by none other than Mr. Leo Lerman himself.

I was introduced to Mr. Lerman, the legendary arbiter of style and taste for Condé Nast publications for more than fifty years, by my friend the supermodel Wilhelmina. Wily was herself a legend, not only for her beauty but also for her enterprise. The Modeling Agency of Wilhelmina was the first of its kind, illustrating that she truly was more than just a pretty face. Mr. Lerman asked me to write a one-and-a-half-page article with two pictures discussing our travels to Papua New Guinea and the forthcoming exhibit of art.

It was my first and only appearance in *Vogue,* and I am happy that it occurred as a writer.

Our venture into the art world was not without its speed bumps, and we had quite a few. The worst hiccup had to do with our long-awaited shipment, which had sat far too long on the dock in the rain and sun before departing Papua New Guinea. In the course of the delays, our crates and the packing materials inside had become an attractive dwelling place for countless creepy crawlers, who wound up taking a free ride to the United States.

At Bloomingdale's, we were given a corner of the home furnishings floor adjacent to the bedding department as a staging area for unveiling the art. As Richard and I began to open the crates and undo the sometimes soggy wrapping meant to protect the pieces, we encountered some astonishingly large members of the insect family. These critters took one look at us and sent a message to their friends, which brought them ALL scurrying out of hiding into new and uncharted corners where the Sealy Posturepedics lived.

For years, Richard and I wondered what happened to those life-forms in such an unusual environment: Dare I ponder the thought that they might have prospered?

The show was a huge success, and in the process, our friends Gail and Chuck Feingarten kindly offered their gallery in West Hollywood to show some of the pieces we held in reserve in Los Angeles. What a privilege to share space with bronzes by Rodin and Degas.

W.A. Stefrick Imports Ltd. was indeed launched.

DURING BILL'S YEARS in Hong Kong, he had a favorite spot he would visit from time to time. He shared his special place with me on one of our trips. The location overlooked the bridge at Lo Wu, which was the demarcation point separating the no-man's-land between the colony of Hong Kong and the People's Republic of China. Bill had filmed on that spot when he'd appeared as host of a CBS *White Paper* at the request of his friend William Paley.

The White Paper was part of a series of TV specials produced by the CBS news department. It was considered serious, in-depth documentary reporting. Hollywood movie stars were never employed as presenters. When Paley decided to do a *White Paper* on the phenomenon of Hong Kong, he asked Bill to be the host. He chose Bill not because he had filmed two highly successful movies in Hong Kong (*Love Is a Many-Splendored Thing* and *The World of Suzie Wong*) or because he owned an apartment there. He chose Bill because he was regarded as a respected China hand.

At the end of the documentary Bill was scripted to say that if such remarkable results could be obtained from the enterprise of the people in Hong Kong, imagine what was waiting to be achieved across the nine hills of Kowloon in China. The program was filmed at the tail end of the 1950s and the McCarthy infamy, during a period when our foreign policy was simply not to acknowledge the existence of the then 700 million people in the People's Republic of China. In fact, because Bill mentioned the name China in reference to the People's Republic of China, the program was banned from airing for nearly two years. During all that time the flames of Bill's curiosity had only been fanned. In the mid-1970s the armed soldiers that stood guard on both sides of the bridge at Lo Wu presented an extremely sinister presence.

The bridge was passable for only a very few with special documents, none of whom were Americans. Beyond the bridge were the hills of southern China, standing as a symbol of forbidden fruit in a land that intrigued both of us. With each visit, Bill's craving to finally taste this long-awaited delicacy increased, and it became our constant subject of conversation. When Richard came to us with an opportunity to fulfill our desires, we jumped at the chance.

Nixon's visit to China in 1972 not only began the lengthy journey toward "normalization" of relations between the United States and the People's Republic of China but it also unlocked the door to the first stages of trade. The Chinese, historically wary of foreigners, considered Americans the new kids on the block and, as such, still an unknown quantity whose "friendship" needed to be well seasoned before we could enjoy privilege. With that in mind, early commercial entrepreneurs were relegated to the restrictions of the Canton Fair, recalling the history of British traders in Canton before the first opium war in 1838. Clearly the floodgates were open to accommodate only a trickle of commerce, not the deluge that was yet to come. If you were granted a visa to the fair, you would forever be categorized at that level of trader, and it was highly unlikely you would ever get a visa to the regions of Shanghai or Peking. As luck would have it, a client of Richard's had the distinction of signing the first one-million-dollar contract with the Chinese government–backed agency called China Light Industrial Products. The products in question were for the most part plastic flowers, but nonetheless it was the biggest contract of its kind at the time. As a reward, the Chinese government invited Richard's client for a visit to Peking, Tien Sing, and Shanghai. They were wined and dined in the famous Chinese custom of banqueting and taken to see large warehouses of antiques and antique reproductions, which they were invited to buy.

The porcelain store in Tien Sing was piled high with lovely pieces that could be purchased for a song. With Richard's client to act as our sponsor, we applied for visas to China as the W.A. Stefrick Imports Ltd. Company.

The four of us—Richard, Ani, Bill, and I—met in Tokyo and traveled together to Peking, which was yet to be called Beijing. We were obliged to use the China state airlines, whose business and first-class services had not even begun to evolve. In 1977 travel to China required an invitation, thus the passengers on our flight consisted only of those who were expected guests. In fact, the airport closed after our plane landed.

The customs and arrival halls were spartan in design and decor, with nothing but the most utilitarian of necessities. Awaiting the new arrivals were representatives from the agencies hosting their clients. In our case, the agency, or *cadre* as they were called, was section 5 of China Light Industrial Products. Because the W.A. Stefrick Imports Ltd. Company was a first-time visitor, we were not of high standing and were therefore assigned a guide/interpreter of equally low rank. Our driver never looked us in the eye as he efficiently loaded our luggage into a car that resembled a prewar model, straight out of a Humphrey Bogart gangster movie. The automobiles in China were leftovers from their onetime friendly relations with the Russians, whose design concepts were still frozen in the 1940s.

We were running on sensory overload, absorbing every sight, sound, and smell.

If you read Chinese history concerning the way foreigners were dealt with going back hundreds of years, you would note that nothing about the way we were handled had really changed very much. All foreigners were relegated to one hotel and one guesthouse. Other than sidewalk emporiums for fast food, there were only two restaurants where foreigners were allowed to eat outside the guesthouse and hotel.

We were lodged at the famous Peking Hotel, an imposing structure in three joined sections, constructed under different regimes: the old wing, of European influence; the middle wing, of Soviet cold war influence; and the new wing, influenced by recent exposure to Hong Kong. The hotel lobby had no desk. In fact, it had nothing but a cavernous marble expanse and doors leading to the bank, the offices, and the reception rooms, all of which were open only during designated hours.

We arrived late and everything was closed, except for a small room, where we sat for tea with our guide, who discussed our schedule for the following day. After agreeing on our activities, we were shown to our floor, where the uniformed matron/desk clerk looked up our names and gave us the keys to our rooms, all executed with a decided lack of charm. Our rooms were identical, down to the two tiny squares of once white, now graying, towels, which would have to suffice for all purposes. A large thermos of incredibly hot water was on the bedside table, and it became the greatest feature of the room. We had been forewarned, so we'd come equipped with instant coffee and cream, which also came in handy.

In the morning we found our way to the dining hall, whose gigantic doors had been shut the previous night. It was indeed a hall of enormous proportions filled with mostly empty tables. The few that were occupied were in various corners of the room, making any contact with the other guests impossible. We ordered breakfast, scrambled eggs on toast and coffee. When it arrived, the eggs had been cooked in oil. It was most unappetizing. Just as we were about to feast on our toast, someone passed our table, and Richard looked up and said hello. It was Ahmet Ertegun, the owner of Atlantic Records. We watched as Ertegun joined his table companions, among whom was another recognizable face—the soccer player Pelé, who had just signed with the New York Cosmos. Then it dawned on us: Ahmet Ertegun owned the Cosmos! We discovered that the Cosmos were in Peking to play the all-China team Saturday night. Our hosts kindly arranged tickets for us at our request, much to the delight of our young guide.

Not quite a year before our arrival, China had suffered two devastating events: the death of Chairman Mao and the largest earthquake in the twentieth century. The earthquake was centered near Tientsin (now called Tianjin) and killed more than 250,000 people. In addition to the human devastation, the physical loss of infrastructure created by the 8.3 magnitude quake left the population fearful. As far away as Peking, people were still living in shacks on the streets, afraid to return to their high-rise apartment buildings. Among the structures in Tientsin that suffered extensive damage was the warehouse containing the huge store of pottery and porcelains, where we were hoping to make our purchases.

One of the conditions of our visas was a guarantee that we would spend a minimum of $50,000 acquiring objects from the large variety of inventory offered by our hosts.

Our first exposure to the porcelain collection at the warehouses outside of Peking was, to put it mildly, a colossal disappointment. The patina on the porcelain was dull, and there were cracks rather badly mended on many of the pieces. Our guide/translator was most disturbed when we did not respond to the display with enthusiasm. How were we going to meet our contractual obligation when we could not buy what was not resalable? We moved on to the jade room. To our equal dismay, most of the pieces were reproductions of low quality in both jade and carving. The Cultural Revolution had attempted to remove artistry, considered a bourgeois value, from the hearts, hands, and minds of the people, so the carving of the jade was primitive at best. The echo of the Cultural Revolution was still audible.

Our guide was polite but clearly not happy that our day had passed without a purchase. After an early dinner, he organized our entertainment for the weekend: Saturday night the soccer game, Sunday a trip to the Great Wall and the Ming tombs.

The Cultural Revolution must have taken a page from Nero's Rome, which gave the people bread and games; in this case it was rice and soccer. The stadium in Peking accommodated around two hundred thousand people and had what looked like a moat around the playing field that separated the standing-room-only section from the players. We were in a second balcony, overlooking the best seats that were directly behind and above the people in the standing-room-only section. Periodically, the standing crowd would become overexcited and throw things into the seats behind them.

For the most part, it was an extremely reserved crowd, so much so that we were able to hear the players on the field shouting to one another in between polite applause. Every once in a while, when the Cosmos would get the ball, from somewhere below us came the sound of a trumpet and a hearty cry in English: "Charge!" It was certain that there were other Americans in our midst, but who were they? The game ended in a tie, so detente was preserved.

SUNDAY WAS INDEED a day of rest—certainly for most government workers—so the roads were empty and we sped to our destination.

We all have our own reactions when encountering a structure as iconic as the Great Wall. Mine was simply awe. No photo can truly capture the magnificence of this edifice.

There were quite a lot of local visitors on the wall when we arrived. Most of the people were dressed in uniforms, some official, others as part of their normal wardrobe available for purchase in the government stores. Mao-style jackets, trousers, and hats were available in two colors, gray and navy blue. Western clothes were not available for purchase. The public only had access to government-issued fashion.

The only other foreigner we saw on the wall was one of the Cosmos, who was equally speechless in the presence of such an overwhelming man-made construction.

For the rest of our day everywhere we went we were the only foreigners present. There was no exchange with the local tourists, who made an effort to act as if we'd been invisible. Only the children dared to glance at us, instantly reprimanded by their parents. It made us feel as if they still regarded us as *gweilo* (foreign devils).

It was still light when we arrived back to our hotel in Peking. Ani and Bill wanted to go to their rooms, but Richard and I were dying to take a walk. No one said we couldn't walk on our own, so we took off with our cameras in the direction of the Forbidden City. Looking at Beijing today, it would be impossible to imagine it as it was on our first trip. The streets were a constant symphony of thousands of ringing bicycle bells, accompanied by the occasional whooshing sound of an electric-powered bus and hardly ever a car. The police sat in a kiosk in the middle of the intersection, shouting orders through a megaphone to direct traffic. Again we saw not one foreigner on the street, but this time the locals dared to take a long look at us, more as a curiosity than as a gesture of friendship.

The Tiananmen gate, the main entrance to the once revered Forbidden City, was open, and there was light foot traffic in and out with no guards, so we went across the bridge and through the gate.

Since the time of the Ming, who built the royal enclave, immediately inside the gate on the right was a military billet. As we entered and looked to the right, we saw a platoon of Red Guards going through a drill in the dirt yard in front of their post. We stopped to watch, and as we did, the drill instructor shouted a command and the ranks closed. They then began what looked like a martial arts routine, but in such unison that they appeared to be one mind, one body. At another command each of the guards dropped a short dagger down the sleeve of his jacket, into his right hand, and proceeded to repeat the choreography of the drill. They did this with such precision, and it was impressive, to say the least.

Almost simultaneously Richard and I realized that we were interlopers, with cameras hanging from our shoulders. Attempting to conceal our equipment, we discreetly backed away and moved on deeper into the grounds within the outer wall. The entire structure was under construction and restoration. The wear and tear of centuries had taken a hefty toll on the buildings.

As we stopped to look at a residential area over the outerwall, whose traditional roofs were as old as the Forbidden City itself, we encountered two rather elderly gentlemen. The men turned to look at us. With our newly acquired Mandarin phrases, we said good evening and they said good evening back to us. I had my trusty pack of Marlboro cigarettes with me and I offered them. To our delight, each man took a cigarette and smiled, saying thank you. Then suddenly they looked around in fear and scurried away.

The sun was setting and we decided to make our way back to the hotel. We were a few blocks away, walking on the wide sidewalks that lead off from Tiananmen Square, and Richard was on the outside closest to the road. I remember saying something about how one day we might be asked, "Wow, you were in Peking in 1977, what was it like?" Suddenly Richard looked beyond me to a man rushing out of the bushes on my side of the sidewalk. He could have been running for a bus, but he wasn't; in his right hand we both recognized a short dagger, which he lifted as if intending to attack me.

Richard reached across, grabbing the man's arm, and they both went down in a scuffle. Everything seemed to be in slow motion, and there was no sound, no shouting.

In an instant I realized that if I jumped in it might appear that we were attacking the man instead of the opposite, so I grabbed the first person near me on the street and shook him, screaming for him to help. When our helper reached to pull the attacker off Richard, the man with the knife took a swipe at our helper and ran up the street, at which our helper began shouting and running after him with others following.

Richard was still on the ground. He said, "I've been hit." He pulled up his shirt, and there was a clean in and out wound in his pectoral muscle, and underneath his arm was a puncture that was bleeding badly. Fortunately, I had a scarf around my neck. We tied a tourniquet, snapped up all our gear, and ran as fast as we could to the hotel. When we arrived in the so-called lobby, there was no one there and all the doors were closed. Richard was very cool and collected, so he sat down and I began running around calling for help at the top of my lungs. The only response to my desperation was a small voice saying, "Can I help you? I speak Chinese." I turned around and saw, but didn't register, a young blond girl with a younger boy, wearing Baskin-Robbins T-shirts and carrying a skateboard.

"Yes," I said, "this man has been stabbed and we have to get him to a hospital."

The girl said, "Well, I can't go, I have to babysit."

"Never mind," I said, "we'll take him with us."

Just as I was about to kidnap the two youngsters, the doors to the dining hall opened and the elevators disgorged their hungry passengers, one of whom was a colleague of the children's father. Everyone rushed over to help us. Someone put us into a taxi and someone else went to inform Bill and Ani. We were taken to the Capital Hospital, a teaching hospital built by the Rockefeller family in the 1930s that contained the foreigners' clinic.

It was dinnertime, so most of the lights were out. We found an examining room, and while I began to wash the blood off Richard's arm, our Good Samaritan went to find a doctor. Richard was taking it all with amazing calmness and control, but I was frenetic. A man, presumably a doctor, appeared in the doorway, carrying a small tray, upon which was a glass syringe with a long needle. It looked as if it belonged in a museum, perhaps a museum of torture.

The once white gown he was wearing had the stains of far too many meals on it. In what was one of my most embarrassing displays of stupidity, I addressed him in pidgin English. The doctor responded with, "Please, madame, will you wait in the hall." I was mortified by my behavior.

As I slunk out of the examining room, I looked down the hall. Arriving en masse was Bill with his arm around Ani, followed by a phalanx of police, a group from the Revolutionary Committee of Peking, some Americans attached to the embassy in Taiwan . . . and reporters.

The Good Samaritan who'd helped us to the hospital had called for backup, phoning the restaurant where overseas diplomats and the press gathered. Peking was such a small town at the time, at least for the foreign community, that news traveled fast. While Bill took Ani in to see Richard, I was guided by the Americans into a room nearby, where we could talk. The six Americans were in Peking to make all the arrangements for the American Legation offices. The men had been stationed in Taiwan and spoke perfect Mandarin. I couldn't help but think that they must have been CIA. They debriefed me, and I was able to describe the look of the man and what he was wearing. All those years of acting classes, where we were taught to observe all details of a character, came in handy. The CIA boys quickly told me what to expect, what to say, and who would interrogate me.

I was taken to another room, where the press, the police, and the representatives of the People's Revolutionary Committee of Peking were waiting for me. As I was finishing my description of what had happened, Bill arrived and the press went mad. The Chinese were completely disoriented by the attention we were getting. Bill brought sanity to the moment by producing an eloquent statement to the press saying that this was a random act and it could have happened anywhere in the world. As far as we were concerned, it had no reflection on our good and friendly relations with our hosts or the Chinese people.

Not until later did the officials discover that the company called W.A. Stefrick Imports Ltd. Company included one world-famous movie star and an American actress whose TV series was on in Hong Kong.

The news of the incident got around the world in less than twelve hours. First to call was Ani's agent, Eileen Ford, who was a newshound. She even had her own teletype machine in order to pick up breaking news from around the world. I was concerned about my mother hearing a report, and Richard was worried about his parents as well.

For a moment, the incident was newsworthy, coming as it did at such an early stage of diplomatic relations with China. Bill did his best to defuse the press, and in the process the Chinese government, which had already lost so much face by the incident, was grateful.

When I rang Mom, she had indeed heard about the incident, and she was relieved that Richard was not seriously hurt and that I was all right. Ani called Richard's parents and explained that he had been wounded, but it was not life threatening, and that he was in the hospital largely because the government was so worried there might be complications. We eventually discovered the identity of the Good Samaritan who'd helped us. It turned out he was American, and he and his colleagues were the ones yelling "Charge" at the soccer game. They were with the Kellogg Chemical Company, setting up fertilizer plants for the government as part of Mr. Nixon's friendship diplomacy.

A full report of our incident obviously arrived in the appropriate hands in Washington, and our government showed their concern in the form of a phone call from the ambassador designate to China, Leonard Woodcock, who rang from the U.S. embassy in Tokyo to express his support. Suddenly, as if in acknowledgment of our new and elevated status, we received a more sophisticated and higher-ranking group of guide/translators from section 5 of China Light Industrial Products, and their protocols began to become clear to us.

After Richard was allowed to leave the hospital, we were invited by our hosts to see some of the quality merchandise reserved for their longtime, good customers. We were shown lovely carpets, antique porcelains, and jade-encrusted screens, all with no obligation to buy anything. Nevertheless, we were happy to do so.

As part of the face-saving formalities offered by the Chinese government, we were given dinners hosted by the mayor of Peking and by the head of the People's Revolutionary Committee of Peking. We were also taken to visit the tomb of Chairman Mao, a privilege reserved for very few at the time.

In the end, the incident was explained as a thwarted attack by a traitor loyal to the Gang of Four, who had come to Peking to kill a foreigner. The man had been apprehended after he'd run away from us and attacked someone up the street who'd tried to stop him. My description and those of other witnesses matched the person they caught, so he was summarily tried and executed.

As we prepared to leave China, cutting short our visit, we were invited to return at any time and for many years to come. It was made clear to us that we would be received as "good friends" and the encumbrances of the many visa formalities would be waived. Our trio of companions from section 5 became good friends, and after all these years I am still in touch with one of them, Mme. Wang Fu Heng.

We were accompanied by our very own "gang of three" all the way south on our way out of China by train, and the tears that filled their eyes and ours as we said good-bye were real. As if preordained, our train came to the end of its journey at the bridge at Lo Wu, and we had to cross by foot to the Hong Kong side. It was sad to wave back at our new Chinese family from a border they could not cross.

Of course, the China of those days no longer exists, but it was only yesterday that it was so very different.

BILL AND I had shared a major event in both of our lives, and it had brought us together in a complicity unlike any other relationship either of us had experienced. We would forever love and appreciate each other for what the military acknowledges as *performance under fire*.

When we returned to the States, I was feeling very much not myself.

After further examination by my doctor, I was told I had contracted non-A, non-B hepatitis.

Bill drove me to Palm Springs and ordered me to bed, where I stayed for nearly five weeks. Around the beginning of the fifth week, when I was almost ready for the loony bin, I received a phone call from my agent. I was offered a film, costarring with Roger Moore, Elliott Gould, David Niven, Telly Savalas, Sonny Bono, Richard Roundtree, and Claudia Cardinale, to be shot in Greece on the island of Rhodes. I got well in record time.

Bill and I traveled to London together, where the preproduction for the movie was being done. When the film and cast left for Greece, Bill left for Kenya. As we were finishing the movie, Bill joined us in Rhodes, and the director convinced him to do a cameo.

In the movie, Elliott and I played two USO entertainers shot down in Nazi-occupied Greece and taken to a concentration camp whose commandant was none other than Roger Moore, everyone's favorite German. Since the director was besotted with the film *Stalag 17*, he contrived a moment with Bill that recalled that film.

Bill was placed outside a wooden barracks smoking a cutoff cigar. Elliott walks by and does a double take, saying to Bill, "Are you still here?" Bill replies, "Why not? It's three square meals a day."

OUR INCIDENT IN China was still fresh in our memory, but it did not discourage us from wanting to go back. I was eager to experience China in transition. I was always envious of Bill's having traveled around the postwar world while it had been in the midst of recovery and rebirth. It is a rare privilege to spend time in a place that's in transition, where you can still see the remnants of its individuality before it is lost.

Bill understood my curiosities because he had them too, and he always encouraged me to pursue my interests in the spirit of exploration.

I would have many trips alone to China during its transformation and even buy a house in Hong Kong as Bill had in his day, all the while being encouraged by him, my mentor, my love, and my best friend.

But even as enthusiastic as he was for my determination, and as proud as he was of his protégée, I could feel some unrest in him.

THIRTEEN

Too Soon Old . . . Too Late Smart

In 1978 I was faced with a dilemma that plagued me most of my life. It was my inability to easily recognize when opportunity knocks. In fact, true opportunity has been even more difficult for me to identify.

Take, for example, the case of *Cyrano de Bergerac* versus *Hart to Hart*. I was given what I thought was a perfect opportunity to open the door to Broadway by playing Roxanne to Stacey Keach's Cyrano. The production was to open in Long Beach, then play San Francisco before going to New York. While we were well into our rehearsals, and about to open to preview the play, I received a call from three old friends, Tom Mankiewicz, Robert Wagner, and Aaron Spelling. They were about to do a pilot for a new TV series called *Hart to Hart*.

Tom was a longtime friend and a successful screenwriter. He had been coerced by Aaron Spelling's partner, Leonard Goldberg, to rewrite and direct a property they owned called *Double Switch*. Tom was at last forced to step into the role he was born for, and the pilot was his opportunity to do so.

I had a long history with Aaron Spelling going back to when he was married to the actress Carolyn Jones, coaching our girls' softball team, and working as a staff writer for *Dick Powell Presents*. When Aaron and Leonard formed their company, the first TV movie they produced was called *Five Desperate Women,* and they cast me as one of the women long before housewives were desperate.

By the end of 1978 Spelling-Goldberg Productions already owned most of TV's prime time, and they saw *Hart to Hart* as an opportunity to en-sure their position as the most successful independent production team in television history. At one time, there was actually a rumor that ABC was an acronym for Aaron's Broadcasting Company.

I first met Robert Wagner, with his wife Natalie Wood, when they visited the set of *West Side Story.* Years later I guest-starred on his series *It Takes a Thief.* RJ, as his friends call him, had a contract with SGP to do a new series. He saw Tom's script as an opportunity to play a role that suited him perfectly. When the network pressured him to cast the role with either Lindsay Wagner, *Wagner and Wagner in Hart to Hart,* or Suzanne Pleshette, with whom they had a series development deal, RJ remembered me and the special affinity we'd had when we'd worked together. He be-came my champion, and in the end it was RJ who took the stand that he would not do the series without me.

However, I was in the middle of doing *Cyrano.* After a wonderful meet-ing in the pool house of the Wagners' Beverly Hills home, it was not only clear that we all had a great rapport but it was also clear that I was suffering an embarrassment of riches.

What was I to do? Each of the productions carried its own risk, and neither the play nor the pilot contained an absolute guarantee for success.

Aaron arrived at a reasonable solution: there was a rumor of an impend-ing newspaper strike in New York City. Newspaper strikes at the time were notoriously lethal to newly opened shows on Broadway. If it were to hap-pen, it was highly unlikely that *Cyrano* would be brought to New York. Everyone agreed to wait a few weeks to see what would happen.

Cyrano opened to good reviews. Bill came backstage with roses on opening night, and I think he was more nervous than I was. So was my mother. The production moved to San Francisco and the newspapers began to negotiate with their unions. We were all on tenterhooks for days. Finally, it was decided: they went on strike for eighty-nine days. I will forever be grateful to those unions for one thing: in voting to strike, they gave me the opportunity to clearly see where my true opportunity lay.

———— ∞ ————

WE BEGAN FILMING the *Hart to Hart* pilot at the La Quinta Resort, only a few miles from Bill's house in Palm Springs, so I had an easy drive to work. The guest stars in the cast included Roddy McDowall, Stella Stevens, and Jill St. John, all mutual friends of RJ's, Mankiewicz's, and mine, which made it seem more like a reunion than a job. "Mank" wore a T-shirt I gave him on the first day that read I AM the Director, and he created an atmosphere on the set that made every day filled with jokes and joy, the likes of which I had not experienced at work in many years.

It is absolutely a fact that when a script and a part are well conceived and well written, it makes the job almost easy. There was one added piece of good luck that surprised us all. The chemistry between RJ and me on the screen manifested itself with far greater depth than anyone had anticipated. I must admit, though, that the circumstances of the first scene we filmed together were a bit disconcerting. The scene entailed my climbing into a room through a window, unzipping the jumpsuit I was wearing, and letting it fall to the floor. The camera panned down to my bare legs, then I climbed into the bed under the covers, snuggled up to RJ, we kissed, and Jonathan and Jennifer Hart were born—all in the presence of an entire film crew plus Natalie Wood holding the hand of her four-year-old daughter, Courtney.

———— ∞ ————

It took months before postproduction was completed and the finished pilot was presented to the network for them to determine whether or not it would be purchased as a series. Bill suggested we go to Kenya, which was a good way to distract me from the nervous anticipation of the waiting period.

Bill's involvement in Kenya was changing. Ray Ryan, who owned the controlling interest in the Mount Kenya Safari Club, was under investigation for tax issues in the United States, and he needed to divest himself of his foreign holdings. Carl Hirschmann, the other partner, was also under financial pressure and wished to sell his interests. So with a heavy heart, Bill agreed, and the club was sold to the famous entrepreneur Adnan Khashoggi.

Shortly after the sale, Ray Ryan was murdered in the parking lot outside his health club in Evanston, Illinois. It was a classic gangland-style slaying, perfectly designed so that as he turned over the ignition key of his car, it ignited both the engine and the dynamite packed inside.

With Ray's death a chapter in Bill's life ended. While it was a relief not to have the concerns of the hotel, it is never a happy situation to live next door to a property you once owned, and the game ranch surrounded the club. Don and Iris, who lived on the ranch, had built a guesthouse that was at Bill's disposal. Bill appreciated the offer, but it made him uncomfortable not to have his own place. He had to confront the unavoidable unpleasantness of reassessing his priorities and reevaluating his options, something we all avoid like the plague.

It is inevitable that at certain points in our lives we must go through the pains of taking a personal inventory that includes recognizing our age and how we wish to spend the rest of our days. Bill had to confront not only his changing role in the movie industry but also the changing landscape in every aspect of life in the world around him.

I think that facing this was so difficult for Bill that, rather than including me in the process, he excluded me, isolating himself from me and the realities of his choices. However, there was one thought he did include me in: his idea of building a house for us on the game ranch. He even showed me what he thought would be the perfect site for it, in a grove of thorn trees we both loved.

⊗⊗⊗

ONCE WE WERE back in the States, his isolation increased and Bill began to console himself with an occasional drink, not always and not continually, but for lost weekends that became increasingly more frequent. Although the game ranch and his involvements with wildlife conservation were in many ways Bill's proudest achievement, acting was still his source of income and the only compelling reason for him to reside in California.

He had a lot to think about, and I did not envy him the chore.

Around the same time we began the pilot of *Hart to Hart,* the tenants at one of the houses I owned in Benedict Canyon wanted either to buy the house they were renting from me or leave to find another they could purchase.

Having made what I thought of as a good investment, I chose to let them go on their way. After attending to needed repairs, I decided to move in, at least until I knew what was happening with the pilot. I collected some of my furniture from the storeroom at Bill's house and my stepsister's spare room and did a cursory decorating job to make it comfortable. By now my little family was growing. Senor, the fabulous feline, was the prince of the house, followed by Papuga, the amazing yellow-naped Amazon parrot, who remains my feathered companion throughout thirty-seven years. BB, the bouncing bush baby, was a small prosimian we brought back from Kenya, and Bear was simply the most loving and loyal German shepherd ever, who some fool dumped off in the hills of Beverly and I was lucky enough to rescue. We were joined by my foster son, Silvano, from Italy, who finally was able to come to the States on a tourist visa.

I was still partially living at Bill's house in the desert, and we were working on our relationship and his "problem." It was clear that we loved each other very much, but when he sought solace from his depressions in alcohol, it was as if he had a mistress who at times was so demanding that, try as I might, I could not get between them. What was even more hurtful was that on two of the three occasions he proposed marriage, he was drinking and forgot all about our plans by the next day.

My mother was my constant and great support, always there to look after my menagerie when I was away with Bill or working. Eventually, when her apartment building was going to be torn down and the tenants received notice to find other quarters, it seemed only practical that she should move in with me in the new extension I constructed.

By the time *Hart to Hart* was in production we were all well ensconced.

At times Bill enjoyed my little family and embraced it as his own, but on other occasions the constant lack of privacy made him claustrophobic. Bill was basically a loner, and having his own space was very important to him. I not only understood him but I too was somewhat of a loner, a more gregarious loner than he, but nonetheless a loner.

Thus, on the pretext that my house was too crowded for him, Bill installed himself in one of the apartments at a building he owned a large share of in Santa Monica. I should have sensed something was afoot, but I was so preoccupied with my long working hours that I failed to recognize Bill's lifelong pattern and contest his decision.

When Bill flew to Hawaii to join Paul Newman, Jacqueline Bisset, and Ernest Borgnine in the cast of the last of Irwin Allen's spectacular disaster films, I was able to join him for a few days. It was an amiable cast, all living in a cluster of condos in the big island, which made for a congenial social environment and somewhat compensated for the lack of quality in the script.

One day, after the company returned to film in L.A., I received a call asking me to come to the studio and take Bill home. Bill had been drinking at lunch and was unsteady on his feet. They had been filming an escape sequence with the cast on a suspension bridge erected twenty feet overhead on a soundstage. Bill's unsteadiness was putting the other actors at risk.

They decided to shoot around him so Bill could be excused early. I came to drive him home. It was a Friday with a long weekend ahead.

As luck would have it, visiting the set was a friend of one of the cast members, who happened to be a therapist familiar with alcoholics. He suggested I take Bill to Dr. Joe Takimini, who operated a clinic at St. John's Hospital that specialized in addiction. I spoke with Dr. Joe, and we agreed to give Bill the choice to either spend the weekend "recuperating" in his care or going home with me. Knowing that Bill had a great respect for doctors, we convinced him that he could get his needed "rest" better under Dr. Joe's care.

Bill responded positively to both the clinic and Dr. Joe. He thought the clinic was a place for a cure similar to the ones he knew in Europe; actually it was a detox center. Dr. Joe treated not only the body but also the mind, and Bill absorbed both, even agreeing to go back into a program. The treatment Bill chose was at the clinic run by the famous Dr. Persch, who was the cornerstone of the Betty Ford Clinic, yet to be constructed.

After filming was completed on Bill's movie, I drove him to Dr. Persch's clinic. A week went by before I received my first call from Bill, who sounded wonderful and full of enthusiasm. Dr. P wanted to see me. I arrived at the clinic and Bill was waiting in the lobby, looking so good and so happy to see me. When he lovingly embraced me, my heart was filled with hope. He introduced me to the doctor, handed me a present, and departed for his "class." I assumed that the doctor was going to ask me some questions about Bill and his history with alcohol, but instead he turned to me and said, "So, tell me what's wrong with you." I was taken completely by surprise. "Why are you with an alcoholic?" he continued. I understood that the famous doctor practiced tough love, but this was a direct attack on me, telling me that I was an enabler and that if I really loved Bill as I claimed I did, then I would "break the plate" so that he could not dine out on me or my support.

Suddenly my hopes faded. What did "break the plate" mean? And for how long? According to the doctor's instructions, Bill and I were to remove our possessions from each other's houses and give back the keys, symbolically disconnecting ourselves. In addition, we were not supposed to see or speak to each other. I didn't ask if Bill had agreed to this; I just assumed that he had. If this was what the great guru required of his patient and I was in the way, I had no choice but to give it a try. I was heartbroken as I left.

I opened the present Bill had given me. It was a small hook rug he had made in one of his occupational therapy classes.

It said, "Too soon old . . . too late smart."

AS UNHAPPY AS my personal life was, my professional life was joyful. We worked long, demanding hours on *Hart to Hart,* and the first season was not a runaway hit. It was only the clout of Spelling and Goldberg and the star power of Robert Wagner that kept us going for another season.

RJ was simply the most charming, naturally funny, and endlessly caring friend a person could have. Lionel was an anarchist at heart and a champion of anyone who questioned the status quo. Mank was always there to shepherd his flock and make sure we had good scripts that maintained the stylish essence of the show. He was also honing his directorial skills with us, and we were the grateful recipients of his talents.

If *family* is a term for a group of people who band together against all odds with a common bond and a mutual admiration, then the *Hart to Hart* "family" more than qualified in that category. As our ratings went up, our insecurities diminished and the producers' confidence grew, allowing us to go on lavish locations, such as Vail, Colorado, in the height of the skiing season.

After a time that seemed an eternity, Bill and I began to talk again. While the romantic part of our relationship had been bruised, we still had a deep connection as soul mates. We began to see each other again. It was fragile in the beginning, but then we found a comfortable groove that seemed tolerable. Bill still maintained his apartment in Santa Monica, which he decorated beautifully, reflecting his impeccable taste and fastidiousness.

When Bill read the script of *The Earthling*, he saw it as a message he identified with and very much appreciated. However, the timing was not good as far as AA was concerned. Filming would take place far into the outback of Australia, away from proximity to anything that remotely resembled an AA meeting, and Bill was still in a fragile state. He was given self-help tapes by his AA sponsor to support his sobriety, and against all odds, off Bill went across the Pacific.

To make matters even more challenging, the film crew and cast were to live on location in a camp of mobile homes arranged in a circle, like covered wagons. With little, if any, privacy, Bill would call me on a radio phone, shouting into the handset, making it possible for everyone to hear his end of the conversation. In spite of the difficulties, Bill loved the script and his costar, young Ricky Schroder, whose affection for Bill led him to name his sons Holden and William.

In addition to the uncomfortable living conditions, increasing unhappiness began to result from the director's temper. It eventually was revealed that, much like the character Bill was playing in the film, his director was suffering from terminal cancer. After collapsing on the set, he was evacuated to a hospital in Sydney, where he sadly died. The direction was taken over by the film's screenwriter, John Strong, who was, by coincidence, a longtime family friend of my mother's and mine. Fortunately Bill and John bonded and they worked hard to finish the film, all the while Bill keeping his resolve to remain sober.

On his way back to the States, Bill stopped off in Hong Kong and chose to stay at a hotel where the manager was an old pal he used to kick up his heels with. It could not have been a worse environment. I tried to keep in touch with Bill by phone, but after a few days of his not returning my calls, I knew he had lost the fight. I asked my close girlfriend Elaine Forsgate to pay a call on Bill, and what she reported confirmed my suspicions.

Bill eventually returned to the solace of his apartment in Santa Monica, where he hid himself. I knew there was nothing I could do until his sojourn on the dark side had run its course, so I carried on with my work and my life.

Eventually, when Bill did call me, I made no reference to his "hiatus," nor did he. I was just happy to hear sobriety in his voice again. When he began filming *S.O.B.* for Blake Edwards, Bill was in great form. He was delighted to join the cast with Julie Andrews and Robert Preston and to be working with pals. I visited him on the set several times. As with all of Blake's productions, the atmosphere was permeated with his special wry humor and wit, which was contagious. One night after I finished work, I paid a visit to the set in Santa Monica where they were night shooting. I obviously surprised Bill, who reacted strangely to my arrival.

Then I smelled it.

By now, I had developed the olfactory skills of a bloodhound, and I could smell the alcohol on his skin. My disappointment was palpable, so much so that the following day Bill called to apologize for not having been more attentive, making some excuse that neither he nor I believed.

Whether it was a conscious decision on his part or not, Bill had chosen his own path, and it was not up for discussion. When he felt the need for a binge, he would leave the desert and lock himself in his apartment near the sea. When he had satisfied himself, he would emerge looking remarkably well. It was these incredible recuperative powers he depended on throughout his life that had given him the arrogance to feel he could always bounce back.

It was more than clear to me that Bill wanted no more confrontations or recriminations concerning his habits, and I had no other course but to respect his wishes. Somewhere in the back of my mind I thought that he was so strong willed that he just might be able to tolerate his schizophrenic existence, at least for a while.

IN THE BEGINNING of 1981, after we celebrated the new year together, Bill left for Kenya to do a documentary for NBC. On his way to Africa, Bill stopped in Hannover, Germany, to have a thorough physical examination from the famous cancer specialist Dr. Hans Neiper. Dr. Neiper had successfully treated our good friend Chuck Feingarten. Bill, being a heavy smoker, as well as a hypochondriac, was anxious to be examined using all the cutting-edge methods the good doctor was reputed to have. The tests' results, amazingly enough, produced a clean bill of health. What Bill did not know was that some paparazzi had seen him enter the clinic and caught him on film.

One week after Bill arrived in Kenya, the rag sheets all over Europe carried a story with photos and the "shocking news" that Bill was fighting terminal cancer and seeking treatment in Germany to conceal his illness. I was called by reporters and naturally denied the entire story.

When I tried to contact Bill, the phone lines were constantly busy, which usually meant out of order, and it lasted for days without repair. Because of the eleven-hour time difference between California and Kenya, I asked Mom to try calling throughout the day, as I was filming on location with no phone. Finally, Mom got through to Don Hunt, who told her that after Bill finished the documentary and the crew left, he went into a funk and began to drink heavily. Bill was meant to attend the premiere of *S.O.B.* in New York on his way home, but Don said he tried to convince Bill to go straight to Palm Springs and check into a hospital.

Bill followed part of Don's advice, only instead of a hospital Bill opted for his apartment. When Bill did not answer his phone, I assumed he was on a toot and would not be done until he was done. Usually there was some point where his survival mechanism would pull the rip cord, ending the binge.

When Bill called the following week he was filled with a new determination to go back to AA. I rang his former sponsor in Palm Springs to alert him that Bill was returning and seemed to be asking for help. For the next few months, Bill was deeply involved in recovery. When I visited him in the desert, he appeared to understand how life-threatening his illness was.

That weekend we had some good and meaningful talks for the first time in a long while; at least they appeared to be meaningful. Bill talked again about building a house for us on the game ranch, where he wanted to spend more time and begin an education program for the youth of Kenya so that they could learn to value their wildlife.

Around the same time, Bill had an invitation from President Ronald Reagan and Nancy to visit them in the White House. Bill had been best man when they'd married, and he'd also served as vice president when Reagan had been president of the Screen Actors Guild. When he'd separated from Jane Wyman, Reagan had slept on the Holdens' couch; they were good friends.

Bill had so many wonderful options in life, ones that most people only dreamed of, but the trick was getting him to see the positive side as a more desirable state of being.

Easier said than done.

———

DURING MY BREAK between the end of the first season of *Hart to Hart* and the beginning of the second, I traveled to China and Hong Kong, returning to L.A. on the fourth of July. Bill was always so proud of my interests in the Far East and Africa, as if he took personal pleasure in his prize student's accomplishments.

Bill picked me up from the airport, looking tanned and sober. We drove up the coast to the beach house of Billy and Audrey Wilder for a barbeque. The house was filled with old friends, all commenting on how well Bill looked.

That weekend Bill talked about his plans to visit the Reagans, and then go on to Kenya for Don Hunt's fiftieth bash. This time he wanted to look at Kenya from a different perspective, one as a full-time resident.

After that weekend he never revisited that idea.

In the fall of 1981, *Hart to Hart* traveled to Hawaii to film. Bill was having his ups and downs, but I was working such long hours that I couldn't go on those rides with him. We were always in touch by phone during the highs, and we would see each other when he was able, even if Dr. Persch would have disapproved.

A few days before we returned from Hawaii, Bill stopped answering the phone at his apartment. I knew he was off the wagon.

I left countless messages but received no answer. We arrived back in L.A., and the following morning we filmed in the ocean just off the Santa Monica Pier. It was Friday; I was going to spend the weekend in the guesthouse of the property I was renovating in Malibu. I drove past Bill's apartment building and rang his bell from downstairs. No answer. I rang the manager of the building, but no answer there either. I had no key, thanks to Dr. Persch.

I left messages all weekend long, begging Bill to answer if only to tell me he was alive. How prophetic. I reported to work that Monday morning in Malibu Canyon. I was driving to the next location in town with the news on in my car.

When I heard the first words, "Veteran actor William Holden . . . ," I was suspended in space and time. The reality of that moment was caught in isolation, as if I could rewind the tape and it would be all right. I heard a sound from the bottom of my soul, "No, don't let it be true. Please, don't let it be true, it must be some mistake."

I don't know how I got there, but I drove home holding my breath, as if that would make time stop. Mom was at the door in tears. "Is it true?" My secretary, Jann, was fielding phone calls. I rang Bill's lawyer, Deane Johnson, whose velvet voice embraced me in consolation. It was true. Bill's masseur, Chet, called me to tell me that he had visited Bill on Saturday to give him a massage. Bill was trying to pull himself together, but he had the shakes so badly that Chet couldn't work on him. Bill tried to stop the shaking with a shot of vodka, but it didn't work, so Chet suggested Bill lie down and they would make another appointment when he was in better condition.

It might have happened shortly after Chet left the apartment, or it might have happened later that night. They couldn't state the exact time, but Bill tripped on a Chinese throw rug we had bought on our first visit there. The rug was perilously laid atop wall-to-wall carpeting, on the side of his bed.

He caught his foot on the rug and fell onto the sharp corner of the bedside table with such an impact that it cut a deep wound in his forehead and severed the artery. "He bled to death in twenty minutes," the coroner said.

I was in a daze, functioning, but in a fog. The house began to fill with friends. RJ and Natalie were in the first wave, and they held on to me, trying to give me strength. I remember a montage of phone calls, flowers, platters of food, and a train of people passing through the house. Don and Iris were fishing in Australia when they heard the news, and they jumped on the first plane for L.A.

The papers were all over the story. Oh, how they salivate when there's any hint of sordid details. The details become exaggerated, and the life becomes secondary to the death. Everyone is there to jump on the bandwagon. People come out of the woodwork. Opportunistic journalists who claim close friendship take it upon themselves to write biographies, using a jilted girlfriend and an alcoholic former accountant as sources of information.

Misinformation, after time, seems to become fact, and it shapes the character of the person and tinges the legacy with scandal.

Then there is a book, written by a self-proclaimed expert, filled with direct quotes from people the author could never have met or spoken to, because they were all dead by the time he wrote his book.

Bill did more in his life, on and off the screen, than most people do in three lifetimes, and he did it with style and talent. *That* is his legacy, not his flaws.

Given his lifetime consumption of alcohol, it is almost superhuman that he could have accomplished all he did.

That too is his legacy.

And the legacy he left me is my greatest treasure. My devotion to his memory is not clouded by denial but seen in the clear light of day, for the great man he was, and for what he passed on to me.

In Kenya, where his memory lives on unsullied, I see his legacy in the animals he helped to preserve and the people whose lives he bettered.

I see his legacy every day.

FOURTEEN

Where Do I Go from Here?

———◆◆◆———

During the two weeks after Bill died, it seemed as if I lived a full spectrum of emotions condensed into each moment. Loss, remorse, anger, abandonment, love—it's like a bitter cocktail that nothing can prepare you for. Some days, it was a blur, whose mist enfolded me, postponing reality until some future time when I could cope with it.

Each person's journey is uniquely his or her own.

There was to be no funeral. Much to our surprise, the executorship of Bill's estate was taken out of the hands of his attorney, Deane Johnson, and myself, by the disclosure of a two-page notarized will that postdated the elaborate estate planning Deane and Bill had collaborated on for several years. Unceremoniously, Bill's family collected, cremated, and disposed of his ashes with no notice to Deane or me.

We were shocked and hurt. Neither Deane nor I were able to do anything to execute the wishes Bill had so painstakingly explained to us. But after all, Bill was gone, and the rest was the shoddy business of postpartum.

Funerals and memorials always made me feel they exist to comfort the living, and indeed they do. All of Bill's friends and I were in need of emotional closure.

With a great deal of help from my friends, we created a gathering at my house, one that informally encouraged no speeches but many stories. Some of those who attended were a brilliant reflection of Bill's career. By chance, Bill's former girlfriend Capucine was in town and able to attend, touched by the invitation that opened the door to our good and long friendship.

The following week was shortened by the Thanksgiving holiday. With RJ's great support, I went back to work on *Hart to Hart*. Early Sunday morning after Thanksgiving, still digesting Mom's vegetarian turkey feast, the phone rang. On the other end of the line was a distraught Roddy McDowall.

"Tell me Natalie is all right," he said, but I didn't know what he was talking about. In an instant, Roddy told me what he had heard on the radio and that no one was answering the phone at the Wagner house. We agreed to meet at Natalie and RJ's house in Beverly Hills, and as we entered, so did the rest of the world.

It was RJ and Natalie's world of friends, some of whom had visited my house the week before. Of course it was different, but it was also very much the same. As the news trickled in, and the pieces of the puzzle coalesced, we learned that Natalie, RJ, and Christopher Walken had gone to Catalina on RJ's boat, the *Splendor,* for the weekend. While moored in Cat Harbor, Natalie had fallen overboard and drowned. The rest of the details are factually revealed in RJ's memoir. It was unbelievable and unimaginable. Natalie was so vibrant, talented, beautiful, and such a good mother and friend to those she loved.

Then the blur returned, surrounding the unspeakable pain of both tragedies only two weeks apart.

After Natalie's funeral, RJ returned to work. We were like a couple of shell-shocked victims, but somehow the comfort zone of Jonathan and Jennifer Hart and their fictional family had a medicinal effect on both of us.

When *Hart to Hart* went on hiatus after completing its second season of shows, I went to Africa. Don and Iris not only made me welcome but also made me feel that I was a part of the ranch and the work that Bill loved. As a result of the ambiguous interpretation of his wishes regarding the game ranch, expressed in Bill's two-page will, notarized by Frank Schappe, his on-again, off-again accountant who at times doubled as his drinking buddy, I had to defend the game ranch in court twice in the months following Bill's death. I was also in court to retrieve my possessions that remained in Bill's house. Except for those items removed by his family, I was able to salvage most of them.

While in Kenya Don, Iris, and I spent many days and nights reliving their adventures with Bill and the creation of the game ranch. After much discussion, Don and Iris came up with an idea as a memorial to Bill. By the end of my stay, we had created a template for what would become the William Holden Wildlife Foundation, inspired by Bill's idea to build a wildlife education center as a backup to the ongoing conservation work at the ranch.

None of us imagined how big our little idea would become. Fifteen acres of land that belonged to the game ranch but had been separated from the ranch by a road into the forest was an ideal place for the education center. Don suggested that before my next visit, he would have the property cleared of low-lying bush so we could better view the terrain and conceptualize the layout of the site. My job when I returned to the States was to set up a public charity and begin raising funds.

It all seemed so logical, a living memorial to Bill and the child we never had. It somehow made sense out of our unconventional relationship in a way I know would have met with Bill's approval.

———— ∞∞∞ ————

THE SUCCESS OF *Hart to Hart* in no small part paved the way and opened doors that made it possible for me to create a 501(c)(3) not-for-profit public charity. It was through the inexhaustibly benevolent collaboration of far greater minds than my own that the bylaws were meticulously written and the legal documents drawn. I was receiving a crash course in a business education that would change forever my attitudes and perspectives toward the financial world.

When you grow up as an actor in film, television, or the theater, it is automatically assumed that you function largely with the help of the right side of the brain. Indeed, agents, business mangers, lawyers, and financial consultants assure you of the fact that they should be given the responsibility for handling all those tedious left-brain chores for you so that you need not worry. All you have to do is keep working to pay their fees.

In most cases they are right; the universes of finance and the law ensure their indispensability by making their professions as incomprehensible as possible. I was incredibly fortunate to have in my arsenal a business manager, a lawyer, and a financial consultant who were cut from a different cloth and magnanimously were more than happy to help me demystify their professions, creating a climate of partnership from which I have greatly prospered. I am eternally grateful to those mentors, Paul and Leo Ziffren, Mini McGuire, Barbara Tarmy, Henry Bamberger, Linda Judd, and Jon Lovelace. Of course it helps to be audacious and highly motivated. At last I had found an outlet for the boundless energy and curiosity that had been my albatross.

Once we received our IRS status as a charity, I was allowed to begin fund-raising. Easier said than done. Asking people for money is always a very difficult thing to do, but I soon discovered that what I was never able to do for myself I had no qualms about doing for the foundation. My first big check came at a dinner party. Leonard and Wendy Goldberg sat me next to Gordon McLendon, who owned a chain of radio and television stations in Texas and the Midwest. Gordon had been an acolyte of the writer Ayn Rand, so he respected women with a mission. After listening to mine all through dinner, Gordon pulled out his checkbook, wrote me a check for $10,000, and in true Texas style waved it in front of everyone, saying, "Well, here's my check, where's yours?" The next day at work, RJ slipped me an envelope containing his check for $10,000. We were on our way.

Fund-raising events are now and were then a euphemism for social life, and fund-raising in places like Hollywood is usually the domain of the wives of the rich, famous, and powerful, who exchange large checks to buy tables at one another's events. I was clearly not in that league; all I had was a TV show and determination. Together with my secretary, Jann, and some well-meaning friends, we began to look for a venue where we could create an afternoon of fun for the entire family. We found an attraction called the Kingdom of the Dancing Stallions, where thirty-two Andalusian stallions performed in the manner of the Spanish Riding School, in a chandeliered, theaterlike arena located near Disneyland.

The husband and wife who were the owners and principal performers could not have been nicer or more enthusiastic about our proposal to take over their show as a fund-raising event. With the help of the studio art department, we designed and printed five thousand invitations, which forty volunteers from Hughes Aviation helped me fold, label, and pack over a weekend on an empty soundstage at Warner Bros. Studios.

Sunday afternoon, after packing the last of the mailbags of invitations, I bought everyone a drink, thanked them profusely, and loaded the bags into Jann's car for the early-morning drop-off at the post office.

I then raced home to change for dinner with an actor friend, Robert Logan, who had been under contract to Warner Bros. at the time I was under contract to Columbia. I hadn't seen Bob for many years, since he had more or less given up his acting career to pursue his love of polo. I was barely out of the shower when the phone rang. I could hardly hear the person on the other end of the phone for all the noise in the background. The caller apologized, saying things were very chaotic there and that he was from the Kingdom of the Dancing Stallions. That afternoon the riders and horses had performed their Sunday show and, as was their tradition after the show, they all joined the boss and his wife for a meal.

Shortly after the late lunch, the husband retired to his room, presumably for a nap, put a gun to his head, and pulled the trigger. The poor man had been diagnosed with incurable Alzheimer's disease. I was shocked and saddened, but I also couldn't help thinking about my five thousand invitations that were on their way to the post office in the morning. I immediately phoned Jann to stop her from mailing them. The doorbell rang, and I must have looked like a deer caught in the headlights when I opened the door.

I explained to Bob what had happened. Not only was he sympathetic but over dinner he also came up with an alternative. The newly opened Equestrian Center in Burbank was featuring professional indoor polo matches on Friday nights. They were also encouraging amateur games and polo lessons. I had not revisited the world of polo since the days when Lance Reventlow exchanged flying lessons for workout sessions to get his horses fit for the Santa Barbara season.

Bob Logan rang up Suzanne Peika, who came from a legacy of polo at Oak Brook, Illinois, just outside of Chicago, and was organizing the games at the Equestrian Center. We made a date to see her after work on Monday. Suzanne was like a ray of sunshine.

Overnight we redesigned the invitations, drafted a celebrity polo team from friends, and the world of polo opened its generous arms to help create a better event than I could have dreamed of.

Stacy Keach, my Cyrano, had taken polo lessons for a film role, as had Alex Cord, with whom I'd appeared in the movie *Stagecoach*. Both were excellent riders. Pamela Sue Martin, who was on *Dynasty* at the time, was married to Manuel Rojas from Chile, who was an excellent polo player. After a bit of arm-twisting, she agreed to join our team.

That gave us four celebrities, plus Manuel and Bob, who would keep the ball moving for our exhibition "chukkas." Our celebrity team would play two chukkas before the proper game of polo that Suzanne organized with real polo players, who would give our guests an exciting taste of the fast and furious game of indoor polo.

We had forty celebrities who agreed to either ride a horse or a hay wagon in our celebrity parade, including friends like Sammy Davis Jr., Lorne Greene, Buddy Hackett, Jennifer O'Neill, William Shatner, David Hasselhoff, Ernest Borgnine, Merv Griffin, Red Buttons, Sidney Poitier, Bo Derek, Zsa Zsa Gabor, Larry Hagman, and Ricky Schroder. Our *Hart to Hart* cast, complete with Freeway, rode in a convertible car. We created a Western set as a background to our chuck wagon buffet, and we fed fifteen hundred people and raised $150,000. We were not only on the map as an organization, we had a bank account that was growing.

In the following years, our celebrity polo ranks would grow to include William Devane, Stewart Copeland, Jeffery Lewis, Jameson Parker, Mickey Dolenz, and Tommy Lee Jones, with regular supporters such as Dolly Parton, Sylvester Stallone, Mohammad Ali, and Paul and Joanne Newman. I have never known a more generous and encouraging group of people than those in the polo world. Once they open their hearts to a cause or a newcomer like me, they never stop giving. Through polo events, we raised the bulk of what has endowed our project in Kenya. I can never show my appreciation enough to those people who made our events possible. Maggy and Alan Scherer and their son Warren created weekends of polo games, lunches, and parties in Palm Beach and Palm Springs that were spectacular in every way as only they could, and Suzanne Peika and Jann Rowe dazzled all comers with the elaborate scale of each of our events in L.A. True to form, Mom was my biggest cheerleader. She even bought me my very first polo pony, Weasel, as a birthday present. "It's cheaper than a psychiatrist," I told my business manager, who, after my fourth horse, said, "Not anymore!"

At the top of my game I had fifteen playing ponies, four in L.A, six in

England, and five in Kenya. I am now down to seven playing ponies, four riding horses, and nine retirees.

———⊗⊗⊗———

WHEN I VISITED Kenya in December 1982, we broke ground and began working with the architect on the site plan for the education center. The wildlife clubs of Kenya were active in the urban schools of Nairobi and Nyeri, but they had no location in the bush where they could continue their studies of the natural world, so our facility made an ideal partner for them. The alliance helped us form a curriculum for the education center compatible with those of the wildlife clubs as we began to develop and define our own. I knew that I had made a lifelong commitment to the foundation, and I was determined that our donors be treated as partners in our venture with full recognition from our students, who would come to learn that the names on all the tiles cemented to our buildings were those of the people whose generosity made everything possible.

I was also dedicated to the idea that 100 percent of every donor dollar would go to our project in Kenya and nothing would be taken out for the overheads of the California office or even my airplane tickets to Kenya. In order to make sure I could look our donors in the eye and maintain the integrity of our organization, I committed to pay all of the overhead costs in the States. None of our directors receives a salary, and Don and Iris oversee our Kenya operations when I am away. All the visiting groups of students and adults pay nothing except for a reservation fee, which is refunded on their arrival. Since hosting our first group in 1983 we have welcomed more than five hundred thousand Kenyans at our education center. Beginning the foundation made me grow up very quickly.

One of the greatest additions to my life and my ongoing education was my introduction to Mr. Jon Lovelace. Because of our Chinese experiences, Bill and I had become friendly with T'ang Shu Suen, a filmmaker, artist, and cook extraordinaire, and her husband, Shaw Sing Ming. Sing Ming worked for a large mutual fund company called CRMC (Capitol Research and Management Corporation), which created and managed a family of mutual funds called the American Funds. Today the American Funds rank among the top three world mutual funds. Jon Lovelace and all the Lovelaces are some of the most benevolent people I have known. Their endless support and nurturing of worthwhile causes reflect their broad spectrum of concerns. Not only did Jon enlighten me regarding the management practices of institutions but he also helped me define my needs, trust my intuitions, and interpret my observations.

On one occasion I met with Jon after returning from a trip around the world visiting my haunts and houses in Hong Kong, Kenya, and London. I was filled with questions and was interested in finding an investment for our growing endowment account. As I traveled around the world, I was newly sensitive to local economies and business opportunities. I thought it would be interesting to find an investment that would take into consideration the highs and lows in a variety of investment sectors in order to offset losses by gains in other parts of the world while increasing growth and yield and ensuring the lowest possible risk. Globalization was still only a whisper of an idea. CRMC had no funds with the parameters I described. I would never be so bold as to say that they created CIB (Capitol Income Builder) for me, but Jon Lovelace has said that I was its inspiration. I currently sit on the boards of three of the American Funds, and I am as faithful to the concerns of our shareholders as I am to the careful husbandry of donations to the William Holden Wildlife Foundation.

As huge an issue as wildlife conservation is, those actually working in the field on grassroots issues are a small and tight community. Even though we might sometimes compete with one another for donations, most of us know or know of each other, and the best of us are promoters of one another's work. A special cause for me is the work of my dear and good friend

Biruté Galdikas, who is the third member of the trio of women originally sponsored by Dr. Louis B. Leakey to do behavioral studies of our closest relatives, the great apes, in the wild. Biruté is one of those whose life's work I support and promote. She is a warrior in the battle to save enough habitat in Indonesia for a remnant population of orangutans in Borneo. There are other echo warriors who put their lives in jeopardy in West Africa protecting the forgotten ape called the bonobo, and closer to home we in North America battle constantly to ensure the preservation of our iconic mustangs.

It is a fight that can never stop. Despite bans on the killing of endangered species, there is a new wave of poaching. Rhino horn and ivory, encrusted with fresh blood, is being smuggled out of East Africa in diplomatic pouches destined for the newly rich in the third world. All we can do is hope to produce an army of apostles to preach the gospel of preservation. The Catholic Church started with only twelve and look how far they got. I hope that some of the eleven thousand young people who come to us annually will make a difference one day.

I think Bill would be amused to know that students all over Kenya refer to our education center as "the William Holden."

In fact, I think I can hear him laughing.

As THE FOURTH year of *Hart to Hart* came to a close, plans were made to begin the fifth season with two episodes filmed in Greece. Lionel Stander and his wife and daughter were going to Europe as they did each year, ending their trip in Rome, where they had once lived. RJ was taking his daughters to Europe and would also end his trip in Rome, where he too had once lived. I was coproducing my first movie for television, *Family Secrets,* which I also cowrote with my producer/writer partner, Lee Thuna. When I was finished filming I was going to Rome to see Silvano, before traveling on to Greece.

Since we would all be in Rome at the same time, RJ suggested that we try to get an audience with the pope. In the summertime, the pope leaves Rome for the papal country house, Castel Gandolfo. He only comes to Rome on Wednesdays, for a public audience in St. Peter's Square, where he stops briefly at a reserved VIP section and leaves the pope mobile to shake hands and pose for photographs. RJ knew the American ambassador to the Vatican, so he was going to use his connection there to try to obtain passes to the VIP section for all of us. As a backup, I was going to use my connections with the Polish mafia to see what I could do in case RJ's man failed. Being of Polish heritage and having established my connections with Poland in 1977 when Mom and I traveled there to do a concert in Katowice, I hoped I might be able to pull some strings to see our Polish pope.

Filming on *Family Secrets* went extremely well. We came in three days ahead of schedule and $30,000 under budget. The story was about three generations: mother, daughter, granddaughter—Maureen Stapleton, me, and Melissa Gilbert. We needed two young men as secondary characters, who were pivotal to the story. I had the very good fortune of casting two actors at the beginning of their careers. The roles required actors with a quality we were unable to find in any of the boys in L.A., most of whom looked as though they had just stepped off their surfboards.

After watching some tapes from casting people in New York, we bit the bullet and paid for one of the actors to come to Los Angeles. He was perfect for the role and came to the audition as the character we'd written. I always humor myself by saying that he was my discovery. His name is James Spader, and he has become one of the finest actors of his generation.

The other young man had one scene in which he tries to pick up Melissa while she's in her car waiting for me. We were filming that scene in Chicago, and we needed a young actor who was based there. The actor we found was exceptional. One of the toughest things that an actor can do is to come on the set of a film that has been shooting for weeks and do a one-page scene with two of the stars of the movie. When the scene was finished, I asked this young actor how he got to be so good, and he said that he worked in the theater and was in fact helping to start a young theatrical company in Chicago by the name of Steppenwolf. I said I'd look out for him, and I still enjoy watching Mr. Gary Sinise.

THERE WERE NO direct flights from Chicago to Rome. Mank was flying to Rome from New York, so we made plans to travel together on that flight if I could make the connection. Fortunately, there were delays leaving New York, so I just managed to get on the flight, but our delays made us arrive after the time designated for us to be in St. Peter's Square. Both RJ's Vatican connection and mine had come through with arrangements for us, but sadly TWA fouled our plans.

By the time we arrived at the Hassler hotel at the top of the Spanish Steps in Rome, RJ, Lionel, and all the girls were returning from the Vatican with photos in hand. Crestfallen, Mank and I, both of Polish heritage, had missed our great opportunity. Never daunted by defeat, I rang the telephone number for Father Sokolowski, who was the head of the Polish hostel in Rome and my contact.

The good father patiently suffered through my mediocre Polish, peppered with Italian and English, and finally said that he would do what he could for us and would call me back at the hotel. We were all scheduled to leave for Greece on Friday morning and the arrangements were written in stone, so the Friday departure was unmovable. On Thursday I received a call from Father Sokolowski, who said, "You have to go to confession."

"Why?" I asked.

"Because on Friday morning, you are going to take mass from the hand of the pope!" I was speechless. "Do you want to confess in Polish, Italian, or English?"

This was no time to overestimate my capabilities. "English!" I said.

There is an American Catholic church in Rome, but because it was summertime, there was only what might best be described as a skeleton crew on duty. I phoned and asked if I could arrange for a priest to take my confession because I was going to be given mass from the pope! They were decidedly unimpressed, or maybe they thought I was lying. In any event, far too casually for my taste, they said that if I wanted, I could come now.

I raced to the church, where I met a young priest called Father York. He asked me if I wanted to go into the confessional or do the deed in his office. Opting for the air-conditioned comfort of the office, we began.

"Father forgive me for I have sinned. Since my last confession, which was . . ." A long pause . . . "Let's just say a while ago. Quite a while ago."

What ensued was a two-hour discussion on organized religion, on corruption in the church, on the scandals of the Banco Ambrosiano di Milano, Cardinal Marcinkus, etc. At the end of our long-winded session, being a clever Jesuit, Father York used the unarguable rationale that only God is perfect and mankind is corruptible, so as long as I had my faith, I could be absolved.

So after a good Act of Contrition, I retired to the church to say my penance and was prepared for the following day. Mank preferred not to take communion, so he did not go to confession, which I'm sure would have resulted in a session far longer than my own.

As promised, Mank and I arrived at the rear entrance to Castel Gandolfo promptly at 7:00 a.m. to meet Father Sokolowski and a group of twenty-five pilgrims from Poland. The Swiss Guards ushered us through a small doorway, and up a narrow staircase that led to a long, covered balcony overlooking a garden. At the far end of the balcony was a simple table with a long white tablecloth and a gold crucifix. As we assembled, the pilgrims began to sing in Polish with voices like angels, which resounded off the antique fresco-covered stone walls. Father Sokolowski pushed Mank and me to the front of the group, next to the temporary altar. With no fanfare whatsoever, and in the simplest white attire, the pope arrived, accompanied by a small entourage.

To be in the presence of a holy man is an awe-inspiring experience that cannot be denied even by nonbelievers. Pope John Paul II radiated such abundant compassion, it was as if he filled the space with light. As I suspected, the mass was in Polish. Thankfully, my mother taught us most of the essential prayers when we were children, so that from the deep recesses of my brain's recall center spewed almost all the words. It was a good thing too, because the pope kept glancing over at me, as if to check on my participation.

Was it because he had been an actor? Was it because there were not very many American actors of Polish heritage? Or was it because, as I later learned, he watched *Cuori Bati Cuori* (*Hart to Hart* in Italian).

Anticipating that we might have an opportunity to exchange words with the pope, I was determined to do so in Polish, as I rehearsed my speech over and over again, *"Jestem aktorka Amerykanska. Moje prawdzie nazwisko to Federkiewicz. Chociasz jestem urodzona w Ameryce, moje serce jest nadal Polskie,"* which, translated, means "I am an American actor. My Polish name is Federkiewicz, and although I am born in America, my heart is still Polish."

At the end of the mass, as the pope turned toward me, a memory flashed into my head. It was a memory from many years before, when I was working in England at ABPC Studios and I received a hand-engraved invitation to meet the queen, delivered by a chauffeur-driven Rolls-Royce. ABPC was a very small studio, so word traveled fast. When Mom and I arrived in the dining room for lunch, Roger Moore and Michael Redgrave were waiting to give me lessons on how to behave.

Sir Michael took me aside and said, "Don't fret, dear girl. Let me tell you about the first time I met the queen. It was this queen's mother and my first Royal Command Performance, so I felt the need to rehearse myself. 'Ma'am, *my* name is Michael Redgrave and I play the part of the captain . . . Ma'am, my *name* is Michael Redgrave and I play the part of the captain . . . ' Ma'am, etc. Over and over again. But when the curtain came down and the receiving line was formed, the queen walked straight up to me and said, 'Oh, you're Michael Redgrave and you played the part of the captain.' And I said, 'Ma'am, my name is Michael Redgrave and I play the part of the captain.' "

Likewise, when the pope came up to me and spoke to me in English, I spoke to him in Polish.

I have photographs of us talking away like mad, and I have no idea what he said, because I was determined to speak in Polish and he spoke to me only in English. There is also a photograph of the pope pressing a rosary into Mank's hand, and the expression on Mank's face made him say that he looked like a William Morris agent trying to offer the pope a two-picture deal. It was an unforgettable experience.

DURING EACH HIATUS from *Hart to Hart,* I would make my usual trek around the world: to Hong Kong, where my house on the beach at Discovery Bay was finally completed; to China, where, among other things, I would go to collect biographical material from Muril Hoopes Tu, hoping to publish her story; and to Kenya, where the education center was beginning to receive its first students.

I would make this pilgrimage twice a year, with Mom joining me for a part of it each trip. By now our relationship was not just mother and daughter; we were best friends as well.

At the end of our fifth season *Hart to Hart*'s ratings had slipped a bit, but we still had extremely respectable numbers. Aaron Spelling and Leonard Goldberg ended their long partnership, and Leonard took over the helm of our show. It was his job to fight for us with the network, which had just appointed a new head of programming.

RJ wanted to begin the sixth season in France, with two shows: one featuring the fashion world and one that would have Freeway falling in love with a French poodle, disappearing and leading us on a merry chase. As it happened, I was in France filming the miniseries *Mistral's Daughter* with Stacy Keach and the divine Lee Remick. It was a fateful Sunday night when I received a call from California: RJ, Mank, and Leonard were on the line giving me the bad news that we were not on ABC's schedule for the next season.

It was a crushing blow. The head of programming had canceled six hours of ABC's prime-time shows along with us, eventually causing ABC to drop to the bottom of the network ratings. I cried all night and went to work with a very puffy face. The rug had been pulled out from under our feet.

For five years I'd had the security of knowing where I was going every day and the comfort of knowing that I would be in the protected bosom of my *Hart to Hart* family.

I was now a free agent, but I felt lost, as if my ship had been adrift.

FIFTEEN

Travels with Mom

⬤⬤⬤

After completing the filming of *Mistral's Daughter,* I left Paris for London. Some of my greatest and most enduring friendships are within the borders of the United Kingdom, and I have always felt at home there. On this occasion I needed my pals around me. Their attempts to console me by assuring me that the loss of *Hart to Hart* was merely the opening of a new chapter in my life were very touching. That's when real friends show their true colors.

One of those very good friends was Lord Aubrey Buxton, founder of Anglia Television, creator of the famed wildlife series *Survival* and the man who brought the World Wildlife Fund to Britain. While having lunch with Aubrey in the House of Lords dining room, who should appear but none other than Mr. and Mrs. Aaron Spelling on their very first trip to England. Aaron never traveled, so this was a huge surprise, and he was just as shocked to see me in this privileged surrounding.

Aaron invited me to their farewell party the following night. At the party he was as ebullient as ever, so I didn't entirely believe him when he insisted that I should be in his next miniseries, *Hollywood Wives,* based on the Jackie Collins novel. With not a word said about the cancellation of *Hart to Hart,* I thanked him profusely and said I would love to work for him again.

A few weeks later, while in Kenya, I received a call from my agent. True to his word, Aaron made an offer, and I cut short my stay in East Africa and returned to California to begin filming *Hollywood Wives*. I was cast to play opposite Anthony Hopkins, which was a complete joy.

Although *Hart to Hart* ended as a weekly series, the afterglow in the hearts and minds of its loyal audiences around the world has lasted even until today. RJ went on to do other series and other films, and so did I, but *Hart to Hart* has always remained a special experience for both of us.

Following *Hollywood Wives,* I worked in a miniseries for NBC called *Deceptions.* When *Deceptions* was aired, the ratings were so good that CBS became interested in signing me to a highly lucrative contract. CBS was offering a full-spectrum deal, which included another television series, several TV movies, and two miniseries. They had no particular projects for me to do, so they encouraged me to create and develop some of my own. I had been nominated by the Writers Guild of America for *Family Secrets* in the category of best dramatic anthology written originally for television, so I had some small credibility as a writer/producer.

Over the next year I spent a great deal of time developing ideas that might pass the CBS criteria. In the course of my contract, Ted Turner began negotiating to buy CBS. When I met him at Jacques Cousteau's seventy-fifth birthday party in Washington, D.C., he was quoted by *People* magazine as having said to me, "The reason I want to buy CBS is so I can have you." I don't recall those exact words, but that night on the *Calypso* we had a conversation that lasted until dawn.

As far as I am concerned, there is truth in the saying that when one door closes, another opens. We actors are always having to reinvent ourselves, and the opening of a new door is part of what keeps us in the game. Life-changing opportunities are often only a phone call away. It is a lifestyle that is incredibly insecure, but for those of us who can stand the highs and lows and the constant rejection, we wouldn't have it any other way.

ONE DAY I received a call from a well-known Broadway producer, Alexander Cohen, and his equally talented wife, Hildy Parks. They were creating a lavish TV spectacle called *The Night of 100 Stars,* and they flatteringly asked me to be in the company of some of the most legendary names in our business. As a result of that night, I met Placido Domingo, who had not yet arrived at his full celebrity status. Because I spoke Spanish, Placido felt comfortable in my company during the long hours we waited backstage. That evening was also meaningful because it began a long and affectionate friendship with Alex and Hildy. When they produced Placido's first TV special, I was asked to be one of the ladies to share the stage with that lovely and outrageously talented man.

One of my favorite moments as a performer can be seen immortalized on YouTube. It is a duet between Placido and me singing "The Rain in Spain Falls Mainly on the Plain," he as a thickly accented Henry Higgins and me as an Eliza Doolittle who switches roles with him, forcing Placido to do the correct enunciation of the words rather than me.

That experience reignited my love of the musical theater, so when Alex and Hildy called on me again, I jumped at the chance. This time it was to join a dancing and singing ensemble they cast for two of the Tony Awards TV specials they produced. It was like a dream to perform with such exceptional theatrical talents as Chita Rivera, Juliet Prowse, Maureen McGovern, Lee Roy Reams, George Hearn, Dick Van Dyke, Jim Dale, and Leslie Uggams. And to sing accompanied by none other than Jule Styne and Cy Coleman was icing on the cake. I rang my mother after the live broadcast, and she was in tears, saying, "Well, you finally made it to Broadway."

While at CBS I was able to broaden the scope and variety of the parts I played. It was a big departure to portray the villainous Frances Schreuder, who coerced her son into the murder of her father in the true-to-life miniseries *At Mother's Request*. But my all-time favorite was portraying the aviatrix Beryl Markham in *Shadow on the Sun*. Beryl Markham grew up in Kenya and was a product of a time and place that produced remarkable women. Not only was she the first woman to fly solo across the Atlantic but she was also the first person to do so in a westerly direction. Even Lindbergh said it couldn't be done against the headwinds, but Beryl Markham, a bush pilot from East Africa, proved him wrong. Almost everyone I knew in Kenya had something to do with Beryl, so it was relatively easy to collect stories about her, but it was extremely daunting to portray her accurately. I'm afraid I was more concerned about their approval than I was of the audiences in the States.

Our director was Tony Richardson. I had worked with Tony years before in a miniseries called *A Death in Canaan,* so I was familiar with his talent and his sometimes contrary behavior, treating anyone in authority with disdain and contempt. As one of the producers, it was not an easy experience to work with Tony, nor was it 100 percent successful, although in hindsight the parts that were good were very good indeed, and I did not lose face with my Kenyan friends.

The greatest compliment I received while filming *Shadow on the Sun* came from one of the men who worked as a groom at the Nairobi racetrack in Jamhuri Park. We were filming in the grandstand at the track, and I had to leave the set for three hours to transform into the eighty-three-year-old Beryl. Having been a successful trainer of racehorses before becoming a pilot, Beryl resumed racehorse training in the last part of her life. She rented a bungalow on the grounds of the race course, where she trained horses from time to time, and where she suffered the fall that led to her death in 1986. She was a well-known fixture at Jamhuri Park and an artifact of a time gone by.

After three hours of makeup, I reappeared on the set as the old woman.

I could hardly walk around in an energetic fashion, so I assumed the appropriate body language the makeup required. Suddenly there was a horrifying scream, and in a panic the man who'd made the scream went running, bumping into a friend of mine who was visiting the set. "What's the matter?" Jonathan asked of Njorogi, the groom. "She is back, Bwana, she is dead but she is here!" he said, referring to me. I was sorry to have frightened that poor man so much, but that is the highest compliment an actor could receive.

DURING THE LAST year of *Hart to Hart,* I had been contracted to appear in three commercials and represent two products. I was thrilled with the unexpected income that would help provide the funds I needed to support the administration of the William Holden Wildlife Foundation. I had a very nice time working with Cover Girl makeup, London Fog used me as their model for women's outerwear, and Sears shot me for the cover of their catalogues with some fashion pages inside. Sears was thinking of producing a line of upmarket women's apparel that could be featured in their more modern stores, most of which were situated in shopping malls. In finding an image for their fashion statement, my name was tested along with many others in their copious marketing research, and I seemed to score the highest in the categories they were seeking.

After a lengthy negotiation to clarify my role in the venture, we came to an agreement, and the "Stefanie Collection" brand was born. Once we were in full swing, we manufactured two clothing collections per year, featured in 690 stores, which amounted to seventy-four thousand pieces two times a year for five years. Whew!

I was dying to read Sears' marketing research. I always thought it was crazy that as actors, we never really know—or can afford to spend the money to find out—what the perception of us as "product" really is. When

Hollywood had a studio system, the star they created had their own niche. In effect, the studio presented their stable of actors, "products," within the context of the images created for each one that would guarantee the audience an anticipated response. Eventually Sears kindly allowed me to have a copy of the research report, which revealed that in creating a new TV series for CBS, the character the audience might respond to best was someone like Jennifer Hart but without Jonathan.

I worked with Juanita Bartlett, the writer/producer of *The Rockford Files,* the series that was so successful for James Garner, to create the character of Maggie in a pilot for a series of the same name. Using the strength of the U.S. dollar against the British pound, we could get so much added production value filming in London that we placed the show there and surrounded Maggie with a cast of wonderful characters.

With the help and influence of director John Huston, Ava Gardner was made to feel sufficiently secure to accept our offer. I promised her that we would have the best lighting/cameraman for women in England and that her wardrobe would be made by her favorite designer. Even though I knew Ava, she was gun shy about working in TV, due to a bad experience she'd had as a guest star on *Falcon Crest,* mostly caused by a jealous leading lady.

I adored Ava and wanted her to look and feel her best, and I am both happy and sad to say that *Maggie* remains the last piece of film ever shot of Ava, and she looks magnificent. Jeremy Lloyd, whom American audiences first met on *Laugh-In,* played our recently landless lord, and Ian Ogilvy, who followed Roger Moore in the remake of *The Saint,* became our extremely attractive tax collector. Herb Edelman rounded out the cast as the wisecracking American expat who lived next door.

Sadly, *Maggie* was never shown on television. We were victims of the bad luck that comes from network infighting, and the conflicting personalities of a newly appointed head of programming and his former boss, who was made the new head of Warner Bros. television—the studio that produced the pilot. The excuses for not picking up the show were so convoluted that the only explanation that made sense rested with the acrimonious relationship between these two men.

BUT OTHER DOORS were opening to new and exciting ventures, not the least of which was my first involvement with the publishing house of Simon & Schuster. My girlfriend and neighbor, Judy Balaban Kantor Franciosa Quine, was involved with the unlikely enterprise of bringing the sport of full-contact karate into the clear light of commercialism. With the fitness industry on the verge of an international explosion, Judy had the foresight to think of combining the physical disciplines of karate with user-friendly techniques that could be translated for popular consumption.

Together, we created *Stefanie Powers: Superlife!*, a hardbound, photo-filled book containing exercises with easily understandable text that gave a new and different perspective on working out. Simon & Schuster editor Dan Greene was the book's godfather, and I still look at the pictures of me "assuming the positions" and wonder how the hell I got into all those poses. Years later I authored another exercise book, which Simon & Schuster also published. This time its theme approached the techniques of Joseph Pilates as body therapy rather than exercise. That book was called *Powers Pilates*.

How nice that I'm still being published by Simon & Schuster after all these years.

DURING THE DECADE after the end of *Hart to Hart*, there were a few gentlemen callers who came across my threshold; the best of them still remain friends. Whether it was bad timing, or inappropriate choices, no one seemed to fit with the life I was creating for myself. At times I wondered if

I had deliberately built a moat around my vulnerability to a relationship. I had, more or less, gone from my mother's house to my relationship and marriage to Gary, and when that ended I moved into Bill's life. Having been a working actor all my life, I was always too busy or too inhibited to participate in the "sowing of wild oats" that my contemporaries took advantage of. I was always a late bloomer. During my ten years of "bachelorhood" I wasn't exactly making up for lost time, but I did have a few dalliances that gave me a great deal more confidence about my sexuality. I always appreciated discretion, so accordingly I never wanted to impugn my reputation or compromise my privacy, which I value enormously. I was also on a quest, pursuing curiosities that took me away from Hollywood and gave me an unorthodox education with a rich spectrum, making deposits in an imaginary bank for which there was no conventional balance sheet.

While developing two projects in Paris, one with my *Mistral's Daughter* producer Steve Kranz, I stayed in the house of the artist and director Just Jaeckin, who is like family to me. Just was living mostly in New York City, so I looked after his lovely house and his extraordinary dog PamPam. Mom was able to join me in Paris, and she delighted in the spontaneity of our daily activities and the variety of our impromptu travels through the countryside. On the spur of the moment, we went to visit the chateaux of the Loire Valley. We completely improvised our tour, discovering wonderful places to eat and to stay. Fortunately we were just at the beginning of the tourist season, so we found accommodations. It was often observed by others that our relationship was a rarity in show business. Of course my mother and I did have our moments, but most of those were now ancient history and by now we had made peace with each other, allowing us to appreciate and view each other as individuals, warts and all.

Whereas Europe was a familiar destination for my mother and one that she had also explored without me, when it came to Egypt, Southeast Asia, and Africa, she felt comfortable only with me as the tour guide. Regardless of where we were, Mom was always a good sport and a willing companion.

Each year, the station manager for Pan Am Airlines in England sponsored a team to travel to the Chitwan Valley in Nepal to compete in a tournament of elephant polo. I had been asked twice to join them, but the timing usually conflicted with our annual Christmas migration to Kenya, carrying with us my dogs, Jackie and Russell, presents, food supplies not available there, and what seemed like a mother lode of luggage for the two months' stay.

Since tradition held that three strikes you're out, the third time I was invited I thought I had better accept or forever hold my peace. Knowing that the trip to the lowland forests of southern Nepal might be more adventurous than comfortable, I proposed that I go on ahead, then meet Mom and our menagerie in London after the polo, and fly on to Kenya. It was then that I heard the memorable words that my mother had never before, to my recollection, uttered. "I have always wanted to visit Nepal."

"Great," I said, worrying about how I was going to manage the transport of the circus I was bringing to Africa for the holidays. With the help of Tony Morris, who handled PR for Pan Am, and his darling wife Sue, anything was possible. Roger Moore gave me Tony and Sue, and they were the best present I have ever received. As long as we were going to Nepal and had to pass through India on the way, we couldn't miss the opportunity of going to see the Taj Mahal. We were joined on the trip by our family friend Geri Bauer, who lived in New York. Together we planned to hire a driver and visit some highlights on the way to the great monument to love. That would give Mom a taste of India, however brief.

The Pan Am team met at Heathrow Airport and, after a scheduled stop in Frankfurt to change planes, we embarked on our odyssey. Our first stop was New Delhi, where we had a day and a half to stretch our legs after the long flight and see some of the sights. The one "must see" in the city that once represented the seat of power for the British Raj was the famed Red Fort. The imposing design of the fort was purposely intended to intimidate all who would pass through its portals, and it succeeds. Flying into

Kathmandu at what seems to be a respectable altitude and looking up to see Mount Everest is truly a breathtaking, if not unnerving, experience.

When we finally arrived at Tiger Tops in the Chitwan National Park, we managed to change and meet the other teams at the first night cocktail reception before we crashed underneath the warm duvets in our "rooms."

Tiger Tops is a fancifully designed hotel in a magical location, deep inside the forest. The construction is highly unconventional. While it appears to be a solid structure, it is actually made of bamboo framing covered with woven grass matting that serves as the "walls" for the structure. To say that it was drafty is an understatement, and privacy was limited, so earplugs were an absolute necessity. That is not to say that it was uncomfortable—on the contrary, it was very comfortable, just rustic. Mom never complained.

Solar panels heated the water for the rooms, so a clever strategy was essential in order to be assured of a hot, or even a warm, shower. But we had not come for comfort, we had come for elephant polo, and that is what we had. At the end of the logging season, the elephants and their owners, or mahouts, leave the forest for their villages, but before they go they have one big celebration and make wagers with the money they have earned during the working season, betting on which of their elephants will triumph in the game of polo.

The game is played with very long sticks, but the ball is regulation size and the rules are largely the same as polo on horseback with the exception of "elephants may not stand on the ball." I thought that was logical. I soon learned that while the smaller elephants might be faster, they would never challenge the adult females, because it was not proper in elephant behavior, and these elephants knew their manners.

We had a great time, and the Nepalese were lovely people. Mom, ever intrepid, enjoyed her game drives atop an elephant, going off in the tall grass "as high as an elephant's eye," with her own "driver," to look for tigers or Indian rhinos. Mom was seventy-nine at the time and looked every bit of ten years younger. It was difficult to leave Nepal, but India beckoned, and so we said a fond farewell to our hosts and departed for New Delhi, to begin our tour of the Mogul palaces and the Taj Mahal. Mom loved all of India, and she began to run out of adjectives with which to express her wonderment.

Returning to New Delhi, we were invited by the family of the owners of the Oberoi Hotel for our farewell dinner. Most of the planes that leave India for Europe do so at the ungodly hours of the early morning in order to arrive in time for passengers to make connecting flights. Knowing we were to depart at 1:00 a.m., the dinner was a protracted entertainment graciously hosted by the family of Mr. Bicky Oberoi, who had known Bill from his time in Ceylon filming *The Bridge on the River Kwai*.

The dinner table was a long one, filled with gregarious strangers, with Mom and I at opposite ends. At a certain point Mom got up, as did a group of women, who all departed with her saying they would be back shortly. Two hours later, I was in my room. When there was a knock on the door, I opened it and there was my mother looking a bit pale, with a diamond in her nose! I said the only thing anyone in my position could say: "What on earth possessed you to do a thing like that?" The role reversal had begun.

To this day I find Mom's explanation beyond adorable. When she was a girl, her uncle Leo had a subscription to *National Geographic* magazine, and she remarked how she loved looking at the pictures of India with all the beautiful fabrics in "vivid colors." And she thought a nose ring was the most exotic adornment a woman could have, fantasizing that one day she would have one.

The interesting thing was that *National Geographic* magazine was not published in color until the 1960s.

So Mom, her diamond, Geri, and I left India, but not before we had spent three hours waiting on the tarmac with all the passengers loaded in the plane until we were cleared to take off. We landed in Frankfurt to change planes for England and were met by the nice Special Services man, who had looked after us on the way out. Only this time his face was not smiling. We were ushered into a small private room, and after he sat us down, we were told that there had been a terrible accident. The plane we would have connected with had we not been delayed was Pan Am 103, and it had gone down over Lockerbie, Scotland, that morning. We would have gotten off in London, but Geri would have gone on to New York City. She would not have made her destination. We were speechless, devastated and shaken by what we were told and what would eventually cause the end of Pan Am.

There were many more trips and many more adventures, but the gravity of this one would remain with us forever.

⸺ ∞ ⸺

WHILE I WAS traveling the world at a dizzying speed, pursuing all sorts of interests, back home life was changing. The changes were largely in the way business was conducted, but it would influence society in every aspect of our existence, as we entered the age of globalization and computerization.

By the early part of the 1980s, most U.S. corporations had embraced computers as a means of organizing payrolls and data, but it was not yet the essential piece of office equipment that is now seen on every desk. In fact, for many in senior management, the dreaded computer made them feel their jobs were in peril. They were mystified by how it worked and intimidated by anyone who could operate one.

At the same time, business schools were turning out graduates with master's degrees, who were becoming evangelists for a new order. The philosophy that was proselytized generally reinvented business procedures, superimposing an entirely new and universal lexicon that could be applied to any and all types of businesses, regardless of what they produced.

Whether you were selling cars, furniture, clothing, heavy equipment, widgets—or movies—the idea was that you could sell them all over the world with the same business vocabulary. Using this theory, you could find employment anywhere.

Wall Street was hiring all the MBAs they could get and placing them on the fast track to middle and upper management. For a while, everything was going extremely well and lots of money was being made, which always translates to more funds becoming available to make movies and television. But then in October of 1987, things changed.

Computers were set up to execute high volumes of trading and programmed to sell when shares reached a certain criteria. "Circuit breakers" had not been employed to prevent the cascading effects one huge sell-off would cause, so there was a financial disaster. The cover of *Newsweek* magazine said it all: "The Crash: After a Wild Week on Wall St. the World Is Different."

Wall Street recovered much faster than other businesses did. While we were in the midst of preproduction, we were notified that CBS had to reduce the licensing fee for *A Shadow on the Sun*. The licensing fee amounted to our entire budget for the series, and so reducing it would make it impossible to produce. The "crash" did not have such devastating effects in Britain, so like white knights, London Weekend Television came to our rescue with the three million dollars we needed, more than they had ever paid for rights to an American series. We were back in business. But *Newsweek* was right when it printed that "the world was different."

My professional world would become unrecognizable.

───⊗⊗⊗───

AFTER WE COMPLETED *A Shadow on the Sun,* I returned to L.A., and my darling Roddy McDowall invited me to a screening at the Directors Guild of a movie he had worked on. The Directors Guild was the best screening room in town, and usually every seat was filled with someone you knew in the "biz." Very few outsiders gained access to those hallowed halls. It was always fun to catch up with people after having been away, but that night was different.

As the industry began to file into the theater, I looked around and didn't see any familiar faces. I asked Roddy if he knew the people filling the room and he said that he only knew a few of them. The odd thing was that they all seemed to know each other.

Hollywood, that small town I had grown up in, was now a big city. The studios were bought by large conglomerates, no longer run by movie moguls but by corporations.

Henceforth decisions would be made by committee, creative ideas would be tested for public reaction, "branded" concepts would override imagination, and product placement would account for one of the largest sources of financing.

I understood change; in fact in 1970, I was a party to a revolutionary change impacting television. I was invited to join Walter Mirisch, head of the Producers Guild; Edward Anhult, head of the Writers Guild; Robert Wise, head of the Directors Guild; Charlton Heston, head of the Screen Actors Guild; Sidney Poitier; and Jack Valenti, head of the Motion Picture Association. We all testified in front of the FCC for discontinuing the three-network monopoly of the airwaves in favor of what was then called "family choice" television. Today it is known as "cable TV."

But what I experienced at the Directors Guild that night with Roddy was not just change—it was metamorphosis.

SIXTEEN

Life in London

As with all careers that span a few decades, there are bound to be highs and lows. The film and TV projects I was being offered were less and less interesting. In a way it really didn't matter to me, because I was spending so much time in Africa and Southeast Asia in my other life that I was well employed.

The William Holden Wildlife Foundation's education center was evolving extremely well under the guidance of Heather Eves, my favorite protégée. With boundless enthusiasm, Heather took on the chore of revamping our education programs and created the basis of the curricula we use today. Don Hunt's brothers gave us four llamas from Chile to use at the education center as a dramatic example of biodiversity, and our library/ lecture hall was built and fully equipped with hundreds of books and videos. Our reputation as an institution was beginning to grow in popularity, and our yearly totals of students served rose accordingly.

I am happy to be able to say that to date we have hosted more than five hundred thousand Kenyan students and adults at our center. We have an ongoing outreach program that consists of libraries built at primary and secondary schools in rural communities, which we stock with books, maps, and charts that help elevate education standards, while providing needed information concerning relevant environmental issues and wildlife concerns. We have five libraries serving roughly three thousand students on a continual basis. We also construct water-catchment facilities at the schools and build mess halls with fuel-efficient stoves capable of cooking lunches for three hundred students on less than two kilos of wood.

Almost all the teachers and students from our rural schools come for a visit to our education center, where they can see functioning uses of solar energy, biogas production, water recycling, companion planting for pest control, alternative fuel briquettes, solar cookers, bush refrigerators, tree propagation, and composting of biodegradable waste. We also offer video presentations that promote the understanding of the vital role animals of all kinds play in the balance of nature and in our quality of life on this fragile planet.

The groups that visit the center may come for a day trip or a three-day stay, during which time they receive lectures, nature walks, and game drives on the neighboring Mount Kenya Wildlife Conservancy (formerly the game ranch). Each group has lessons tailored to suit their needs and levels of comprehension. We make a great effort to encourage their enthusiasm to evangelize and join the crusade to save our precious wildlife and the environment we share with them.

While in the process of earning my stripes in the field I became acquainted with an entirely new group of people. Don Hunt had spent a lifetime dealing with wildlife and zoos around the world. Through him I began to know many of the great innovators who were changing the look and the purpose of zoos. I accepted a position on the board of the Los Angeles Zoo and was invited to the boards of both the Cincinnati Zoo and the Zoo Atlanta. At the Cincinnati zoo I met Dr. Betsy Dresser, who has become a lifelong friend. Betsy taught me about the concept of a frozen zoo. With the use of cryonic freezing methods, both flora and fauna species can be preserved. Precious samples of DNA and tissue, along with sperm and ova, are frozen in the hopes of ensuring against the disappearance of species, largely due to human impact.

I also learned about Betsy's leading-edge research with embryo transfers, and I had the privilege of assisting her in transferring embryos from an antelope called the East African bongo into a host female of another species of antelope. The bongo is extinct on Mount Kenya, and the only captive herd in East Africa exists at the Mount Kenya Wildlife Conservancy. Those bongo were captured when Bill and Don began the ranch. In order to help propagate more of the desperately endangered bongo, Betsy was using the same techniques that began long ago with the dairy and cattle industry and are now employed in human reproduction.

Today, Betsy is in New Orleans and heads the Audubon Center for Research of Endangered Species, and I am on the board of the Species Survival Program for the East African Bongo, operated by Dr. Ron Surratt at the Fort Worth Zoo.

With Dr. Terry Maple, the director of Zoo Atlanta, and the man responsible for the transformation of that zoo from one of the worst in North America to one of the best, I traveled to Java and Sumatra. We had a wonderful expedition on the Awash River for five days, studying flora and fauna and hacking our way through rain forests, climbing slippery hillsides to visit orangutan sanctuaries and walk with Komodo dragons. We sailed into the caldera of Krakatoa, the site of the largest volcanic eruption in modern times, all the while making a documentary of the trip and cementing our friendship.

I became involved with other documentaries that made me lose my heart to that wondrous medium for storytelling, where the truth is better than any fiction imaginable.

Alan Root is one of one the finest documentary filmmakers to have captured African animals on celluloid. Alan's footage exploring the unique relationship of lionesses in a pride is one of his seminal works, and I had the honor of narrating the story for the *Survival* series.

When the BBC decided to do a "World Safari," broadcasting live from remote places around the planet linked by satellite, I was standing up to my knees in the Chilkat River in Alaska, surrounded by bears, bald eagles, and salmon swimming upstream between my legs, while talking to Sir David Attenborough in London. And when Microsoft experimented with an online nature magazine called *Mungo Park,* named for the great explorer, they asked me to be their wildlife correspondent, beginning with a trip beyond the Arctic Circle to film and report on the caribou.

It was easy to lose my way, seduced by the wonders of the natural world, and it was equally easy to join the battle to protect them.

The only way my peripatetic lifestyle was possible was because my mother not only kept the home fires burning but she also continued to maintain a stable base for me, looking after all my critters as if they'd been her grandchildren, and pestering my agents to get me a job that would force me to stay home.

<hr />

WHEN A. R. Gurney wrote a play called *Love Letters,* he had no idea what a sensation it would become. This two-character play about the letters a man and a woman write to each other throughout their lives was like a gift to all the actors who played it, and the list is long and impressive. In hindsight, it seemed only natural that RJ and I might be a good team to tour with the play, but at the time it was proposed, neither one of us had done a play for some time and we were a bit nervous about whether our rapport would translate to the stage.

Because the play was essentially read by two actors seated at a table, there was no real rehearsal period scheduled before we opened at the Wilbur Theater in Boston. So, to pluck up our courage, RJ and I performed the letters in front of a select group at his home in Brentwood. The audience consisted of his mother, my mother, his secretary, and our mutual friend Sidney Guilaroff, the famed hairstylist to all the iconic stars at MGM.

You might say that the audience was predisposed to love us.

It had been seven years since *Hart to Hart* had ended, yet we seemed to find that old groove without much effort. We had one day of rehearsal with the director, John Tillinger, in Boston, and the next night we opened. My dear friend Father Ed McCabbe, a local parish priest, said a few prayers for us, and we walked onto the stage.

When we walked off, it was to a standing ovation. Our mutual friend Robert Osborne wrote in his *Hollywood Reporter* column that we broke all records for a one-week run at the Wilbur Theater. It was the beginning of many record-breaking engagements that surprised us more than anyone else.

Perhaps *Love Letters* came at the right time for both RJ and me. It gave us both a shot in the arm and rekindled the desire to work. Over the next few years, from time to time, we would tour with the play for five weeks at a time all over the country, in Hawaii, and in Canada. Then, the pièce de résistance—London's West End. The night we opened in the gorgeous Wyndhams Theater, mounted police were called to control the crowds. We had never been seen as a couple on the stage in England, and the reaction was overwhelming. Naturally we were only a professional couple, but that didn't seem to matter. I've never been in love with RJ, but I have always loved him, and the public loved Jonathan and Jennifer Hart.

—◦◦◦—

I HAVE ALWAYS been respectful of the many fans who have so loyally stood by me and who have so generously contributed to the William Holden Wildlife Foundation. Thousands of dollars have come from my "girls," who are an international gang of wonderful women whose financial sacrifice is considerable and whose bighearted benevolence I can never thank enough. Whether it was the tours of *Love Letters,* or the many subsequent theatrical appearances I have made both in England and in the States, the "girls" find a way to get to where I am, and we always have a fond reunion. Kathy Bartels was the first to form a fan club, and as her enduring friendship and trust grew, she began to play a much greater role in my life and in the operations of the foundation. Kathy is the secretary/treasurer of the foundation, and as with my late business manager, Mini McGuire, she too would know the bank balance if I woke her in the night. Nancy Dugan keeps my archives, and she knows more about my career than I do. Thank you all now and forever.

On January 15, 1991, we began a five-week tour of *Love Letters* with an opening in Seattle to a sold-out house of twenty-seven hundred people. The play had never before been presented in a theater of such size, and we worried that we might appear as tiny dots seated behind a large desk in the center of an enormous stage. There was something else that worried us about that night. Half a world away, our troops and the might of our armed forces were poised for the "witching hour" in Washington, D.C., when, for the first time since the day after Pearl Harbor, the United States would declare war. The curtain would be coming down on our first act at approximately 9:00 p.m. PST, and one minute later, at 12:01 a.m. EST, our president would sign the proclamation of war.

In effect, we and our audience would go to the intermission in peacetime and return for the second act at war. What were we to do? Was it appropriate to make an announcement and have a moment of silence for all those whose lives would be lost that night? Were we to let it go by as if it were a non-event?

RJ rang his publicist, who called an official at the White House for advice on the protocol. We were told that we were not to make any announcement.

When the play ended, we received a standing ovation and an opening night party, and then we rushed back to our hotel to turn on the late-night news. Another precedent was being set that night, one that involved CNN. That early morning in Kuwait, CNN transfigured itself. By that morning, graphic designs like the titles of a movie announced the blow-by-blow transmissions from the front lines, with reporters live in the epicenter of the battle.

It was like a media event.

The next night the theater was once again full, and the audience was wonderful and enthusiastic. Afterward we signed autographs, then we again rushed back to our hotel to watch the war. The Nielsen ratings for that night included a TV movie I was in called *She Was Marked for Murder,* which came in at number 12 for the night against *The War, Day 2* on CNN, which came in number 1. It was like a scene written by Paddy Chayefsky, from the movie *Network,* which Bill had acted in. We were competing with the war as entertainment!

WHILE WE WERE still on tour, I received a call from Bryan Morrison, one of the fabled rock 'n' roll manager/producers during the height of the English pop scene in the 1960s and '70s. Bryan was also a committed polo player who owned a very glamorous club called the Royal Berkshire Polo Club, where I was a member. Bryan had optioned a musical play based on a concept album by Tom Jones, called *Matador.* The music was sensational, and they wanted someone to play the "Ava Gardner-ish" female lead. It was a great chance to return to the West End in my first love, the musical theater, and it would be an added incentive to be working with friends. The offer was irresistible.

I installed myself in the lovely Kensington house of my girlfriend Elaine from Hong Kong and her husband, Anto, who lent it to me for a few months until I could find more permanent housing. Rehearsals were a dream, as was the cast. My longtime friend Nicky Henson, whose talents are an asset to any production, played the manager, and the newcomer John Barrowman played the young bullfighter. The director was Elijah Moshinsky, one of England's best. The "bull" was to be played by five flamenco dancers from Spain.

Mom came to England for the opening night, along with my business manager, Mini McGuire, and my lawyer, Leo Ziffren, who was making his maiden voyage abroad. These were the captains of my support team, along with my devoted right arm and housekeeper, Albertina, on the home front.

Mom always defied the aging process. No one ever believed how old she was and always took her for at least ten years younger. Her energy was boundless and her humor irreverent. But on this trip something was different. Six months before I left for England, Mom had an "episode." That is a euphemism for what is medically termed a transient ischemic attack, a very brief alteration in the blood flow to the brain, usually caused by plaque dislodging from the wall of the artery. After an overnight stay in the hospital, she came home and resumed her usual pace, which was one that would make a quarterback wilt. When she arrived in England, I knew she was suffering from jet lag, but she seemed uncharacteristically detached. When we came home after the opening night party, changed into our robes, and sat down to do a postmortem of the night, she was not her usual self, although she did manage to make her predictable critique of my hair.

When I asked her if she felt well and mentioned that she seemed to be distracted, she acknowledged that she did feel sort of out of focus. There was nothing that she could define, and she didn't feel unwell, only that she wasn't sharp and her reactions were dull. When I look at the photos taken of us that night, I can plainly see the vagueness in her expression. She promised to see her doctor when she returned to L.A., but I don't think she did. I was not yet aware that I had to assert myself with her concerning her health.

You never think a parent needs parenting, but the time inevitably comes when we all must assume that responsibility.

Matador did not receive rave reviews, but they were not a death knell, so at the very least, we were assured of the short run of three months I was contracted for. One of the things I began to miss terribly was Jackie and Russell, my Jack Russell terriers. The stage door manager had a very large Jack Russell, and I used to bribe him with treats in order to get my fix of fur. One evening as I arrived at the stage door and bent down to give Buster his treat, someone popped his head in the door and asked us if the dog running around the street was our stage door dog. Seeing Buster, he guessed it was only a lost Jack Russell. Like a heat-seeking missile, I jumped out the door and caught a glimpse of a small white dog running between the traffic across the street to what we affectionately called "glue sniffers park."

I raced after her and called her. She stopped, turned indignantly to look at who had the audacity to distract her, and, after a brief second pondering the thought of coming closer to me, she changed her mind and darted off. I was determined, so I cornered her and had one chance only to sweep her up into my arms, which worked. I felt her actually heave a sigh of relief at not having to run anymore. Appropriately, we called the police, and two officers came by the theater and into my dressing room to look at the dog. They said she was probably a vagrant's dog, judging from her condition and lack of tags. They also said I could either keep her or they would take her to the Battersea Dogs Home. Without a moment's hesitation, I took her.

Miss Laura Jane Wilding was the character I played in *Matador,* and the name suited my new little friend to a tee. After a good scrub and a nice meal, Laura Jane was part of the family. Sleeping on the high-thread-count sheets and the soft duvet of my bed was a far cry from the back alleys of Soho. Miss Laura Jane was on her way up the social ladder.

Just before *Matador* came to an end, I was approached by the director Frank Dunlop to play the Sadie Thompson role in a revival of the play *Rain,* based on a Somerset Maugham short story. Frank had spent the previous fifteen years successfully directing the Edinburgh Festival, and this was to be his first play after resigning from the festival. I was very flattered.

The play was to open in Plymouth and then come into the West End. It was scheduled to begin rehearsals in May 1992, almost ten months from the end of my contract with *Matador*.

I had been looking for a house to buy in London with the hopes that *Matador*, and now *Rain*, would lead to more West End projects. I found a perfect but very small mews house in South Kensington and began negotiations. Even with the house, I would still have to find a place Laura Jane could stay in whenever I had to leave England. England's quarantine laws make it near to impossible to easily transport dogs back and forth, so once she left England, she was never coming back.

One day I was invited to play tennis at the estate of the king and queen of Jordan. Laura Jane was amusing everyone with her favorite impression of a soccer player, kicking the ball forward with her front feet and tossing the ball up in the air to hit it with her head. It was uncanny. The queen asked me if I had found a place to board Laura Jane for the months I would be away, and I said I was still looking. The queen then mentioned that they would be away for the next six months at least and that their housekeeper had a dog and . . . It was too delicious an offer and the height of Laura Jane's social climbing. But alas, her chances at a royal position were dashed. As we played tennis, Laura Jane ran around the outside of the court, incessantly barking in a shrill pitch so irritating that when the game was over there was no further mention of her staying. LJ had committed the ultimate social gaffe.

Laura Jane eventually came to California, but her energy was too exhausting for Mom when I was away. I was worried that Mom might trip on Laura Jane when she was chasing around the house, in typical terrier fashion. In addition, our other babies, Jackie and Russell, had become very jealous and their noses were permanently out of joint. I farmed LJ out to an English girlfriend of mine, Liz Radley, who could appreciate the personality of a Jack Russell. Liz only agreed to take Laura Jane from time to time when I was away, but gradually they became so attached to each other that her stays with Auntie Liz became longer and longer. Laura Jane's epic journey from the alleys of Soho to the playing fields of Windsor ended in sunny California, where she lived for eighteen years, mostly in the loving care of Liz. Hers was a great success story.

THE LAST TWO weeks of *Matador,* many well-meaning friends in the theater stopped by to see the show and console us, including Placido Domingo and the director John Schlesinger. Yes, the show was flawed, but no one in the theater wants to see a show close, and the Brits are particularly supportive when it comes to fellow performers.

During the final week of our run, I received a call from my girlfriend Marie in Paris, who was asking for a favor. A friend of hers was coming to London and he was interested in playing polo in England, and she thought I could help. She described him as substantial, intelligent, attractive, and someone who it would be nice for me to know. With such a recommendation I suggested he come to the show and we could have a drink afterward. His name was Patrick de la Chesnais.

The night Patrick came to see the show, my dressing room was, as usual, filled with people. John Barrowman always used the shower in my room, as his had none. John would always entertain my guests by emerging from the shower still wet, wrapped in nothing but a towel, much to the awe and admiration of any guest, male or female, who might be there. Laura Jane had a young walker who was my fan and devotedly arrived before the end of the second act every night to take her out to do her business. Then there were the friends who came to see the show and stopped by for a glass of wine afterward. It was always Grand Central Station, and I loved it.

After everyone left, I waited for the mysterious Frenchman, but he never arrived. As I prepared to leave, the phone rang from the stage door saying

I had another visitor. In keeping with tradition, most of the older theaters in the West End were constructed to have the stage below ground level; accordingly, the one "star" dressing room was always on that level next to the stage, so it was necessary to descend two sets of stairs to arrive at my room.

His footsteps echoed as he negotiated the cement steps. I poked my head out the door and called up to him to encourage his progress, and soon I saw his feet. Then the reveal of the rest of him replicated a slow camera move, panning up to a tall, dark-haired man with broad shoulders, a lovely accent, and a charming smile. I had done two shows that day, and I was tired. The theater was empty and about to close. With Marie's recommendation I felt safe to invite him back to my house for a drink.

We managed to navigate the adoring but demanding fans at the stage door and board my awaiting car. I had just moved into my little abode, so the sitting room furniture was yet to arrive. We popped a bottle of champagne, sat on the floor, and spoke of horses, polo, England, and life. When we said good-bye, I watched his silhouette disappear down the end of the mews and felt a little twinkle of attraction, which I immediately dismissed as a momentary fantasy and a symptom of too much champagne.

A few days later I received some flowers and a note inviting me to come to Patrick's estate, called La Salle, in Burgundy, for his annual August polo tournament. It was a nice thought but completely out of the question. When *Matador* ended, there was still a bit of the polo season left and a women's tournament to be played at our club, so I stayed on in England. The ladies tournament was an international one, and players came from all over Europe and the United Kingdom. I happened to be teamed with two women from France, who were not only good players but also great fun. The coach for our team was an American 5-goal-rated player called Warren Scherer. Warren was like my little brother, and he had a great flair for the theatrical, along with an outrageous sense of style.

When my new friends mentioned they were going to play at the tournament in La Salle and I mentioned that Patrick had invited me to play, before I had time to say no, Warren had organized our entire team, the transport of the horses, and airline tickets. He drafted one of his patrons who lived in Geneva to not only play with us but also to provide cars for our drive from Geneva to La Salle. Patrick's property was located an hour from the Swiss border, between Cluny and Mâcon, in the heart of the Beaujolais, Pouilly-Fuissé, Mâcon-Villages, and Puligny-Montrachet. The estate was twenty-five hundred acres of woodlands, with two polo fields, an equestrian center, an eighteen-hole golf course with driving range, and the centerpiece, a Burgundian-style Gothic-revival château built in 1823.

The polo tournament was much more laid back than in England, but the atmosphere was warm and friendly.

Patrick was a generous host. His lineage descended from old nobility on his mother's side and Industrial Revolution wealth on his father's. All this heritage, however, had seen better days, and while his family owned many châteaux, most of them were in great need of repair. Patrick's was no exception.

But that was neither my concern nor my preoccupation at the time. The five days of the tournament were filled with delightful activities in the bucolic loveliness of the countryside, which enchanted all of us. While there was no wife or girlfriend in the picture, there were Patrick's two young daughters, who lovingly hung around his arms and his shoulders, showing a tenderness in him that was extremely seductive. The attraction between us was palpable to everyone, and we never seemed to find ourselves more than an arm's length distance from each other.

Yet when the weekend ended and we all returned to our real lives, I was glad we had not started something that was so far from possible. But then again, I suppose, love conquers all . . . or something like that.

AT THE TIME I met Patrick I was entertaining the notion that I was no good at relationships, so I had taken a sabbatical from romantic involvements. It had been ten years since Bill died, and the more time I spent in Patrick's company, the more I thought of trying it again.

In the beginning, Patrick expressed a desire to live in England. I had many long and well-established friendships in England and always enjoyed working there, so it seemed a good place for both of us and easy to develop our lives there. Our wedding in Kenya was one of my best productions, and eighty-two friends came from all over the world to join us for a safari wedding.

When the wedding was reported in *Hello!* magazine, it took up two issues. I should have known about the curse of *Hello!* magazine before I agreed to allow them to publish the photos. The so-called curse involves the many weddings they cover that then result in divorce.

While Mom was impressed with Patrick when he called her to ask for my hand in marriage, she was worried about the mysterious parts of his life and was insecure about our future. What should have been a love affair became a marriage that was probably doomed before we took the vows. The insurmountable complexities of his life and the incompatible demands of mine never allowed us to find an even ground for our marriage, and the differences between us began to overwhelm any of the similarities. In the end there was no option but to go our separate ways.

Mom's instincts were, as always, impeccable.

SEVENTEEN

One Door Closes, Others Open

While RJ and I were on yet another tour with *Love Letters*, he mentioned that there was serious interest from NBC to resurrect *Hart to Hart* as part of a mystery wheel they wanted for their new season. The "mystery wheel" was a concept created in the 1970s by Universal Television in which four two-hour "episodes" of four different shows would alternate each week in the same time slot, all with a mystery or crime-solving theme.

The shows included *McMillan & Wife*, starring Rock Hudson and Susan Saint James; *McCloud*, starring Dennis Weaver; *The Name of the Game*, staring Tony Franciosa, Robert Stack, and Gene Barry; and *Colombo*, starring Peter Falk.

It was very successful at the time, but then, at the time, there were only three television networks and a more captive audience. The idea that by doing six two-hour shows we could finally put a period at the end of the sentence as far as *Hart to Hart* was concerned was very appealing, especially after such an abrupt cancellation of the series. With two new producers and RJ as executive producer, we filmed five "episodes," but as we went on the air, the other spokes of the "wheel" began to fall apart, and so did the concept.

Something else happened after the fifth episode that was far more important: Lionel Stander died. Our Max was gone. Not enough can be said about his illustrious career on Broadway and in Hollywood movies. Nor can we forget his famously remarkable testimony before the House Un-American Activities Committee during the infamous McCarthy witch hunt, and his subsequent blacklisting, which resulted in his leaving the States to appear in countless European films, including *Cul de Sac,* directed by Roman Polanski.

Lionel was as flamboyant as they come, both in his life and in his work, and if he stood on your side, you could have no better backing. Some people leave a hole when they go; Lionel left a crater.

⊶⊷

IT IS AN inconsolable fact of life that if you know people considerably older than yourself, the odds are you will lose them before they lose you. I was losing my most cherished friends and advisors, and Mom was becoming increasingly fragile. The frustration of doctor after doctor failing to diagnose her elusive pain and excusing it because of her age put me on the warpath. The dismissive attitude of some in the medical profession when it comes to the aged is unconscionable.

In becoming an advocate for my mother, it was crucial that I educate myself as much as possible about her symptoms, as well as her medications and their cumulative effects. Understanding the vortex of treatments and the maze of medical assistance afforded through Social Security, Medicare, and her own insurance was a career in itself. There are no schools that offer courses in how to navigate these waters, and yet they are waters we will all dive into at some point in our lives.

In the midst of our attempt to stabilize Mom's condition and comfort, I was asked to be the grand marshal of the Pulaski Day Parade, taking place down the length of Fifth Avenue in New York City. I thought this might be just the tonic for Mom. That day began with mass at St. Patrick's Cathedral by Cardinal O'Connor, breakfast at the Pierre hotel with the cardinal and one hundred others, then the drive to the starting point of the parade downtown. We climbed onto the giant float that was to carry us uptown to the steps of the cathedral, and there was an unobstructed view as far as the eye could see, with traffic suspended and the streets full of the vibrant colors of the bands and costumed dancers.

I never saw so many Polacks in one place. It was a thrill for both of us. I asked Mom if as a young woman in this city she ever imagined that one day she would be riding on a float up the grandest avenue in town. It was not only a memorable day for us both; it was also therapy that worked to lift her spirits with long-term positive effects.

⟡

WE HAD ONE more shot to do to complete the fifth episode of *Hart to Hart*. It had taken a long time to accomplish, largely due to the difficult schedule of the person who was to make a guest appearance in that scene. Mr. Donald Trump finally had a gap in his schedule, and we rushed to New York to shoot one scene with him exiting his limo. When the show was completed, we sent him a tape, and he sent a note to both RJ and me, which I recently found in my diary. The note said that he waited to see the show when it aired rather than watch the video and his comment about his performance was, "What I have determined is that I had better keep my day job."

While NBC had canceled the wheel and was generally doing badly in its ratings as a network, our reunion shows had done rather well, so they informed us that they wanted to complete our contract to do one more. As the months went on, the idea of our sixth show evaporated. RJ and I were still in demand for engagements in *Love Letters,* and we appeared in Las Vegas at both the Desert Inn and the Sands shortly before they were scheduled to be torn down. Never in my life could I have possibly imagined I would appear on the same stage that the Rat Pack had played on.

As I look back, it really was the end of another era. Those two hotels embodied the old Las Vegas, and once they were both gone there would be little, if any, evidence of the original town that Bugsy Siegel, Moe Dalitz, and Meyer Lansky built. The days when everyone went to the dinner shows dressed in evening gowns and black ties would fade from memory, a vague remnant of the past. The loss of history and elegant style was, however, replaced by a Las Vegas that is truly phenomenal. With the new came Steve Wynn, who gave us spectacles like Siegfried and Roy, who became great friends of mine and were always so kind to Mom—not to mention how good they were to their animals.

While I was in Kenya, only a few weeks after NBC had given us their official termination notice, I received a fax from my agent telling me that the Family Channel wanted to pick up *Hart to Hart* for three two-hour movies.

RJ had been working to get the show picked up by another network, and he was going to produce with his company and a partner who brought in money from Germany. Whatever he did convinced the Family Channel to put us on. We would be squeezing all the blood out of the turnip as *Hart to Hart* was taking its final bow.

The first show was to be filmed in Canada. It would be a tribute to the Max character that explained his death and would guest-star our friend Joan Collins. Prior to going to Montreal, we went to New York to buy wardrobe for the show. While in the city I received a call from the Broadway producers Barry and Fran Weisler, whom I had met in London a year earlier. They were trying to find a project that they could do with me, and what they came up with was a revival of *Applause,* the musical version of the film *All About Eve* that won Lauren Bacall her first Tony. They wanted the show to do a five-month tour before coming into New York, and they needed a commitment a year in advance to do the bookings.

By this time, the *Hart to Hart* franchise and *Love Letters* had made a professional team out of Wagner and Powers. Poor Jill St. John because of her red hair was always being mistaken for me, and it was assumed by the public that RJ was married to me and not to her, which disturbed us both.

Even after the weekly series went off prime-time television, we were on the air in syndication in the States and in sixty-seven countries around the world for years. Our professional association had spanned nearly fifteen years, and with our lives taking us in opposite directions, our rapport was wearing thin.

In show business, as in life, it is not only important to know when to enter but it is even more important to know when to exit, no matter how painful that might be. *Applause* might have been the wrong play and the wrong decision, but it seemed like the right thing to do at the time.

So after the third movie for the Family Channel, I said good-bye to Jonathan and Jennifer Hart and moved on.

***

AS WE WATCHED the flag come down the flagpole at Government House on the Peak of Hong Kong the afternoon of June 30, 1997, it was more than a historic event; it was for me, in many ways, an end and a beginning.

Two years earlier, I had reserved a corner suite at the Mandarin Hotel just for this occasion. The suite had a balcony that overlooked the dock where the Royal Yacht *Britannia* was moored and many of the handing-over ceremonies were staged. The weather at the end of June was always something to be avoided, and most of the people I knew there always did, except for this year. In anticipation of the "handover," which was billed as "one country, two systems," the general insecurity in both the European and the Chinese communities affected both the economy of the colony and the property prices. Most of my friends who could afford it had created bases in other countries in advance of 1997 so they could have a foot in both places "just in case." I stayed up till dawn on the first of July to watch the Royal Yacht sail out of Hong Kong harbor, as Chinese troops in military trucks and tanks drove across the border and through the streets of the city to make a dramatic demonstration of the new order.

It was a diplomatic faux pas that did not engender confidence.

A place is special not only for itself but also for the people and the personal relationships we acquire there.

I entertained a small conceit that in some way a part of me belonged in Hong Kong, but I was beginning to feel like a gate-crasher. Many of my friends, both Chinese and European, were leaving. When a respectable offer came in for my house, I was advised to take it. It was the end of another chapter, and reluctantly I had to turn the page. *The Mandarins and the Barbarians,* the miniseries I wrote with Nigel Cameron, based on his book, remains one of the fruits of my time in that very special part of the world, along with my enduring friendships, and I will always feel that I left a piece of my heart there.

Change, regrettable as it may sometimes be, is a fact of life, and accelerated change is a primary ingredient of present times. But the one prevailing axiom in my life that has held true is that doors close and others open.

———— ∞ ————

MY GREATER INVOLVEMENT with environmental and wildlife issues and working in the theater in England distracted me from the collapse of my marriage to Patrick. Even though we had agreed to divorce and I drew up the papers with my lawyer, Leo Ziffren, it took Patrick more than a year to sign them.

Patrick had begun a relationship with someone else, but I was held hostage by my old-fashioned principles, which required a formal dissolution before I felt free to pursue my own personal life.

While I was still waiting for the papers to be signed, a friend of mine in

London gave me a belated birthday present that he said would be a remarkable experience.

His gift was an appointment with his new clairvoyant, who lived in the Midlands of England and came up to London once a month to visit clients.

My friend Tomasz assured me that he had only told the woman my address and that she would be seeing a female friend of his.

The woman arrived in a taxi, and as I opened the door, she entered, quite flustered. I showed her to a chair and offered her a glass of water, which she took and drained in one go. "Well," she said, "I usually travel from one client to another in a taxi so that I can clear my mind and have a moment's rest before I see the next person, but I couldn't do that, could I, because Bill was always there nagging me. Nag, nag, nag, he did, saying that I have to tell you to get rid of the Frenchman, that he was no good for you! There is someone in a cowboy hat, and he is going to love you very much, but he will let you be who you are! Does that make any sense, dear?" I was startled to say the least.

I certainly knew who Bill was, and I certainly knew who the Frenchman was, but the man in the cowboy hat, that was from far left field.

MOM'S PHYSICAL PROBLEMS were slowly returning, and the exasperation the pain in her body caused manifested itself in bouts of temper that were not at all characteristic. For some time it had been necessary to have someone in the house looking after her exclusively, and she progressively resented anyone's help. Each time I would arrive in L.A., Mom would miraculously recover, and the only person she would listen to was me. I would sort everything out for her, and perhaps it was the confidence my presence gave her that made her respond so well. In any event, it was clear that I needed to spend more time in California. With that in mind, imagine my surprise when I received a call from my mother, while I was in Africa, announcing that she was leaving my house and that she and my aunt had decided to move in together.

In early 2000, darling Uncle Howard, the man who taught me to do a soft shoe to the tune of "Sunny Side of the Street," died. Uncle Howard and Cioci Helena had a love affair for the fifty-eight years of their marriage. They were the proverbial two peas in a pod and the only members of our family to live in California. They never had children, so they doted on my brother and me, and naturally we loved them. Uncle Howard had been married when he was very young and that marriage had produced a son called Jack, who'd grown up with his mother, so I only knew him as my cousin, the highly decorated ace pilot in Vietnam. Later in life, Jack would realize his dream of becoming a woman, a feeling he had harbored his entire life.

I met "Jackie" when she came to the funeral and stayed with me. Her heartrending story of emotional and physical pain was shared with such love that all I could do was embrace her as my newfound cousin.

When Uncle Howard died, I offered to help my aunt sort out the papers that comprised the postmortem requirements of the government. I knew that she had not been the partner who'd dealt with bills, taxes, and the "business" of life in their marriage, so I rightly thought my aunt could use the help. When she turned me down, I thought that eventually I would have a great deal to sort out for her, but I realized she needed the time to find her way. My aunt, my mother, and I had a "meeting" to discuss the ramifications of their decision to cohabit. Just because they were sisters and had once lived together, it did not follow that they would be able to share the same space, unless it was sufficient space.

Our conversation was like a scene out of *The Golden Girls*, with the most unrealistic ideas of who, what, when, and where life would be once they were on their own. The principal requirements of the condo they wanted to buy was that, first, they would allow my mother's dog, Marilyn, and, second, that it should be walking distance to the shops near the center of Beverly Hills. At this point, they were ages eighty-nine and eighty-seven, my aunt being the elder. I asked them if they intended to carry the groceries home.

"No," they said, "we'll buy a shopping basket with wheels." I was able to at least convince them that they should have a three-bedroom condo, and with that in mind, we began to look. Naturally, nothing was just right for one or the other of them, as you might guess. The prices, of course, were outrageous to people who had not shopped for property for more than twenty years. So we kept looking.

In the meantime, I rented a house in the desert for one month during the polo season, where we would all move in together, thinking it might be an interesting trial run on neutral ground. My aunt and uncle had lived in the Coachella Valley near Palm Springs, and I knew they loved that environment, so the idea met with the "girls' " approval. We packed up my car with three dogs, a parrot, horse equipment, and luggage, and the three of us moved out, looking like the Beverly Hillbillies. The month had its highs and lows, and after our return to L.A. the deadline for my mother's moving out suddenly became more flexible.

I WAS OFFERED a small job in London, and on the way I stopped off to sing at a benefit in New York City being organized by a friend who entertained lavishly in his West Side apartment. In order to keep the peace, he invited the neighbors in his building, including them among his enormous number of other guests, most of whom had recognizable faces. The centerpiece of his evening was a musical presentation with stellar performers, to the delight and amazement of all his guests. He was a showman and did everything on a grand scale.

The night of the benefit I received a call from David, the host, who asked me if I would come to his apartment early, and then informed me that he had fixed me up with a date, who was a fellow tenant and the chairman of the board of the building. His name was Tom Carroll. Upon my arrival, I found David in his bedroom on the floor, looking as if we should call 911. He had gone in for hemorrhoid surgery that morning and was bleeding from his rectum. He said he would be fine, but he needed me to act as hostess and receive his guests at the door.

I knew David had a flair for the dramatic, but the circumstances were such that I could hardly refuse his request. As the guests arrived, I dutifully greeted everyone on David's behalf, making his excuses. The apartment had been transformed into a nightclub, and it was incredible how many bodies fit inside, with only a few spilling out into the corridor.

I was standing at the door when I heard a mahogany-toned voice say, "Hello, I'm Tom Carroll." I think I saw his smile before I saw his face. It was a very attractive smile, and it belonged to a very attractive face. He was the all-American boy, healthy, fit, a Notre Dame Irishman. Clear-eyed, and unattached, he looked like a movie star in his suit and tie. We squeezed into our seats and attempted to have a conversation over the din of the crowd and the festivities. Somehow or other, we managed to make a date to go sailing the following day, where we could talk and enjoy getting out of the city on a hot weekend. Tom was an excellent sailor and looked just as good in his sailing gear. As attracted to him as I was, I still had the battle scars from a failed marriage that had taken too long to dissolve, and I was not anxious to jump into an involvement. Tom did not seem to me to be someone interested in just a one-night stand.

If there is one thing I have learned in life, it is that whenever I say "never," I am usually wrong. Not only was there a physical chemistry but there was also something we touched in each other that made us know we could trust one another. There is an abiding decency in Tom that makes him a rare and special person. And he makes me laugh even if we fight like cats and dogs.

I think the cowboy that the clairvoyant saw was Tom, and I am so grateful I did not miss the chance to have him in my life.

The week before my birthday, my mother and my aunt had finally agreed on the apartment I'd found. It was only a rental, but it met all the criteria and had three bedrooms, so there would be enough room for them to have privacy and for a helper to live in when needed. It would be their last stab at independence, and I was trying to make all their dreams come true.

Tom was in the habit of running in the New York marathon each year, and the marathon is usually run on the first weekend in November. To complicate matters, my birthday is on November 2, so a sacrifice had to be made, and it was clearly mine to make. Attempting to be a dutiful new girlfriend, I made plans to celebrate my birthday early. The Thursday before the marathon, a small group of friends, including my aunt and my mother, gathered at the Hotel Bel-Air for my pre-birthday dinner.

My friend Michael Butler volunteered to drive my aunt, so he delivered her back to her apartment complex after dinner. Michael let my aunt off at the front of her building, and she waved at him as he drove away. Apparently when she turned to enter the building, either she fell and broke her hip or she broke her hip as she turned, but she wound up on the ground with a broken hip.

The security in her complex was excellent, and they found her almost immediately and called 911 to take her to Cedars Sinai Hospital. I drove home with my mom and we said good night, knowing I would be leaving early the next morning.

Sometime in the middle of the night, my mom got out of bed to go to the bathroom, and on the way back to bed, she turned and fell down, breaking *her* hip.

Not wanting to disturb either me or the caregiver who lived in the house, Mom did not ring for us; instead, she crawled back into bed and somehow passed the night.

The car arrived at 6:00 a.m. to take me to the airport. There was not a sound in the house, so, thinking all was well, I left for New York. When I arrived, the driver of the car that met me gave me a message to call my secretary in L.A. My heart leaped.

When I called Kathy, I heard her say, "Now, don't worry, everything is fine, but your mother fell and broke her hip and is in Cedars Sinai Hospital." She went on to say, "But there is only one problem—we can't find your aunt." Kathy said she had rung Cioci Helena's apartment several times but didn't get an answer. I asked Kathy to call the security at the complex and have them break down the door if need be. In the end, the girls wound up not only at the same hospital but on the same floor and in the same ward, ten rooms apart.

I was beside myself, and Tom was almost as upset as I was. He had spoken with my mom but never met her, yet he was already emotionally involved, which was very touching to me. I was on the phone with the doctors most of the night and they assured me the girls were stable and comfortable but under sedation for pain, because they could not be operated on until Monday.

I returned to L.A. the following day. My aunt and my mother quickly became the favorites of the ward, and the nursing staff was endlessly amused that the two sisters, on the same night, had had the same accident and wound up being treated on the same floor. They became a curiosity, and all sorts of people stopped in to see them, which also helped garner more medical attention. They were soon moved to adjoining rooms, and their sense of humor earned them the nickname "the hipsters."

———— ∞ ————

THERE IS SOMETHING about falling that always seems to begin the slippery slope for the aged. When they fell, my aunt was ninety and my mother eighty-eight, but when you saw them they both appeared to be much younger. I am eternally grateful for being in their gene pool. All three of us were determined that they were not going to let this setback bring them down. The operations went well, but they had to stay in the hospital for two weeks before moving to rehab, where they spent the better part of a month.

Tom had to go to Tokyo on business for a few days, and it seemed a good opportunity for the two of us to get away, knowing that the girls were under the watchful eyes of the hospital staff. En route to Japan, Tom stopped in L.A. to meet my girls for the first time. Tom charmed them, and it pushed their flirtatious buttons. I never saw so much batting of eyelashes as on that day. Their generation employed coquetry, peppered with volleys of clever banter, in the game of seduction, and time had not diminished their skills. Tom became the focus of their attention, and he delighted in the game.

The minute they were able to get up and onto walkers, their competitive spirits engaged. When I visited them in the rehab clinic, I found them doing laps of the hallway, comparing how many they did over the other. I thought it was a very healthy pursuit and was amazed at their tenacity. They were, after all, from what Tom Brokaw called "the greatest generation," and the recipe for whatever chemistry created them is long forgotten.

It was apparent that any thought of them living on their own unsupervised was now out of the question. I began to rearrange my household to accommodate both ladies and the phalanx of healthcare workers and therapists that would be needed to manage their recovery. It was a comedy, to say the least. My house was not designed for what they required. Although I removed as much as I could from the path of their traffic, each day was a symphony of shuffle, shuffle, bang! "Oh, sorry dear!"

Not to mention that my door would be answered by total strangers asking who *I* was. Just as my housekeeper, Albertina, and I were considering taking heavy tranquilizers, one of our former nurses called to say that she had converted her mother's house in North Hollywood to a care center that would accommodate a maximum of four senior people with their own rooms and a twenty-four-hour staff under her direction.

If Mom and Cioci Helena were to reside there, they would be the first and only clients and would have the house, staff, and garden virtually to themselves. I went to look at the premises and took the girls, who, to my surprise, approved. Maintaining the schedule of therapy, doctors' visits, hairdressers, and personal needs for both of them was a full-time job and even more demanding than raising children.

Since I was also gradually taking over the financial responsibilities of my mother and my aunt, I needed to work. I had been offered to take over the role of Anna in the West End production of *The King and I,* which we would open in Edinburgh, and my commitment would be a run of eleven weeks. With the girls in good hands, I was relieved of worry. They would have everything they needed, so I breathed a sigh of relief and took off to England to begin rehearsals.

For any actress who has had the good fortune to play the role of Anna in that most glorious of musicals, each night is a gift. When the curtain comes down, there is usually not a dry eye on the stage or in the audience. The night Tom came to see the show, he too came backstage with tears in his eyes, and I asked him when he began crying. "When I left the hotel," he said. Mrs. Anna and her hoopskirts would be in my life for two years, and the night I hung up the hoops was one of the saddest good-byes I ever had to say to a role.

TEN DAYS FROM her ninety-second birthday, my aunt was awakened by her caregiver, smiled, rolled over to take a few more winks, and never woke up.

Finally she was reunited with the love of her life and the person she longed to join, my uncle Howard.

Mom returned home to our house and we installed a full-care unit that was the rival of any professional operation. Osteoporosis was the principal cause of Mom's discomfort, which should have been diagnosed earlier, but even as little as ten years ago, early diagnosis and treatment were nowhere near what they are today. The team we put together consisted of four nurses and a night man. When Omar came for his interview as the weekend and nighttime helper, I took him to Mom's room for them to meet. Mom was in her wheelchair watching a musical on the television, and when she saw Omar she asked him if he could dance. He said, "Yes, can you?" Mom raised her arms for him to lift her out of her chair and said, "I could teach you a thing or two."

It was obvious he was the man for the job.

In June 2007, Tom and I were on a large yacht cruising the Adriatic with members of the "Save Venice" society. At five o'clock in the morning there was a knock on the cabin door. The captain had an emergency call for me from my mother's doctor. Mom had developed a bad infection that overnight had turned into pneumonia, and she'd been admitted to the ICU, not expected to survive. I became manic to get off the boat and on the next plane.

We were still in international waters off the coast of Sicily, and the yacht was obliged to dock where customs officers could clear us before I would be allowed to disembark. With the time difference, it was difficult to communicate with L.A., but I was able to contact Kathy and Jackie, my right and left hands, and magically they obtained plane tickets from Palermo to Rome to New York to L.A. The connections were close, however, and if I missed any one of the flights, it would cost me a day.

The angels must have been with me that day, because after twenty-six hours of traveling, I arrived at LAX, where Kathy and Jackie gave me the updates and drove me to the hospital. From the look on their faces, the end was near.

The ICU nurse took me aside before he would take me to Mom's room, to prepare me for the worst. When I saw Mom, she was close to being in a coma. I stayed in the room overnight, holding her hand and listening to her labored breathing, thinking each breath might be the last.

In the morning, a doctor came to speak to me about a procedure that might alleviate some of Mom's pain. Putting a needle into her lung to remove some of the liquid was a risky business, but it seemed worth the risk. I was asked to leave and return in two hours. I was disinclined to go, but they insisted, so I went home to bathe and change.

When I returned to the ICU, I walked into my mother's room and there she was, wide awake, being fed applesauce.

When she saw me she said, "Where have you been?"

Mom was back, but I was a wreck. It took another week and the insertion of a feeding tube before she was given permission to leave the hospital. In the meantime, I learned everything I could about what it took to take care of her in the condition she was in. I remembered the lessons my stepfather had taught me about taking care of horses. I had to learn everything from the bottom to the top, or else how would I know if the people working for us were doing it correctly? I even learned how to suction her lungs of the fluids that would collect there, preventing her from breathing easily. I was the one she trusted most to do that uncomfortable procedure, after which she would relax.

That July 21 was Mom's ninety-fifth birthday. Twenty-five friends of ours, not just mine but hers as well, came to help us celebrate. There would have been more but for those who were out of town. I hope I will have twenty-five friends to help me celebrate my ninety-fifth if I get there.

As we toasted her with champagne, Mom looked up at me and said, "Where's mine?" So, in front of God and everybody, I took as many bubbles as I could out of my glass, pulled about 20 cc's into a syringe, and injected it into her feeding tube, to great applause. The effects were immediate, and she flushed as the alcohol did its thing.

She had a very happy birthday, and that night, she slept like a baby.

EIGHTEEN

Sitzfleisch

In the summer of 2008, I committed to doing two plays back to back in England. Mom was stable, our system of care was working, and I needed some gainful employment. The first play to be done was a Christmas musical called a "panto," which is an art form quintessentially British. A "panto" is less pantomime and more what we in the "colonies" would call burlesque. It consists of excessively broad humor set to music with themes very loosely based on children's fairy tales, and including quite a few men dressed as women. Couched in this traditional premise are cues for the audience participation part of the program, which everyone awaits with great anticipation. When called upon, they react with classic responses that have carried on for generations.

I couldn't resist becoming the Fairy Godmother in *Cinderella,* especially when I would costar with England's anointed Panto Queen, my adorable friend Mr. Christopher Biggins. The play was being produced by a wonderful West End producer called Michael Rose, who spared no expense with costumes, sets, and special effects.

When Michael said he was going to open the show with me flying around the twenty-five-hundred-seat theater while singing Stephen Sondheim's "Putting It Together," I asked how he was going to do that. "I flew a car in *Chitty Chitty Bang Bang,* darling, surely I can fly you!" I didn't know whether to take that as a compliment or not.

The musical would begin rehearsing in mid-November and play for six weeks over the holiday season. That schedule fit perfectly, as it would dovetail into rehearsals for the drama *Pack of Lies,* which I was asked to do by another well-known West End producer, Bill Kenwright. This was the play that Dame Judi Dench had won awards for, and it was based on a true story of spies in suburban England during the Cold War.

It was a wonderful way to end one year and begin another.

For years I have kept to a schedule of having my annual physical checkup at the end of each January. Since I was going to be away doing the plays, I thought it might be a good idea to have it done in November before I was to leave. As a normal part of each checkup, I would have a CT scan of my chest, having been a smoker. For each of the five years that test had been done, we'd kept track of a tiny spot, no, not even a spot but what they called a "fleck" on my right lung. My fleck never seemed to change, so I naturally assumed that I would pass this checkup with the same flying colors as always.

Ten days before I was to begin rehearsals in London, my trusted friend and doctor Paul Rudnick called and said that he wanted me to have a PET scan. "What's up, Paul?" I asked.

"That fleck on your lung has changed shape, and we want to have a look at it."

I had absolutely no symptoms indicating there was anything amiss with my body, and I try to take good care of the thing I walk around in. Maybe I was in denial about the potential seriousness of a PET scan, or maybe I just didn't want to anticipate the worst, so I went along to Cedars Sinai Hospital for the test.

As I was packing for my long stay in England, Paul rang and said, "The PET scan lit up." After a lengthy explanation of what that meant and the probability of what I had, Paul told me to go see Dr. McKenna, who was the best man in the city to deal with my condition.

The word *cancer* was never mentioned.

Dr. McKenna looked at all my tests over the years and determined that my fleck was very slow growing but not located in a place where a biopsy was an option. Looking at the cells, from the scans, he was 99 percent sure that it was something he should remove by taking out the entire upper lobe of my right lung.

"Does this thing have a name?" I asked.

"Oh yes, it's called alveolar carcinoma, cancer of the lung."

Finally it sunk in, but I was very calm and I told him about the gainful employment awaiting me. He said that since there was every evidence that this was a slow-growing carcinoma, if I had to, I probably could do the first play but very definitely not the second.

I was not in a panic as I drove home, and when I arrived, while collecting the mail, I saw my neighbor Hal, who told me that his wife had just come home from surgery, having had a part of her lung removed. "Really," I said. "Who did the surgery?"

"Dr. McKenna," Hal said. "He's the best!"

I rang Tom and he, being a hypochondriac, suggested I send all my tests to his friend Dr. Sam Waxman at Mt. Sinai, one of the top cancer researchers in the country, for a second opinion. On my way to England, I stopped in New York and saw Sam, and the pulmonary specialist he recommended. Both confirmed Dr. McKenna's diagnosis and recommended treatment. It was also agreed that I was probably safe to do the first play, but my surgery should be done as soon as possible afterward. I scheduled January 29 as the day, and off I went.

My agent, friend, and soul sister, Alex McLean-Williams, helped me deliver the bad news to Bill Kenwright, who was a complete gentleman and released me from his show.

I really don't know how I was able to function so calmly knowing what was lurking inside my body. I simply did not accept any other scenario but one in which I would have the "thing" out and just carry on. I had to be all right, because who else was going to take care of Mom if not me?

We began rehearsals and, almost immediately, we fused into a company. With Biggins as the company leader and the Kellys, father and son, as the "dames" (the ugly sisters in drag), there was hardly a serious moment. All the dancers and leading players were consummate professionals, and in no time at all a lavish production came to life.

I sent Mom a CD of me flying around the theater with fairy wings and a wand supported by invisible special effects that had everyone baffled. The nurses said she was fascinated by the image and kept pointing at the television, saying my name. So many friends came to see the show, and lots of my girls, the fan club from England, Scotland, France, Germany, Holland, and Singapore.

My dressing room was always full, which is the way I love it to be. Tom came for Christmas and left before New Year's. The week between Christmas and New Year's we double up on shows, because it was the height of the season and short weeks.

The day after Christmas, Mom came down with a cold that was not responding to treatment. At ninety-six, any change in her condition had to be treated immediately, because it could develop into a critical situation very fast. After she was in the hospital on IV antibiotics for two days, her doctor sent her home. She remained stable for twenty-four hours but then began to go downhill.

With the eight-hour time difference, it was difficult to speak with Dr. Miao directly, but we managed to speak on December 30, after Mom had to be readmitted to the hospital.

It could not have been a worse time of the year for an emergency of this kind, because everyone is distracted by the holidays. The infection was lodging itself in the most vulnerable part of Mom's anatomy—her lungs.

Indeed it is said that pneumonia is the friend of the elderly and the illness most commonly seen on the death certificates of senior citizens. I suppose everyone dies of something, and all I prayed for was that after our long journey together, I could be with her at the final moment.

I had two shows on December 31. I spoke with my agent, the producer, and the cast of the show, and they were all supportive of my getting on the first plane to L.A. After the last show I packed up my dressing room and my hotel room, loaded my car, and took off for London.

It was a surreal drive on a deserted highway at midnight on New Year's Eve, with fireworks going off alongside the road the entire way, and me in floods of tears. I arrived at my little mews house, and as if on automatic pilot, I unpacked, repacked, and closed up the house as best as I could, not knowing if I was returning.

The car picked me up at 7:00 a.m. to go to Heathrow to catch the plane for L.A. My entire support team, Sally in London and Jackie and Kathy in L.A., were working together to make the impossible happen. The entire trip to L.A., I had no way of knowing if Mom would be alive or not when I arrived.

Once again, Jackie and Kathy were at the airport to meet me. They told me that Liz, Mom's chief nurse, was with her and that Mom knew I was on my way from England. I called Liz on her cell phone, and she held the phone up to Mom's ear so that I could tell her I had landed and that I was on my way to her.

When I arrived in the doorway of her room, I saw Mom waiting for me with her eyes wide open and a hint of a smile on her face. Although she was unable to speak, she understood me when I told her that I would be with her forever and that I would not leave her. She squeezed my hand, and I could see the fear in her eyes soften.

On the second day of her ordeal, Mom was struggling. I met with all her doctors, who gave me the medical options that would keep her alive. Being men of true compassion, they also allowed me to understand that these were extraordinary methods to maintain a life that would have no quality.

The time had come to face the unfaceable. Two of Mom's nurses, Ruth and Connie, stayed until the end. There was one person from our past who held a very special place in our lives, and he wanted me to call him whenever Mom was in a critical state. John Strong was the man of the hour. He dropped everything in his busy life and came to the hospital, and never left us. What an extraordinary demonstration of loyalty.

I was allowed to order the morphine that would help relieve Mom's suffering, but she had a constitution of steel. We held vigil over her for two more days until mercifully she let go. It had not been an easy passing, but it exemplified the perseverance, or, as the Germans say, *Sitzfleisch* (stick-to-it-iveness) with which she lived.

———— ∞ ————

AS PLANNED, ON January 29, I had my surgery. I am grateful it went well. I am also thankful to Dr. John Levin for coming to my aid when I was in crisis after returning home post op. Dr. McKenna, true to his reputation, did a brilliant job.

My scans have all been clear, and no further treatment has been necessary. The odds are that I will be able to join other cancer survivors in marching for a cure for many years to come.

As the holidays approached, I knew that this time of year would never be the same for me. But perhaps it is fitting that it should be about my mother and the end of our long journey together. The first Christmas, New Year's, and Mother's Day were the most difficult. I had to stay strong for so long that I found myself in tears at the drop of a hat. These are the tears, long overdue, that celebrate the greatness of our bond and the enormity of our loss.

In December 2009, I attended a pre-Christmas candlelight ceremony graciously offered by Forest Lawn Cemeteries for the loved ones of the recently departed. Being in the company of hundreds of strangers with whom I was bonded by our mutual losses gave me a profound sense of the life and death experience.

Intellectually, I understand that life has a beginning and an end, but emotionally it is inconsolable to have to let go of a parent, a child, a sibling, a spouse or a partner, and even a pet.

The cycle of life reminds us of our own mortality, and in reflection comes the inevitable question, "What's it all about?" The only idea that made sense, as I looked around at the hundreds of lit candles at Forest Lawn, was love.

Love.

Perhaps our sole and most important role in life is to love one another and help each other through the trials of the life experience. If not love, what else?

Beauty fades, success has its ups and downs, someone always has more than you do, and lots of people have less. Political and social ideals are corrupted by self-centered ambitions, popular culture panders to the worst of human instincts and doesn't encourage the best, technology is replacing conversation and imagination, and on and on and on.

But still the question remains the same, and in the end, our lives are a reflection of the love we have given and the love we have accepted.

I am grateful to all the people and all the animals I have loved, who have loved me. They have made my life worth living, and I hope that I have returned their love sufficiently for them to feel the same way about me.

That's about all I have to say.

Excuse me if I carried on a bit too long with a thought or a theme. I hope some of what you've read was amusing.

Thank you for taking the time.

Acknowledgments

———⚬⚬⚬———

If we are a combination of genetic inherited traits and environmental influences, then I have to thank everyone I have ever known. That being impossible, for all who are not mentioned below, I apologize. My mother was the inspiration for this book and most of the good things I have done in life. My other teachers who have shared their knowledge along the way are: Leo Ziffren, Jon Lovelace, Mini McGuire, Henry Bamberger, Linda and Bob Judd, Barbara Tarmy, L.S. Barksdale, Don and Iris Hunt, Julian McKeand, Charles Wolf, Aubrey Buxton, Maggy Scherer, Geri Bauer, Rodney Gould, Page Cavanaugh, Jann Rowe, Eddie Collins, David Galligan, Sharon Weisz, Armen Guzemilian, Alex McLean-Williams, John Sobanski, Kathy Bartels, Jackie Edwards, John Strong, Kate Johnson, Larry Fuller, Sally Vaughn, Greta Morrison, Suzanne Lobel, Tessa Kennedy, Tomasz Starzewski, Martin and Stephanie Brown, Rahul and Linda Currea, Robert Wagner and Tom Mankiewicz.

To my darling Mexican family, Betty and Marina Ros, I thank them for all their support over the years. I am grateful for the assistance provided by Richard Buskin in connection with the preparation and writing of this book. To my housekeepers Albertina Duran, Omar Tejeda, Grace Daudi, and to Richard, I thank you for your constant loyalty. To my mother's loving nurses: Liz, Ruth, Connie, Clara, and Maureen. To John Strong—a better friend no one could have.

To David McConnell and our loyal staff at the William Holden Wildlife Foundation Education Center, thank you for your patience with me during my writing of this book. And to all of those whose invitations I've turned down because I was writing.

To my talented and long-suffering editor, Mitchell Ivers, whose taste and wisdom shaped each paragraph of this book.

To all of my wonderful animal companions, who have supported me with their love throughout my life; I couldn't have done anything without you.

And last, but certainly not least, my love, Tom Carroll, whose patience during the journey of this book deserves a medal for valor.